DISCARDED

SEARCHING FOR THE SOUND

SEARCHING

∾ FOR THE ∾

SOUND

My Life with the Grateful Dead

PHIL LESH

LITTLE, BROWN AND COMPANY
New York   Boston

Little, Brown and Company
Time Warner Book Group
1271 Avenue of the Americas, New York, NY 10020
Visit our Web site at www.twbookmark.com

First Edition: April 2005

The author is grateful for permission to include the following: Lyrics to Grateful Dead songs © Ice Nine Publishing Company, Inc. Used with permission. Lyrics to "Music Is Love" by David Crosby © Stay Straight Music. Used with permission. Lines from "For the Grateful Dead" © Robert M. Petersen. Used with permission of Hulogosi Publishers.

Library of Congress Catalogueing-in-Publication Data
Lesh, Phil.
      Searching for the sound : my life with the Grateful Dead / Phil Lesh. — 1st ed.
         p. cm.
      ISBN 0-316-00998-9
      1. Lesh, Phil. 2. Grateful Dead (Musical group) 3. Bass guitarists —
United States — Biography. 4. Rock musicians — United States — Biography.
I. Title.
ML419.L43A3 2005
787.87'166'092 — dc22   2005000149

10 9 8 7 6 5 4 3 2 1

Q-FF

Book design by Marie Mundaca

Printed in the United States of America

To my brothers in music:
  Jerry Garcia
  Bob Weir
  Bill Kreutzmann
  Ron McKernan
  Mickey Hart
  Tom Constanten
  Keith Godchaux
  Donna Godchaux
  Brent Mydland
  Vince Welnick
  Bruce Hornsby

And to my wife, Jill, and my sons, Grahame and Brian, without whose love and encouragement this book would never have been written.

I was permitted to hear an incredible music. . . . I heard the gestation of the new world . . . the sound of stars grinding and chafing, of fountains clotted with blazing gems. . . . Music is planetary fire, an irreducible which is all sufficient; it is the slate-writing of the gods.

— Henry Miller, *Tropic of Cancer*

SEARCHING FOR THE SOUND

have always considered myself a very lucky man. I've been married for more than twenty years to a woman who loves me as passionately as I love her, and with whom I have developed a level of trust and companionship that I never dreamed existed. We are rearing two fine sons, both growing up straight and strong and loving. I survived hepatitis C and a liver transplant. I was born an only child but found my true brothers through the art of music and a series of improbable coincidences. I am blessed with the joy of earning my way by doing something I love — something that is so deep it can never be boring, or run out of challenges.

Music can define life itself, and it has indeed defined my life. In life, as in art, there are recurring themes, transpositions, repetitions, unexpected developments, all converging to define a *form* that's not necessarily apparent until its ending has come and gone.

I was awakened to the power of music early in life, through the magic of radio broadcasts and by listening to my father play, from memory, his favorite tunes on the piano. Music saved me from the worst effects of adolescent angst, partly by giving me a very real sense of accomplishment. It led me into a quest for knowledge and wisdom, for the cultural, artistic, historical, and religious context of the work that moved me so much. It has clarified my feelings as my father lay dying, kept me company in the early light of day as I fed my newborn sons, soothed and transported me during life-threatening illness and surgery, and brought me illimitable joy as I watched thousands of dancers surge and spin to the music flowing through my band.

The Grateful Dead has always been collectively dedicated to many ideals: family, community, freedom, risk-taking — but for me it was always the music. With all its ups and downs, it's an exhilarating experience to improvise — onstage and in life — with one's fellow humans, who after forty years of living, working, disagreeing, and completing one another's thoughts musically and conversationally, are connected by a bond that's "thicker than blood," as Bob Weir likes to say.

*O*h my God, Frank! He looks just like you!" Thus spoke my beloved grandmother Jewel Chapman, known as "Bobbie" to my dad, as she stood before the newborn window at Alta Bates Hospital in Berkeley, California, beholding the newest addition to the family for the first time. Frank's response was not recorded for posterity. Perhaps it was unprintable, as were so many of his asides and exit lines. After all, his relationship with his mother-in-law was fractious and volatile, beginning when he eloped with her daughter to Reno in August 1929. At ages twenty-five and twenty-two, my parents ran away and got married.

My dad was born Frank Hamilton Lesh in New Berlin (now called Canton, the change a result of widespread anti-German sentiment during World War I), Ohio, in 1904, the third of seven children. Family tradition describes an epic journey undertaken in 1919 by Grampa Bill, Uncle Lawrence, and my dad halfway across America, from Ohio to Arizona, then to Oregon, in a Model T Ford. They went west, traveling on what were then mostly dirt roads, to find a new home for the family (or maybe just a little elbow room). My dad's typically laconic description of this trip: "Pretty rough."

They eventually settled in Medford, Oregon, where Grampa opened up a grocery store and bakery. He converted the old Model T into a delivery truck, with the slogan "Lesh's Luscious Loaf" proudly emblazoned on the sides. My dad finished high school in Corvallis, Oregon, and then attended Oregon State University, graduating with a degree in pharmacy. His real gift, though, was working with mechanical things. He had an uncanny ability to visualize the inner workings of any machine and to unerringly diagnose any problems. Does anyone out there remember adding machines? Typewriters? All those clunkity, clackety keys, and little spider arms with letters and numbers on their tips that got all tangled up if you typed too fast? Crippled machines would magically materialize on his workbench; all my dad had to do was breathe on one of them and it would sit right up and start barking. The digital dexterity this talent required also stood him in good stead as an amateur musician. He had played euphonium in high school and college bands, and while I was growing up, we all liked nothing better than to hear him barrel out exuberant versions of his favorite tunes on our upright piano. He was self-taught as a pianist, but you'd never know it to hear him. Perhaps I'm listening through the rose-colored haze of memory, but it seems he could have played in any piano bar I've ever been in. My grampa Bill also played music (I still have his old Albert System clarinet). There's a persistent family legend that he actually played in one of Sousa's bands as a young man, but he would never say one way or the other. We do have photos of him as a clarinetist in bands that played at camp meetings, old-time religious revivals/retreats that took place in communities all over the country from the early nineteenth century up until World War II.

My mom, Barbara Jewel Chapman, was born in 1907 in Winfield, Kansas. When mom was two, her mother, Jewel Schmidt Fuller, known as "Bobbie," separated from her husband and filed for divorce, a very courageous move for a woman in those days. Winning a successful settlement, she lived alone with her child until she married Arthur Chapman, her second husband, and moved to Kansas City,

Missouri. Grandfather Chapman was a bon vivant and restaurateur in Kansas City, and they lived comfortably there until his death in 1928. Bobbie and my mother then moved to Stockton, California, to live with Bobbie's sister, my great-aunt Tillie. It was then that Barbara began commuting to Berkeley on weekends to visit her cousins, and it was there that she met my dad in early '29.

After their wedding in August '29, they found an apartment on Alcatraz Avenue in Berkeley, where they lived for some time. Before I was born, Bobbie came to live with them, and they moved to a series of larger places, culminating in the house on Edgecroft Road in Kensington, a suburb of Berkeley, where I grew up.

After college, Frank had decided not to go into pharmacy but to become an apprentice in the field of office machine repair, where his considerable mechanical skills could be put to good use. He rapidly rose through the hierarchy in the Bay Area, and by the time I came along, he and Mom had opened their own business.

For the first few years of my life, both of my parents were working during the week, first at their business and then, after that folded during World War II, at other similar companies. This meant that I spent most of my days with Bobbie, my grandma, whom I absolutely adored. It was through her sensitive and loving attention that at age four I first became aware of the power of music. It was her custom on Sunday afternoons to listen to the New York Philharmonic radio broadcasts; as the family legend relates, one Sunday during the concert she came out of her room, which was next to mine, and discovered me sitting on the floor with my ear pressed against the wall, entranced by the sounds emanating from the radio. She immediately invited me into her room to hear the remainder of the broadcast. As luck would have it, the next piece on the program was Brahms's First Symphony, an immensely arresting and powerful piece. I felt as if I'd been carried into a familiar, half-remembered realm.

When I was in third grade there was a talent show at my school's

Christmas Assembly; in it, my classmate Johnny played a violin solo. Something about the sound of his playing resonated, and at the next meeting of our music class, I announced my intention to take up the instrument. At that time, we had a music teacher who came in once a week and taught us how to read music notation and sing simple choral tunes. She also taught beginning instruments after school. So I brought a violin home, along with a form for my parents to sign stating that they agreed to maintain the instrument and to replace it if it was damaged beyond repair. This caused no small amount of consternation, for two reasons: One, I had kept my musical aspirations more or less to myself, so this development came as a surprise, and two, the instrument was valued at thirty-five dollars, not a small amount in those days. In the end, reason and kindness triumphed, and so my musical odyssey began.

I progressed fairly quickly on the violin, although it's accurate to say that I was no prodigy. The fingering and coordination of left hand and bow arm is extremely difficult, not to mention getting the notes in tune (there are no convenient frets to guide one's fingers, as on the guitar). After a year or so, I was able to graduate to a private teacher, and by age ten I was considered advanced enough to audition for the local youth orchestra. The Young People's Symphony Orchestra provided young musicians with the opportunity to play some of the great classics in a relaxed atmosphere while honing their skills as ensemble musicians. While I was a member, we played Beethoven's Fifth and Seventh Symphonies, Schubert's Unfinished Symphony, Wagner's prelude to *Die Meistersinger von Nürnberg,* and many other classics, light and heavy.

I stayed in the Young People's Symphony until about age sixteen, by which time I had switched to trumpet. I had originally been attracted to it by its brilliant and electrifying timbre and by its assertiveness and prominence in an orchestral context, and had wanted to try it since sixth grade, but my braces made it painful if not impossible to even try. When my braces came off, I immediately sought out a trumpet teacher. Bob Hansen, the conductor of the Golden Gate Park Band for more than fifty years, not only taught me the trumpet, but gave me the profoundest possible grounding in principles of musicianship — dynamics, phrasing, tempo, context — fundamentals that were basic to my later study of composition as well as performance. Like other great teachers, he taught by example. I would play my lesson, he would watch and listen, and then he would calmly bring up his horn and play it the right way.

It turned out that I had a gift for the trumpet, and as I progressed, I was able to join my teacher in a local semipro orchestra in Oakland, where we played Sibelius's Second Symphony and Brahms's First. The latter work was a personal milestone for me, since it was the one that opened my heart to music as a child.

By this time, I was fairly accomplished as a trumpeter and began to explore more deeply the way that music was made. Unfortunately, there were no classes in harmony or anything remotely resembling music theory at my high school. I was desperate to learn, and what books I could find were less than helpful. I discovered that the high school in the next town offered courses in harmony as well as the usual performance opportunities. So, in the middle of my junior year, I asked my parents to let me transfer over to Berkeley High School. To satisfy the residence requirements, a friend agreed to let me live with his family for the first few months. I hadn't really thought through what would happen after that, but my parents amazed me by agreeing to sell their home and move into Berkeley so that I could go to school there. Bobbie had passed away the previous year, and I guess they were ready for a change. I can't begin to describe the feelings of gratitude and love I felt for them at that moment; they were willing to leave their beautiful home of fifteen years and move to another town, into a much smaller house, so that I could pursue my dream.

Trumpet and harmony studies at Berkeley High exposed me to a much broader spectrum of music than I had previously encountered, not only classical (Mahler, Bruckner, Richard Strauss) but jazz as well. My first experience with improvisation came at my tryout for the high school dance band; we were playing along through the chart, and we came to a place that was marked in my part "Ad Lib." Everybody looked at me, and I said, "What?" "Ad-lib, man!" "What's ad-lib?" General hilarity and merriment. I was informed that *ad-lib* (Latin: *ad libitum* — at one's pleasure) means to play something that's not written, to improvise. I fumbled my way through the section on a wing and a prayer, but my life and my idea of music had changed forever: Play something that's not written! Something that's never been played before! Yow!

Naturally enough, my first loves in jazz were the big bands; when I was in high school, from 1954 to 1957, we were still close enough in time to the swing era that my folks had old 78-rpm records of Glenn Miller, Tommy Dorsey, Harry James, and the king of them all: Benny Goodman. I played those so often that I wore them out. Later, I got turned on to Basie and Ellington, but my fave rave was Stan Kenton, especially the period of *Contemporary Concepts* and *Cuban Fire,* about 1955–56. I was exposed to West Coast small-group jazz during my last year in high school, and I'd heard trumpeter Clifford Brown, who immediately became for me the model for how jazz trumpet should be played. But it wasn't until I attended the summer music camp at College (now University) of the Pacific, the summer after graduation in 1957, that I heard Miles Davis and John Coltrane for the first time. Miles I didn't much care for at first, though I later came to love his playing and especially the bands he put together, but Coltrane just blew me away. His sound was so radical — not smooth and breathy, but solid and edgy, as if it were carved out of bronze — and his ideas! Chords stacked upon chords, phrases looping over the tiniest fraction of the beat, all with the most soulful inflections and passionate intensity. It was so outside anything I'd ever heard in any genre of music. This encounter with Coltrane was my first inkling that jazz and improvised music could carry the weight and spiritual authority of the greatest classical works.

San Francisco in the fifties was very much like a European coastal city, built on hills and bay fill, with only one building in the downtown area rising more than twelve or fifteen stories. The atmosphere was still that of a small town, and the various institutions of higher learning (University of San Francisco, City College, San Francisco State) reflected that ambience, being smaller and lower-key than places like UC Berkeley or Stanford.

That fall, I enrolled at San Francisco State, where I learned that being the best high-school trumpet player in the state didn't mean much — good enough for maybe a slot in the nether regions of the third trumpet section of the band and for nothing at all in the orchestra. I wasn't getting to play much music, the required introductory theory courses were repeating what I'd learned in high school, and the academics were demanding, at the very least.

In any case, at age seventeen I really wasn't ready for college, let alone living away from home. I had originally planned to live at home my first year, but after a blowup with my dad, I moved out, sharing an apartment in Berkeley with a casual acquaintance. It seemed that everybody at school was older and more together than I was. I was living in three rooms with a roommate I barely knew, and commuting (sometimes hitchhiking) to class every day. For years, I had been anticipating living an independent life: I just couldn't wait to grow up and move out. Well, I'd moved out all right, but I hadn't grown up yet. I didn't even recognize my loneliness and homesickness for what it was until after the middle of the semester, when I dropped out and came home without a clue as to what my next move would be. To my enormous relief, my parents were welcoming and supportive, with never an "I told you so" to be heard.

In those times young men had two choices: wait for the draft to catch up with you, or enlist in the regular services for two years (if you chose reserves, the term was four years). It was suggested, probably by my dad, that I follow the path of so many others who, finding themselves with no foreseeable future, joined the army. As much as I didn't like the idea, it seemed to be my only option. It started to look better when, through my trumpet teacher, I heard of an opportunity to join the renowned Sixth Army Band, stationed at the Presidio of San Francisco. With Mr. Hansen's recommendation, and a successful audition at the Presidio, my future was decided. I would enlist for two years and get my obligation out of the way, at the same time pursuing a musical education in the band. After going through the recruiting process, off I went to the Oakland Army Induction Center to start my military career.

The induction center was a warehouse that operated like a meat-packing plant. The raw material went in one end and came out the other right onto the bus for basic training, so I knew that once I made it through, I was in it for the long haul. Upon arrival, all new recruits were directed into a locker room, where we stripped to our shorts; all our valuables (wallet, cash, glasses) were put into a vinyl drawstring bag that we carried with us. We followed the yellow tape arrows on the floor to various testing locations where we were pushed, pulled, and prodded. I arrived at the eye test; my glasses were in my bag. I was asked to read the lowest line on the chart. I couldn't see anything. I asked, "What chart?" "The one on the wall." "What wall?" "NEXT!"

I still don't know whether it was my bad eyes or my bad attitude that kept me out; I was ushered into an office, where a kindly-looking officer tried to take the sting out of my rejection: "I'm sorry to say, son, that you are unfit for military service." A beat. "Does this mean I'll never be drafted?" "Er, why, yes, it does." I didn't even leave a vapor trail, I was out of there so fast. I had suddenly discovered just how badly I didn't want to be a soldier, no matter what the fringe benefits were.

Sometime previously I had heard about a junior college in San Mateo where there was a great jazz band and an arranging program led by a highly respected teacher, Bud Young. This option began to appear more and more attractive: a chance to learn big-band arranging, study more theory, and play a higher position in the band without the pressure of a four-year school. On my own I hitchhiked down to San Mateo, checked out the school, applied, and was accepted. On a bulletin board in the Student Housing Office I found a card advertising a boardinghouse in Burlingame, run by a Mr. and Mrs. Smith. The house had space for three students, two sharing a loft room and one downstairs. Mrs. Smith's cooking came highly recommended by none other than the freshman dean, who had lived in her house when he attended school there. During my first school year away from home, I shared the loft with Ben, a student from Oregon, while Eddie, an engineering major from Jakarta, Indonesia, took the room downstairs.

My initiative must have pleased my parents, as they readily agreed to foot the bill for my room, board, and essentials. I was also very fortunate to get a part-time job at the college library, where my main task was to audition all the records coming into the library for scratches and pops so that we could then make notes and assess any damage done when the records were lent out. Talk about a kid in a candy store! I couldn't wait to get to work every day to see what new stuff I could treat myself to. In this way I was able to hear the widest possible range of music, from folk to bebop to the symphonies of Mahler (which I only knew from trumpet excerpt books and printed scores), without having to buy the records, which I couldn't have afforded in any case.

Working at the library also led to my discovery of the music and the phenomenon of Charles Ives. My first contact with this great American artist was through a survey of Ives's life and music by Henry Cowell, another American composer, and his wife, Sydney. *Charles Ives and His Music* contained a brief biographical sketch and an overview of the works, with musical examples. The examples introduced me to truly original compositions: the song "The Majority," with its notated tone-clusters and unmetered barring, and the *Concord* Sonata, with its free polyphony for two hands written on three staves. It almost didn't matter what the music sounded like — it looked so cool on the page. The power and freshness of his music, together with the story of his life (neglect, misunderstanding, unwillingness to compromise in order to earn a living as a musician, going into insurance and making a fortune, composing at night, using his wealth to promote new music other than his own), made him, in my eyes, an artistic hero. All this, before I ever heard a note of the music, as there were no recordings available to me until years later. Together with that of Coltrane, the music of Ives was to become the foundation for my personal artistic aspirations, and both artists would exert a tremendous influence on the embryonic aesthetic of the Grateful Dead.

Being a year older helped me fit more comfortably into college life. I made new friends during the course of spontaneous conversations, which would be struck up over meals in the cafeteria. It was not uncommon for classes to be missed because we lost track of time while discussing this book or that poem. Everybody, it seemed, had read Kerouac and Ginsberg, and we were all full of the romance of the American road.

One afternoon, while standing in the cafeteria line, I was introduced to a short, compact man with slicked-back hair who looked to be my senior by about four years. Bobby Petersen, a fellow student and a mad beatnik from Sacramento, was a product of a quasicriminal subculture — he'd already served time in the state prison system for robbery. Perhaps because of this, he had a harder edge than any of my other friends, but underneath he was gentle and laughter-loving, with the soul of a true poet. I'd been very impressed by his piece about jazz that had appeared in the school literary magazine, and I told him so in no uncertain terms.

During our long friendship, Bobby opened my mind and heart to certain twentieth-century literature: Henry Miller, Thomas Wolfe, and post-Beat poets like Gary Snyder, Phil Whalen, and Charles Olson. One of our favorite pastimes was to sit late at night in one of our rented rooms and read aloud to each other — Miller, Wolfe, the Beats, Kazantzakis, and even, on one memorable occasion, Homer. Bobby and I would later collaborate on several songs for the Grateful Dead, among them "Unbroken Chain," which I've always considered one of my best songs. Even more important, he also introduced me to the concept of living in the moment, of expanding the "now" into an eternal present.

Not to mention mind-altering substances: I'd done the usual amount of clandestine social drinking in high school, but I'd been turned off to it after one particularly blinding hangover. Bobby wasn't much of a drinker either, and when he offered me some pot, I was ready to try it. I wanted to break out of the straitjacket of my inherited worldview, to see what, if anything, was outside my little bubble of consciousness, and I sensed that marijuana could be a tool for travel. I saw Bobby as a true artist, following an artistic and spiritual quest, and fully trusted him when he told me "You're gonna love this stuff, Lesh."

One evening, he showed up at my place with a twenty-five-dollar matchbox of weed. I had agreed to chip in on the cost, so he rolled up two tiny pinner joints, stuck one in his pocket for later, and fired the other one up. I had heard stories about various first experiences with this drug, but none more potentially embarrassing than the one about the guy who smokes a joint and then spends the whole evening complaining about how he's not high. Over and over again, loudly: "This stuff's no good; it's not working."

Bobby put Stravinsky's *The Rite of Spring* on the phonograph, turned up the volume, turned the lights down low, and went out with another friend to a poetry reading, leaving me alone with the music.

My first words to him when he returned: "You won't believe what I've been hearing!" Heck, I couldn't believe it myself.

While I was living through them, the fifties seemed like the epitome of bland, vanilla, white-bread culture, a vast wasteland of perfectly organized Stepford suburbs and reactionary inertia. Looking back now, I see that decade as a period of innocence; none of the great events of the time — the cold war, with the Damoclean sword of nuclear destruction hanging over our heads, or the whole McCarthy Red Scare — seemed to have made much of an impression on me or my contemporaries. Mostly absorbed in the time-honored pursuits of adolescents in any era — school, social life, the opposite sex, omphaloskepsis — we grew up blessed, as we thought then, to be living in the greatest country on earth, where we were free to develop ourselves as far as we could imagine. The onrushing sixties were to bring a completely different paradigm, when we would begin to involve ourselves in working toward the realization of what some would deride as a Utopian dream: a nation and a culture built on love, respect, and the quest for spiritual values.

Bliss was it in that dawn to be alive,
But to be young was very Heaven!
— William Wordsworth, "The Prelude"

During the waning of the fifties, the first stirrings of what would become a full-blown counterculture were surfacing in university and college towns all over the country; in Palo Alto, for example, several venues had sprung up where like minded people could meet and share ideas, books, music, and more.

The Peninsula Peace Center, run by Ira Sandperl (who would soon become well-known as Joan Baez's political guru), served the more politicized folk — nuclear disarmament activists, protesters, etc. — mostly a committed and focused bunch; but in order to pay the rent, Ira and his partner, Roy Kepler (owner of Kepler's Books), provided rooms for Stanford students and other itinerants. They also threw huge parties that drew freaks from all over the area, providing stimulating intellectual interaction — and an endless supply of food and drink — to the local bohemians. One of these parties was my first introduction to the "underground," defined as that alternate culture surrounding any great center of learning — mostly composed of former students, perennial students, and nonstudents.

St. Michael's Alley, run by Vern Gates, was the classic bohemian coffeehouse — smoky dive, lots of small tables, real strong coffee, and an occasional open-mike night; most of the time, people would sit at the tables playing and singing together: in short, a very loose scene.

Kepler's Books, in Menlo Park, was St. Mike's plus a bookstore, the same loose atmosphere with one big difference — you could casually pick a book off the shelf, bring it to your table, and quote it in support of some intense point you were trying to make (in the freewheeling discussion group always gathered there), or just sit down and read the whole book while your coffee slowly got cold. I can't overemphasize the importance of poetry and literature at that time. I've always felt that the whole sixties artistic counterculture evolved from the Beats (who were mostly writers — jazz was their music), who had themselves evolved from the great period of English Romantic literature 150 years earlier. Their work shared important themes and concerns with the likes of Blake, Coleridge, and Wordsworth. We were all standing on the shoulders of giants.

I was continuing in school at the College of San Mateo. Unfortunately, there weren't a lot of options in San Mateo for R & R on weekends. My friends from school told me about all the cool scenes in Palo Alto, so off I went exploring — spelunking, you might say, or just trolling in deep waters.

Hanging at St. Mike's, I heard about Vic Lovell, a grad student/ assistant professor at Stanford who had an open house for his students and friends every weekend; he lived on a little street in Menlo Park called Perry Lane — right next door to some guy named Ken Kesey, who was supposed to be a big cheese in the Stanford creative writing seminar (at that time conducted by Wallace Stegner). Fairly soon the word got out that here was a rare place to congregate more or less privately, and I started making regular stops on weekends at Vic's cozy living room with its wooden ceilings and stone fireplace. The place got pretty crowded some nights, with loud music and lots of loud animated conversation. Periodically Kesey would come over from next door and throw us all out. I was a little intimidated by Kesey, who was older, presumably wiser, and already gaining a reputation as a writer to watch. An outspoken, iconoclastic thinker and a champion wrestler from Oregon (built like a *big* brick fireplug), he didn't seem to have a lot of patience with kids like us who were just looking for a good time.

When we couldn't hang at Vic's, we gravitated to the Château, a big shingle house on a large hilly lot in Menlo Park, about a mile west of Kepler's and just down the road from Perry Lane. The Château was owned by a guy named Frank, who rented out rooms there so he'd have some company. It was the temporary home of many who would become good friends and newfound brothers, and also a way station on a new kind of underground railroad: People traveling to or from scenes connected to other schools up and down the coast (Emerson College, in Pacific Grove; UC Berkeley; Reed College, in Portland) would stop at Kepler's and often spend the night at the Château before moving on. At the very least, it's the place where I first met Jerry Garcia. In the fall of 1959, I had come down for my weekend cruise and was directed, as if by an unseen hand, to a party up in the hills.

It was a clear, brisk evening; people were milling about on the lawn, while the house was radiating energy. Several rooms held musicians, and from inside, an alto saxophonist could be heard playing solo over the laughing voices from the front yard. One of the music rooms was crowded with people listening to a bearded fellow play guitar and sing folk songs. I had seen this guy around a few times, at Kepler's, St. Mike's, the Peace Center; everyone seemed to defer subtly to him, and this made me a little nervous — nobody could be *that* cool. This was at the very beginning of the folk revival, and I hadn't heard a lot of the music. I confess my reaction was probably superficial, but it didn't *grab* me right away. I would soon discover that I just hadn't been *listening.* Later that evening, I was introduced to the singer/guitarist: "Hey, Phil, this is Jerry — he's a musician too." I responded with some snotty comeback like "Yeah, well I play jazz, man"; but Jerry just said something like "Cool! You gotta meet Lester, and Jackson, and . . . ," naming local East P.A. guys who played jazz in houses and at parties — even then, he was about furthering the music. He also bore an uncanny resemblance to the composer Claude Debussy: dark, curly hair, goatee, Impressionist eyes.

During that period, there were several cars parked at the back of the Château, being used for housing by people who couldn't afford rooms; one car was occupied by John the Cool (later to become Neal Cassady's drug connection), another by Jerry and Bob Hunter, an aspiring poet. Frank, the owner, kept his apartment in the basement; my good friend Page Browning lived in the pump house outside, and the rest of the rooms were rented to an assortment of students and university hangers-on.

There were two sides of the music scene in Palo Alto — the folkie bunch hanging at St. Mike's and the Château, and the blues/R & B/ jazz party scene in East Palo Alto (and at the Château). "East Paly" was across Highway 101 (a version of "the tracks"), and it was referred to as "the Ghetto" by everyone, including its inhabitants. There was a continual cross-fertilization of musical styles occurring — folkies showing up at the blues bash and jamming with the locals, and the jazz guys hanging at the Château; everyone seemed to be full of music in some way, and eager to share the joys and riches of their discoveries.

So it was that one night I fell by a party in the Ghetto, and right there in the front room was a stocky black-haired dude dressed in Levis and leather playing acoustic guitar and singing the blues, a middle-class white kid with the voice of a sixty-year-old black man. "Who's that, now?" I asked someone. "That's Ron McKernan; everyone calls him Pigpen." Looking closer, I saw that he did seem kind of, um, greasy; but that impression was immediately swept away as he launched into a raucous blues stomp. Pig's dad, it turned out, was Phil McKernan, for many years the number one R & B disc jockey at KRE in Oakland; naturally enough, Pig had been absorbing the blues and gospel right through his pores since birth. Strangely, Pigpen also resembled Debussy, judging from some photos taken in the composer's later years. After that, I kept seeing Jerry and Pigpen around the scene almost every weekend, at the Château, or in the Ghetto, or at St. Mike's. Sometimes they'd play together, and sometimes with others individually, just a coupla guys trading songs.

Meanwhile, I had finished up at the College of San Mateo, and I transferred to UC Berkeley in fall 1961, entering as a sophomore. On my first day in the music department, I was waiting to take an eartraining test when I overheard someone say in a clear, confident voice, "After all, music stopped in 1750 [the year of Bach's death] and began again in 1950 [the emergence of the postwar serialists]." Aha! Someone who knows about the avant-garde! This, I soon discovered, was Tom Constanten; hailing from Las Vegas, he was a freshman majoring in astronomy and minoring in music. He was also a pianist who had actually played some of Boulez' and Stockhausen's piano pieces. I was delighted to find someone who knew of, and cared about, what I felt was the most revolutionary paradigm shift in classical music in two hundred years, the equivalent in music of Einstein's theory of relativity in physics. T.C. and I became fast friends on the spot, and within two weeks he had given up his room in a boardinghouse and moved into my apartment on Durant Avenue, a block from the campus.

My main source of support was still my parents, but stockbrokers Dean Witter & Co. had also hired me as a board marker. My job was to read the ticker tape of transactions from the New York Stock Exchange and post the fluctuating prices on a blackboard for the six hours or so the market was open each day. Talk about dark Satanic mills! But at least I was done early, I didn't have to attend many morning classes, and I still had time to volunteer at KPFA, the local public radio station and flagship for the ultra-alternative (read: liberal) Pacifica Foundation. Pacifica was and is the mouthpiece for the farthest-out political views in the country; at that time it served as a bastion of protofeminist, ultraleftist, embryonic-environmentalist doctrine. The music programmers cast their net far and wide for the most unusual and striking recordings of everything from ethnic to avant-garde; their connections with the state-supported radio networks in Europe provided them with recordings of the newest and most controversial works of Boulez, Berio, Stockhausen, et al. — within mere months after their premières.

Since my interest in avant-garde classical music was peaking at that time, it was a great pleasure to be able to volunteer there and, for six hours or so a week, to be able to learn a little about microphones, control boards, mixing, tape manipulation, and, above all, limitation! The signal *must* be compressed so that the dynamic peaks *don't fry the transmitter!* This was the one law — Don't ya let those needles peak. Everything else was so loose that it was easy to make clandestine tape copies of the coolest new music for further study; thank goodness for that, as this music was so dense that it rewarded repeated listenings handsomely.

As I learned more about the actual workings of the studio, I was able to first assist and then engineer various live broadcasts, from panel discussions to live music, but the cream of the crop was the Midnight Special, a live folk music forum broadcast at midnight every Saturday night, the only open-ended program on the KPFA calendar. I really believe that I got the job of engineering the Special because no one else wanted to break up their Saturday night by coming to work at 11:00 p.m.; nonetheless, it was an ear-opener for me to hear the breadth and variety of the Bay Area folkie scene, and it was very impressive.

I continued to drive into Palo Alto on weekends, borrowing T.C.'s car, and it was at a party in the Ghetto that I heard Jerry Garcia sing an old border ballad called "Matty Groves," and I finally *got* it. The song tells of a love triangle between a feudal lord, his lady, and a serf, Matty, who loves the lady and is ultimately betrayed by her in a most gruesome manner. Jerry's delivery was both spine-tingling and bloodcurdling, presented without histrionics and with a fearless objectivity — just letting the song speak for itself. That was my first intimation that music with that kind of directness and simplicity could deliver an aesthetic and emotional payoff comparable to that of the greatest operatic or symphonic works. Needless to say, I was blown away; and later, in the kitchen, as Jerry and I sat across from each other at the old rickety table, talking and drinking cheap wine as the party was winding down, I had a blinding flash: I should get Jerry on the Midnight Special so everybody could hear how extraordinary he was! Jerry, endearingly diffident as always, was a little reluctant to consider it at first; it wasn't that easy, he said, the usual suspects that perform the show regularly were mostly from Berkeley, etc. "But you have a secret weapon," said I. "Me! Let's make a demo tape of a few songs, and I'll take it to Gert [Chiarito, the hostess of the show]. She'll be blown away like I was; it's as good as done!"

So off we went that same night, back to Berkeley to my place, about an hour's drive; we borrowed the only tape recorder I knew of (T.C.'s reel-to-reel Wollensak), turned right around, and went back to the party. There, we commandeered the kitchen table and borrowed a microphone, and as Jerry sang and played, I rolled tape; we recorded "Matty Groves" and "The Long Black Veil" and a couple of Jerry's other favorites.

That night as we drove, we had talked of many things, profound and mundane: music, art, school, girlfriends, the army, scuffling for food, etc. I was an only child and pretty much a loner; he was more oriented to a tribal way of looking at the world. He'd been playing guitar since age fifteen. I'd been playing trumpet since age fourteen but had given it up to study composition. I'd tried to parlay my trumpet chops into a seat in the Sixth Army Band and failed. He was offered the classic choice of the juvenile delinquent: jail or the army. He'd taken the obvious course and had just been discharged.

I knew I had discovered a kindred spirit, but he turned out to be much more; I didn't know then, or perhaps only suspected subconsciously, that I had found a brother.

Jerry was born in 1942, making him and me the only original members of the Grateful Dead over twenty-one when we started. He grew up in the Mission District of San Francisco, part of an extended family that spanned at least three generations, maybe four — Dad: Joe Garcia, a musician (saxes and woodwinds) and bandleader; Mom: Ruth Clifford Garcia, a hospital nurse; older brother: Clifford, also known as "Tiff." For the first few years of Jerry's life, the family summered in the mountains of Santa Cruz County, where at age four Jerry lost a finger in an axe-idental amputation.

After Jerry's dad, Joe, left the music business, he became partners with some friends and opened a hotel and restaurant on the site of what's now the Maritime Hall in Rincon Hill in San Francisco. The family was shattered by a cruel stroke of fate when Jerry was five: On a family vacation, Jerry watched from the shore as his father lost his footing and drowned in the Trinity River. Ruth sold their house to buy out the partners in the hotel, and Jerry and his brother went to live with their grandparents.

The hotel/restaurant/bar became very successful, and the remainder of the family, back together, moved to Menlo Park; Jerry attended all but one year of middle school there. The family moved back to San Francisco when Jerry was almost fifteen, and it was just about this time that he scored his first guitar — an electric, at that — as a gift from his mom. (Actually, it was an accordion, but Jerry persuaded Ruth to see the light and trade it for the guitar. Although I wonder, what if. . . . No. I dare not go there.)

The next summer, Jerry enrolled in an art program at what's now the San Francisco Art Institute, where he honed his drawing skills. He delighted in producing the most amazingly convoluted, multifaceted images — almost Escher-like, but at once more figurative and more abstract. He also spent time hanging with the Beats in North Beach and continuing to play guitar.

By his seventeenth summer, he was bored with school and began cutting classes. This lasted one semester, until Jerry, out of desperation, like so many kids his age, checked himself into the U.S. Army for a tour of duty at the Presidio of San Francisco. Jerry didn't fit well in the military mindset; after being AWOL more often than was acceptable, he was offered a discharge on a technicality: "not suited to the military lifestyle." O lucky man!

Leaving the army, he gravitated south to Palo Alto, where old friends and a place to stay awaited him; he had determined that he didn't want to go to school or to work. His goal was to goof off, and if your idea of goofing off is practicing the guitar all day and then playing in clubs at night, or raving all night with friends at the local coffeehouse and then going out to frolic in nature, he succeeded magnificently.

Once ensconced in Palo Alto, he had access to all the scenes that were just getting started: the Château, St. Mike's, Kepler's, the Peace Center. To pay the bills, Jerry found work as a guitar teacher. (One of his former students became my older son's fifth-grade teacher, who told the story about Jerry being so discouraged by this particular student's lack of progress that he excused himself to use the restroom, climbed out the window, and never returned. Patience was never one of Jerry's virtues.) He had also moved from folk to bluegrass to jug bands to electric blues to rock, taking from each just what he could use; he was a powder keg of influences jostling and elbowing one another — and the fuse had been lit. I drove back to Berkeley that night feeling really excited about having others hear this enormously talented artist.

I had to wait until the next Saturday to give Gert our tape; I was literally twitching with anticipation to hear what she thought. My hopes were raised even higher, though, when she came back the next week saying, essentially: Sure, he's welcome to come on the show, but this guy is so unique I'd like to do a ninety-minute special just on him. (Yes!) As soon as we could get it together, we gathered at the KPFA studios to make a tape for broadcast. I was in the engineering booth, rolling the tape; Jerry, Gert, and ten or so intimates were in the studio (Gert liked to have a live audience, even for prerecorded shows). Jerry was in really fine form; that session showcased his "public" persona: whimsical, diffident, humorously self-deprecating, full of great stories and zinging one-liners. So it went; he played a song, he and Gert talked a little about the song and related matters, then he played another song, and so on for about two hours. Gert and I then edited the tape down to fit the ninety-minute time slot, and the show was broadcast later that month in evening prime time as *"The Long Black Veil" and Other Ballads: An Evening with Jerry Garcia* — not an inauspicious debut for a guy who was, at that time, known only around Palo Alto and the San Francisco Peninsula.

Meanwhile, I had dropped out of school at Berkeley because I was not motivated enough to complete the academic requirements. Through the good auspices of T.C., I was able to audit the graduate-level composition class at Mills College, in Oakland, conducted by Italian composer Luciano Berio, one of the heroes of the classical avant-garde. It was a revelation to observe Berio at work; it didn't seem as if he was *teaching,* just going on about his work, his students learning as if by osmosis — mostly, though, he took us through analyses of twentieth-century masterworks, Stravinsky's *Rite of Spring* being the most memorable.

Toward the end of the school year, Mr. Berio was invited to be composer in residence at the Ojai Festival, a weekend of music new and old held in Ojai, near Santa Barbara. I had managed to make myself relatively indispensable by serving as sound mixer for Mills College performances of the newest electronic music (Stockhausen's *Gesang der Jünglinge,* Berio's *Thema {Omaggio á Joyce}*) and was invited along to mix the tape sections of Berio's *Differences,* a piece for chamber quintet and tape. The festival also presented a panel discussion featuring Berio and Milton Babbitt, who discussed, most amusingly, the problems of composition in the twentieth century. The highlight for me was an outdoor performance, in the Libby Amphitheater, of Mozart's Piano Concerto no. 25, conducted by Berio and played by Lucas Foss (who later would invite the Grateful Dead to perform improvisations with his orchestra, the Buffalo Philharmonic); the performance flowed like a limpid stream of melody, happily accompanied by some twenty or so birds perched in the trees surrounding the seats.

Just after I returned from Ojai, I was fortunate enough to hear a legendary performance by John Coltrane's new quartet at the Jazz Workshop in San Francisco. That night, the great guitarist Wes Montgomery, who had made his early reputation in the San Francisco scene, joined the band onstage. I stayed for both sets, and to this day I haven't heard a performance in any genre of music that came close to reaching the heights of that one. The band played pretty much continuously, with very few breaks, starting at a peak and climbing: The atmosphere in that funky little club literally turned golden. David Crosby told me a great story about seeing 'Trane one night at that same club; David had gone to the men's room, and as he was leaving, Coltrane ended his solo, left the bandstand, walked into a tiny room offstage, and stood there, *still playing* — all the way through the piano solo and into the reprise, when he returned to the band. That night confirmed, in spades, my earlier suspicions that improvised music could reach the heights and depths of the finest classical music, and transcend time and space.

After the KPFA sessions, I didn't see anyone from the Palo Alto scene for almost a year; T.C. and I had an opportunity to study composition informally with Mr. Berio in Europe, if we could only get there. Not an easy task for scuffling students, but T.C. came through again — his father was the captain of waiters at the Sands Hotel in Las Vegas; surely he could get us jobs for the summer so we could earn our passage. So off we went at the end of the school year, full of promise and hope. When we got to T.C.'s house, I was welcomed at first, but his mother, I soon found out, blamed me for the fact that her son was not going to become a scientist, but a musician. So I was unceremoniously ejected from the house in the middle of the night, with a trunk full of stuff and nowhere to go; luckily, an old friend of T.C.'s, Bill Walker, owned a house not far away. T.C. helped me carry my trunk, and we ended up knocking on Bill's door; he very kindly allowed me the use of his living room couch on an open-ended basis (gratis until I got a job), with the promise of a room when one opened up.

Naturally, the hotel job was out of the question, and after some weeks of increasingly fruitless job-hunting, I was forced to admit that I had no practical skills whatsoever, having failed to secure employment at various local industrial firms. I even hitched a ride seventy miles into the desert looking for work at Mercury, Nevada, the nuclear test site for the Department of Defense; I didn't get that job because I confessed to the interviewer that I'd have to hitchhike back and forth from Las Vegas. I turned to the post office; since the substation three blocks down the road from Walker's was hiring that week, I applied, took the Civil Service Exam, and presto! I was a full-fledged flunky of Big Government.

In an interesting premonition of things to come, I hadn't been able to afford a haircut since before leaving Berkeley, and at least two of my fellow employees took it upon themselves to remind me daily of the general unsuitability of long-haired males for any good at all: "Get a haircut!" "Who's that with the hair?" My feeble rejoinder: "Who's that with the mouth?"

Since I'd missed my chance to go to Europe, my goal became to earn enough money to get back to the Bay Area, where I would . . . I wasn't sure what, but I knew I had to get back there. After working through the fall at the post office, I got bored and switched jobs, becoming a keno teller at the Frontier Casino, home of the world's largest neon cowboy. I worked the graveyard shift six nights a week and thus was privileged to observe the nightmarish underbelly of the gambling culture at close range. It seemed as if only the most hopelessly addicted creatures shambled in late at night, usually carrying a sheaf of old keno tickets thick enough to choke a moose, leafing through them as they stood in front of my station mumbling distractedly, finally choosing one particular ticket and presenting it with a flourish: This is the one — I'm gonna win big tonight! Of course it never happened, but I would see the same pathetic souls over and over, night after night, always driven by the hope of the Big Score.

At age twenty-three, I had had just about enough of Las Vegas by the time spring came to the desert, even with the congenial atmosphere at Walker's. I had finally graduated from the couch to my own room, and was working on a big orchestral piece for 125 musicians and four conductors. So I quit my job, dumped my stuff into my old steamer trunk, and took a Greyhound bus to Palo Alto. Although I was planning to meet up with T.C. and Walker in San Francisco and find a place there, I was hoping to get a room at the Château for the summer. I got off the local bus and schlepped my trunk over to Kepler's; I was trying to manhandle my handicap through the door when two young women threw it open and raced off laughing down the street. A good omen, thought I, recognizing Joan Baez as one of the two. (Lucky she didn't trip over my trunk and break something.) As I'd hoped, there were several familiar faces in Kepler's, and I was able to score a lift up to the Château, where Hunter and John the Cool both had rooms; Jerry was living in the pump house by then.

I had saved some money from my employment in Vegas and was able to rent a room there. The scene was pretty much as I remembered it — lots of people coming and going at all hours of the day and night, intense discussions of deep subjects, parties every weekend —

only now I was part of it instead of just a weekend warrior. For the first time in my adult life, I felt really *at home,* sleeping in a little nook off the living room, while we all shared the bathrooms and kitchen and ate mostly fast food from downtown Menlo Park.

By this time Jerry's musical quest had taken him all the way from folk to bluegrass, the bebop of country music; he (on banjo) and Hunter (on bass) formed a hybrid trio with David Nelson, a guitarist from up the road apiece, and were playing at a new club called the Tangent as the Wildwood Boys. His banjo playing was a revelation to me — since I hadn't heard any bluegrass, my idea of the banjo was pretty much strummity-strum; there was Jerry, playing the most ex-hilarating stream of runs up and down the fret board, popping the notes out like tiny rivets, all at amazing speed and with crystalline clarity. He would walk around the Château in the afternoon playing the most astonishing shit — and *he never seemed to repeat himself.*

Around this time, John the Cool was dealing drugs out of his room, and people began visiting him sporadically at odd hours, notably a man of middle height in his early forties, who was what we'd now call "buff," but ruggedly so, with short hair, and usually dressed in jeans and a T-shirt. This was Neal Cassady — who was, I was told by John in hushed, reverent tones, the prototype of Jack Kerouac's road heroes Dean Moriarty, of *On the Road,* and Cody Pomeray, of *Visions of Cody* and *The Dharma Bums.* Neal was then working in a truck-tire facility in Los Gatos to support his wife and two kids. Some time later, John and I went to pick him up at work; it was amazing to watch him hump huge truck tires off the shelves, roll them two at a time to his station, pop them on rims as if they were bike tires, levitate the whole unit onto the wheel hub, and tighten down the wheel nuts — all in a blur of motion, he was moving so fast ("If a job's worth doing, it's worth doing well," my dad always told me; Neal was the living embodiment of that maxim).

I first experienced Neal's supersensory abilities when John and I rode with him up to San Francisco one day. Neal was driving an old Packard convertible, and we set off up the freeway only to run into early traffic for the Giants game at Candlestick Park. There were three lanes of bumper-to-bumper traffic, moving at a snail's pace if at all, a vast, sluggish river of varicolored metal oozing through a gorge, and sailing this river, steadily *moving* through traffic: our car, with Neal not only driving (magically weaving his way into postage-stamp-size holes in the flow), but carrying on conversations with everyone in the car *and* playing his signature game of Radio I-Ching. Radio I-Ching is played by constantly changing the radio station, not just to change the music played, but to illustrate a node or common thread in the several conversations occurring in real time. This has to be done from a state of "no mind"; if there's any thought put into it, we degenerate into mere channel-scanning. An example: We're on our way back that night, leaving an apartment house somewhere on Potrero Hill; Neal is hurtling this monster Packard down the hill, using all the lanes. We're doing at least fifty through little winding streets; when I force my heart out of my throat, I realize, This guy can *see around corners! He knows there are no cars coming!* Sure enough, just then, Neal hits the brakes and slides into the proper lane — and around the corner ahead comes a mail truck. Whew! Neal's now in full flight; we sail on down the hill toward the freeway, Neal's fingers dancing on the radio buttons. Fragments of music and speech flash by, interwoven with the rhythm of Neal's voice (it wasn't necessary for anyone to answer — Neal could hold up your end of the conversation as well as you could); suddenly, a familiar phrase comes through: the finale to Shostakovich's Fifth Symphony. Totally ignorant of protocol, I say, 'Hey, wait a minute, let's listen to that," but Neal's already moved on; he looks at me, shakes his head, and says, "Show tune, huh? Show-tune Phil." Well, that certainly put me in my place, but it still cracks me up that Neal mistook Shostakovich for a show tune.

The first of our bunch to marry was Jerry, as always the reluctant leader. He had met Sara in typical Garcia fashion, while carrying his guitar across the Stanford Shopping Center parking lot, en route to another shiftless day of pickin' and grinnin' down at St. Mike's; she was riding her bicycle en route from class to lunch, the epitome of the studious Stanford girl. He *hitches a ride on her bike,* and the rest is history. Sara was from a well-to-do family, and they spared no horses for the wedding of their little girl, although the sight of Jerry must have given them pause at first. The ceremony was held in church, with David Nelson as best man; but the real fun came at the reception, as the maids of honor and all of Sara's well-dressed friends and family hit the bar, slugging champagne as if it was the last day before Prohibition. Meanwhile, all of Jerry's scuzzy beatnik friends, myself included, descended on the heavily laden food tables like a plague of locusts of biblical proportions: Free food! And lots of it! The social polarity of the time was never so clearly delineated: The upper class drinks, the proletariat scuffles for bread.

The fun came to a screeching halt when we were told by Frank that he was going to sell the Château. Jerry and Sara had already moved into a place of their own and were soon to leave on a cross-country summer bluegrass tour; after the birth of their daughter, Heather, they would perform periodically in folk clubs around the area as Jerry and Sara. David Nelson and Bob Hunter found a house to share in Palo Alto; I moved to a rental room near the highway to finish the first draft of my big orchestra piece, and then temporarily shared a nice house in Palo Alto with my friend Page Browning. With the closing of the Château, the scene began to spread out and scatter; by the end of the summer I would be living in San Francisco.

By the late fall of 1963, I was more or less settled in a cottage-style house on Eureka Street, just west of Castro, in San Francisco. T.C. came back from Vegas to be my roommate. I had once again landed a part-time job at the post office, this time as a driver — my duty was to collect the rush-hour end-of-business mail from all the drop boxes up and down Market Street, with a detour up Van Ness (two of the busiest and most chaotic streets in the city).

I'd been working hard composing the final score of my big piece for four orchestras, entitled *Foci* (quasi-scientific or -mathematical titles and compositional paradigms were all the rage in the avant-garde at that time). The piece itself was composed spatially: I imagined the music rotating or sweeping around the audience with each orchestral group at a focus of an ellipse — the image was of planetary orbits, I guess. . . .

One brisk fall afternoon, I was walking down Castro Street to catch the N-Judah car to work. As I reached the intersection of Eighteenth Street, my eye was caught by a newspaper stand — screaming at me from the biggest headline I've ever seen are the words *MURDER OF THE PRESIDENT.* I fumbled a dime out of my pocket, grabbed the paper, and read the tragic news from Dallas: A sniper had killed President Kennedy during a political visit. Like many young people at the time, I was a huge admirer of our fallen leader; he had seemed to bring with him the promise of fresh approaches and a more flexible consciousness to the great issues of our age. As I rode to work, I wanted to shout at everyone, "What's the matter with you? Don't you know what's happened?"

Later that weekend, I saw for myself something of what it must have been like after Pearl Harbor in 1941 — people weeping openly on the street, gathered in groups arguing about the causes of it all, staring numbly at TV screens in bars and in store windows. On Saturday afternoon, I picked up the mail on Ellis Street; from inside the bar behind me came the most incongruous sound imaginable — the Funeral March from Beethoven's *Eroica* symphony. I dropped the bag and went in — flickering on the black-and-white screen: Leonard Bernstein and the New York Philharmonic playing that noblest of elegies for a fallen hero. That's when I lost it completely, as a wrenching sense of emptiness stabbed at my heart. Although I only sensed it vaguely at the time, my grief wasn't just for the passing of one man, but for the fact that the whole world I'd grown up in, the America that I loved and trusted, would never be the same again.

For the rest of the winter I toiled in a fog of depression and gloom. I was twenty-four years old, a college dropout with no girlfriend, working at a nowhere job, not making music of any kind. The Kennedy assassination had hit me hard, and I was feeling very much at loose ends. I was definitely in the proper frame of mind, looking for a change, anything, when one day after work I was handed a foil-wrapped cube by one of my coworkers. "Here ya go," he whispered. "Two hundred fifty mikes."

For some time, I had been hearing about magical substances that could open hidden realms of consciousness. Foremost among these were mescaline, a derivative of the peyote cactus *Lophophora williamsii,* and psilocybin, a derivative of the so-called magic mushrooms, *Psilocybe mexicana,* or *Stropharia cubensis.* None of your average disaffected youth or protohippies had access to any of these substances; they might as well have been growing on the moon. In my circle of friends, several books on the subject were widely popular: Aldous Huxley's *The Doors of Perception,* Gordon Wasson's *The Road to Eleusis,* and Alan Watts's *The Joyous Cosmology* — all of which only served to whet our appetites and anticipation. Then we began hearing rumors of a new "superdrug," LSD, in connection with the infamous Harvard psychologist Timothy Leary — who, together with his colleague Richard Alpert, had been dismissed from his professorship for allegedly providing this mysterious psychotropic drug to his students. Leary and Alpert had then moved to Mexico and founded an organization called the International Foundation for Internal Freedom (IFIF), which was dedicated to research and experimentation with all consciousness-expanding drugs.

I knew from my reading that 250 micrograms of LSD was a big dose; I decided on the spot to split the stuff, which was still legal at the time, with T.C., who had expressed interest. When I got back to Eureka Street, however, he wasn't home — then I remembered: He worked the swing shift. Well, I just couldn't wait to try this, so I carefully cut the cube in half, and down she went. I don't remember much after that, just a kaleidoscope of emotional peaks; at one point I found myself outside in the front yard on a beautiful starry night, conducting, with extravagant gestures, Mahler's great Tragic Symphony, which was blasting from the house. Since my wonderful first experience with Brahms at age four, I've found music to be, among many other things, a safety net, a lifeline that remains constant when all other mental constructs are in total Heraclitean flux.

So where were the hallucinations, the scary visions, the cosmic truths? I didn't find any of those levels until later. My guess is that I'd left more than half the dose behind in T.C.'s portion; judging from the expression on his face as I walked in the door the day he did his share, his experience was somewhat more ecstatic than mine had been.

For me and my friends, these drugs (pot, acid, the other "entheogens")[1] were seen as tools — tools to enhance awareness, to expand our horizons, to access other levels of mind, to manifest the numinous and sacred, tools that had been in use for thousands of years by shamans, by oracles, in the ancient mystery schools, by all whose mission was to penetrate beyond the veil of illusion. In short, these experiences were not embarked upon as an escape from "reality" — they were explorations into the super-real, voyages designed to bring a larger sense of reality back into human consciousness, which had become irredeemably bogged down in the material world.

It's been asserted from some quarters of traditional teaching that these experiences were artificially induced shortcuts to spiritual levels that were better attained through long and reverent spiritual work. That's partly true; however, I saw these visions as a sign that we were on the right track. After all, the drugs wouldn't let you *stay* there — you came back eventually to "reality" — but *knowing* that these levels of spirit existed inspired us to search out as many ways as we could to return to these exalted levels of awareness.

With my first psychedelic experience I had broken through my depression and was now ready to seek out less solitary forms of creative pursuit — and guess what? Things started happening. First, I ran into my Mills composition classmate Steve Reich, who at the time was driving a cab in San Francisco and working with the San Francisco Mime Troupe as musical director. The Mime Troupe was as classic an anarchist collective as ever was — a bunch of actors and far-left theorists dedicated to provocateur street theater, their productions of classic farces (such as Molière's *Tartuffe*), both in theaters and outside in the parks, were practically the only rays of light in the otherwise grim and gray cultural atmosphere of San Francisco at that time. Ronnie

---

[1] Albert Hoffman, R. Gordon Wasson, et al., "Manifesting the Divine Within," in *The Road to Eleusis* (New York: Harcourt Brace Jovanovich, 1978).

Davis, the director, and Saul Landau, the manager, were both committed activists of the left; their agenda was basically to put the Man up against the Wall. Two other members of the creative team would also make their mark — actor Peter Cohen, later known as Peter Coyote, and Herb Greene, a photographer who became a world-class portraitist on a par with Karsh or Avedon.

In a great stroke of luck for me, Steve asked if I was interested in writing something for a new music concert he was planning at the troupe's theater space on Capp Street. Of course I was, and I eventually turned out a piece of pretentious crap perfectly consonant with all the current avant-garde clichés. The best thing about it was the title: *6 & ⅞ for Bernardo Moreno,* and the best thing about *that* was the reaction of my parents. Mom, ever protective of her little darling: "Oh dear, I hope you're not hanging around with some pachuco." Dad: "What's that mean, hat size for a pinhead?"

Actually, the best thing about it was that I became involved with the troupe, essentially joining Steve in the music "department." Our function was to provide what little atmospheric music was needed in their bare-bones, no-frills productions; aside from that we could just fool around there with various ideas. Steve was just on the verge of a breakthrough in his compositional approach; in the next year he would emerge with a totally stripped down kind of musique concrète using overlapping rhythmic loops of taped voices, eventually becoming one of the postmodern era's most important and influential composers — the inventor of minimalism, some say. Right then, though, he was still heavily into improvised music, and even as we were taking the troupe's tape recorder around the city to record various sounds for the shows, we were lobbying Ronnie Davis for a chance to do some sort of improvisational music-theater piece. Just before Steve joined the troupe, they had put on a "happening" called Event I, so we decided to call this one Event III/Coffee Break (there was no Event II). The idea was to combine improvised dance/movement, lights, and music/sound to — to — tell a story? Channel our aggressions? *Épater les bourgeois?* Nobody knew. Nobody cared. We just wanted to throw all these elements together, *wail* with 'em, and see what happened. In retrospect, this event, the manifestation of a collective *unconscious,* served as the prototype for what became the Acid Test (at that time lacking, of course, the Main Ingredient), a manifestation of collective *consciousness.*

In fact, Event III was like a precognitive vision of the Tests — broad swaths of colored light sweeping through space; chaotic but hypnotic music (played by Steve, T.C., myself, and a great drummer from Oakland, Wahlee Williams); Ronnie Davis in a cop uniform descending from a ladder in grotesque, disjointed moves as I rise from a trapdoor playing "Twinkle Twinkle, Little Star" on trumpet. It was so crazy we might as well have been on acid. It was tremendous fun to work on that level with the troupe, but when their next production didn't need music, Steve moved on — and so did I.

Things continued to look up; one day when visiting Dennis, an old friend from the volunteer days at KPFA, I was introduced by his wife, Jeanne, to a vivacious brunette by the name of Ruth. She immediately intrigued me with her wide range of interests and her salty sense of humor, and I began hanging out at Dennis and Jeanne's place almost every day, hoping to connect with this fascinating female. It turned out that the three of them were also experimenting — with drugs that were new to me. In spite of my lack of knowledge about these drugs — amphetamines and barbiturates — I ignored my qualms about needles and joined in, admittedly not wanting Ruth to think I was chicken. I soon discovered that the drugs in question, far from being consciousness-expanding, were actually consciousness-diminishing, chaining my mind to the physical plane and making me grind my teeth and sweat profusely.

By this time I had formed my first real long-term relationship — with Ruth — and I eventually moved in with Dennis and Jeanne to be close to her. Even though she was nominally living at home, she would come over every day around midafternoon and hang with me before I went to work. After my shift, we would go out for burgers, or to a movie, to City Lights Books, or to concerts: We saw Bob Dylan in his legendary 1964 concerts with Joan Baez; we saw Ravi Shankar in one of his first Bay Area appearances; we saw Coltrane at the Jazz Workshop. Those should have been wonderful times, but bad drugs were casting a shadow over our lives. Luckily, I was occasionally able to score some acid for Ruth and myself; with those experiences to use as a contrast, I began slowly pulling her away from what I increasingly saw as a very negative scene.

My involvement with music had dwindled to almost nothing after the heady days with the Mime Troupe; oh, I would occasionally think about maybe composing something, or maybe going back to school to study conducting. That period wasn't a total loss, however, as I was introduced to the work of Bob Dylan by Dennis, who turned out to be an old leftist folkie at heart. Sometime around then I bought a transistor radio for the mail truck and began listening to AM radio, just because those were the only frequencies the little box would pull in. Imagine my delight, then, when one rainy night I'm cruising down Mission Street on my way to a mail pickup and I hear Bob Dylan! on AM radio! playing the raunchiest-sounding electric music and singing "Subterranean Homesick Blues"! How totally cool! I can't explain why this was so exciting to me; it just sounded so *righteous* coming out of that tinny little speaker all jungly and slithering. So I come home raving, and Dennis says, "Cool. Check this out," and he puts on *Bringing It All Back Home* — containing, of course, not only "Subterranean Homesick Blues," but five more electric Dylan songs and a side of acoustic stuff, including "Mr. Tambourine Man," thereby blowing my mind even farther out the door. Dennis also played a lot of blues on his monster stereo, so I was getting healthy doses of music I hadn't known a lot about before, especially the Beatles. Steve Reich and I were having coffee on Mission Street one night, and he made me listen to "She Loves You" and "I Want To Hold Your Hand" on the jukebox. They seemed a little bit too *clean* to me, especially compared to the Rolling Stones, whose album *12 x 5* had more grit to it, I thought.

Nineteen sixty-four rolled on, punctuated by the occasional acid trip, with Ruth, at the beach or in Golden Gate Park (the perfect place to relive my earlier stage of evolution as a three-toed sloth) — then one afternoon, on a whim, I went to see a new movie opening up on Polk Street, featuring those same Beatles. I wanted to see just how clean they really were. On the way into the theater, I noticed that there were a lot of teenage girls going to the movie — on a school day. When I got to my seat, it looked as if I was the only male in the place. Hmmm . . . I settled back in my seat, and bang! with that first wide-open suspended chord that opens the title song, "Hard Day's Night," the screen flashed on and we were off — until the screaming started. It hit me like a big soft pillow at about nine hundred miles an hour and never let up until the last credits had faded. Mostly louder than the soundtrack, it would ebb and flow, reaching a peak when one of the four fab mop-tops had a close-up ("Paauuul!" "Geeoooorrrge!") and receding into a dull roar when none of them were on the screen. It was like floating on pink clouds of raw hormonal anguish; at one point in the film there's a scene where the Beatles are performing for TV before an audience composed entirely of young girls. The audience in the theater was screaming at the Beatles *and* at the audience in the film screaming at the Beatles. When I walked out of that theater, I felt as if I'd been granted a vision, a vision of, of . . . I didn't know for sure, but the first thing I did when I got home was to take a shower and comb my hair forward over my forehead, in homage to the phenomenon. Besides, I thought it looked pretty cool. Not so my roommate Dennis, who took every opportunity to give me shit about it, even going so far as to escort people into my room while I was sleeping, transfixing me with the beam from a big flashlight and sucking them in with the come-on: "Want to see a blond Beatle?" Luckily, Ruth loved my new do, so at the tender age of twenty-four I became one of the first long-haired freaks in San Francisco. I got some strange looks at work, but the good old San Francisco laissez-faire spirit prevailed, and there were, at first, no repercussions from management — until, after reporting to work one day, I got the word that the postmaster wanted to see me.

— "The Postmaster? of San Francisco? Oh, right, he wants to give me the Employee of the Month Award."

— "I'm serious, the PM wants to see you in his office."

Off I go, uptown to the old Federal Building; I'm directed to the office of — oh, well, the assistant postmaster (No award? Bummer . . .). It turns out that someone has written a letter of complaint to the postmaster general — of the United States! — about my hair! I make noises of disbelief — and I'm shown a neatly handwritten two-page missive; leaping out at me are the words *disgraceful sight, traditions of the U.S. mail,* and *UNKEMPT MONKEY.* I sputter with inarticulate resentment and receive the Word from on high: Get a friggin' haircut, will ya?

All right already, so I got a haircut, and believe me, there weren't any barbers this side of swinging London that knew how to cut hair the way I needed it cut, so the result was a shaggy mess. The crowning indignity of the whole affair: Inside of two weeks I was invited back uptown, and this time the postmaster himself made it known in no uncertain terms that my hair still wasn't short enough — and that, by my own choice, was my last day at the post office. I didn't even ask if there had been another complaint; I just quit on the spot. Very satisfying, if perhaps a tad precipitous.

In spite of the loss of my job, things continued to improve. Ruth started working at the post office as a clerk, and Tom Purvis, a friend from the Mime Troupe, had invited me to share a flat in a big Victorian at 1130 Haight Street at Baker, right across from Buena Vista

Park. Ruth and I moved in there together, finally freeing ourselves from the doldrums in Needle Park.

The Haight at that time was just beginning to see the influx of hipsters and tripsters that would later culminate in the notorious Summer of Love — but at that time (early '65), it was just a pleasant neighborhood in which to live — smack up against Golden Gate Park and Twin Peaks, with a few blocks of stores and restaurants, and, most important, lots and lots of old Victorian houses that had been divided into flats, one for each floor. On any brisk spring evening we could wander through the residential areas listening to the wonderful variety of music drifting down to the street from open apartment windows; in the course of a single block, one might hear Bob Dylan, Miles Davis, Joan Baez, the Beatles, John Coltrane (and on one memorable occasion, Bach's monumental Mass in B Minor), all blending in a most delightful polyphony of musics. Looking back, it seems as though this experience was a metaphor for the community as yet unborn, the "mingled measure" of which Coleridge speaks so eloquently in his poem "Kubla Khan," promising a rebirth, through music, of spirit and shared awareness of our common humanity.

Meanwhile, persistent rumors had been drifting up from Palo Alto: Garcia and Pigpen had formed an electric blues band with some members of their old jug band and a local rhythm section. For someone like me, who didn't practice music currently but for whom music was still a major force in life, this seemed to be a very exciting development. I couldn't wait to hear Jerry play electric guitar. Judging from what I remembered of his banjo-playing, he would bring a unique perspective to the instrument — and to the music. Ruth and I decided one weekend to cruise on down and check it out; when we arrived, we found that the gig was over, but surprise! there *was* a party. The festivities were in full swing when we walked in the door: clumps of people against the walls, surrounding a roomful of dancers gyrating and swaying to the Rolling Stones, and a constant stream of folks in and out of the kitchen, where the host was holding forth with several jugs of cheap wine. I found Jerry in a corner, talking to the host; he was waiting for his "guitar player" to fall by with some weed. We sat down together with cups of the omnipresent cheap red wine, and I launched into a spontaneous spiel about the Stones and how listening to their song "The Last Time" got me interested in the bass guitar; at the time, I was thinking more about writing for it than playing it. What Jerry told me was that the sound on the record I'd thought was the bass guitar, because it had such weight, was actually played on an electric guitar. Oops.

Just then the word came over: Bobby's here — meet him in the car. We traipse out to the street, where I'm introduced to a baby-faced kid who couldn't be much older than — twelve? Fourteen? But wow, did he have some killer dope; we sat in the car and smoked up a storm, and I learned that Bob Weir was seventeen, still a student at Menlo-Atherton High School, and had been one of Jerry's guitar students before he joined Jerry's jug band, playing mostly jug and washtub bass; he had progressed so far and so fast on guitar that he was now the rhythm guitarist in the new band, called the Warlocks. I remember being thoroughly charmed by Bob's deadpan sense of humor; he also did a sidesplitting Neal Cassady impression.

Bobby was the youngest of the originals, born in 1947 to a single mother and adopted soon after birth by Frederick and Eleanor Weir. Frederick was a very successful engineer and businessman; Eleanor a homemaker.

Bob grew up with two siblings: older brother John, and Wendy, his younger sister. They spent lots of time outdoors in and among the trees of Atherton; Bob remembers the place as a huge sunny oak forest, almost like the Sherwood of legend. Funny he should say that — it sounds very similar to the place where I grew up, although mine was more a "dark romantic chasm," with a forest sloping into a gorge, at the bottom of which flowed a creek.

The first of his generation expelled from both preschool and the Cub Scouts, our hero manifested an irreverent attitude from an early age, especially regarding the various compromises and adjustments required by society. A spinal meningitis infection left him with his psychic edges permanently rounded off, and with the feeling that maybe life is too short to waste not having fun. I think he's proud of his school record, too: expelled from every school except the last, which he quit. (That's not to say that Bob wasn't a good student; dyslexic or not, you can't play the guitar and compose music if you won't *learn*.)

The only athlete among the five originals, he excelled at track and football, which has been his sport ever since. A rabid 49ers fan, he's working out even as I write this with his football team, the Chiefs, for their amateur league championship. Bob's the quarterback: He looks! He throws! Touchdown! General pandemonium from the gallery.

Ahem. Bob's first instrument was piano; however, his parents encouraged him to try another instrument after he'd spent hours one afternoon obsessing at full volume on the same hammered pattern of chords. Then he tried trumpet (how weird would it have been if he and I had met when we both played trumpet?), but that wasn't right either — too loud in the house, too loud outside. But guitar — now there was an instrument worth pursuing. Like the piano, you could do it all yourself — melody, harmony, the lot. Besides, it was so portable and intimate, perfect for cozy surroundings (one guitarist, one cheerleader — shake and serve).

After going through a few middle and high schools in California, Bobby was sent to Fountain Valley School in Colorado, where he met lifelong friend and future songwriting collaborator John Barlow. Bobby and John were kindred spirits, and their antics became legendary — the Great Biology Lab Frog-Parts War being foremost among their accomplishments. Faced with a choice — one of you can come back, but not both — John and Bob spent the summer on

John's family ranch in Wyoming and then parted, John returning to Colorado and Bob to Atherton, where at Pacific High School his curriculum was "guitar and girls."

Moving on to Menlo-Atherton High School after the usual dustup, we find Bobby with "bigger fish to fry" than high school classes or social entanglements: He was actively involved in the pursuit of music, searching out the best local practitioners of blues and folk guitar, notably Jorma Kaukonen, who played locally, and Jerry Garcia, then teaching at Dana Morgan's Music in Palo Alto. With these kinds of connections, it wasn't long before Bob was playing washtub bass and jug in Mother McCree's Uptown Jug Champions, a jug-band collective that also included Jerry and Pigpen.

Back at the party, Bob had to split, it being a school night. We took Jerry's share of the lid back inside, and the rest of the evening passed in a pleasant haze. I do remember being dragged away from the dance floor by Ruth, who reminded me that we had to get back to San Francisco early the next day so she could go to work — at the post office, where she'd started after I quit.

For the next few weeks, we heard nothing from down south, but then the word came in — the Warlocks were playing Fridays and Saturdays at a pizza joint in Menlo Park called Magoo's. Ruth and I scored a ride down for Saturday — the night that was to change my life forever.

The band was in full swing as we approached the door, and so were we. The music was so loud, even outside, and the groove so compelling, that I just *had* to dance. In the door we danced, only to be blown back against the wall by the loudest music I'd ever heard. The band was set up right in the front and separated from the side wall by only the width of the door; we had to fight our way through an almost palpable sea of sound, only to be informed by some fans that there was No! Dancing! Allowed! — something about a permit. This put a damper on our fun for about five seconds, and we all squeezed into a booth to listen. The band finished the rocker that they'd been dis-membering as we came in and started out on a slow blues that I rec-ognized from a Stones album — "I'm a King Bee." When Pig came in with the vocal, I had to look away; it was just so *sexual* — the sound of his voice over the mike delivering slithery insinuations and promises of pleasures beyond comprehension — and when he took a harp lead (backed by Jerry, in a call-and-response pattern), it absolutely ate my mind: Whew, these guys never sounded like *this* at all those parties! What was new, of course, was electricity: Amplification of instru-ments and voices enabled nuances that once would have been lost in the noise floor to be clearly heard and developed further in a seem-ingly infinite progression. I didn't have much time to contemplate those kinds of thoughts; the band went into another rocker, and I spasmodically leaped up from my seat and twitched around the very narrow aisle between the booths and the wall — until I felt a hand de-scend none too gently on my shoulder. This time it was the manager himself: "You can't dance in here!" Oh, all right, already; but by this time the band had finished their set, and Jerry dragged me away and sat me down in a booth, with an uncharacteristically serious look on his face. "Listen, man, I want you to come and play bass in this band. The guy we have can't cut it; we have to tell him what notes to play. I know you're a musician — you can pick up this instrument so easy." At first, I didn't know quite how to respond — this was so out of the blue — of course I'd forgotten about our conversation at the party just a few weeks previously, and to this day I'm not sure whether or not that was a factor in Jerry's offer. Needless to say, he didn't have to twist my arm very hard; having been at loose ends for so long, I was tremen-dously excited, as I'd been waiting subconsciously for some opportu-nity to get back into music on any level at all. Besides, I *knew* I could learn the instrument, and even play it differently than I had so far heard it being played (something I instinctively knew had to happen, given Jerry's unique approach to music); even so, I had to have at least one condition: "OK, man, I'll do it, but I want you to give me a lesson." "A lesson?" "Yep, just one lesson, so I'll have a good idea of the fundamentals." "Sure — come on over to my house after the gig and you got it."

During the second set, I was doing some furiously concentrated listening, trying to perceive the relationships between the various roles — rhythm section, lead guitar, rhythm guitar, voice — and trying to figure out what I could do to fit in in a creative way, no small challenge given the rapport that Bob, Jerry, Pig, and their drummer, Billy Kreutzmann, had already developed. Billy and I didn't meet that night, but he remembers me sitting up front, being "in the band on an energy level." It turns out that Jerry, after our conversation at the party, had actually mentioned me to Bobby right before the gig at Magoo's, saying that he knew someone who could learn the bass fast, a musician, and *he's going to be here tonight.* How could he have known? We had just spontaneously decided to go down late that afternoon.

After the gig I fell by Jerry's little house in Palo Alto. Sara and their baby, Heather, were sleeping, so he and I sat quietly in the living room, where Jerry gave me my lesson: "See this guitar, man? The bottom four strings on the guitar are tuned the same as the four strings of the bass, so borrow a guitar from somebody and practice scales on it until you can get down here and we'll start rehearsing." "That's it?" "That's all you need." It's hard to imagine it being a conscious thought on his part, but it was almost as if he didn't want to influence the way that I approached the instrument, so that I could come to it with only my own preconceptions as baggage. Naturally, as soon as I got back I borrowed a guitar from my roommate, Tom Purvis (who also gave me a very sound piece of advice: Never play an open string unless you really *mean* it), and started with the scales.

It's sobering to contemplate the many events and encounters that lead to such a pivotal moment in one's life. Singly, they seem almost random, and they could have resolved differently. Seen as a sequence, they can evoke the indifferent majesty of predestination. I didn't know or care if this trip would last more than a week — I was going to give it all I had while it lasted.

In June 1965 I'd moved down to Palo Alto to Answer the Call. Jerry had already set up a rental room for me in a communal house until my girlfriend, Ruth, could move down. We needed to get me an instrument pretty quickly. Bob and Jerry were now teaching at Guitars Unlimited in Menlo Park, a large storefront full of guitars with a rehearsal room in the back. There, I found a Gibson EB-1 electric bass (1 meaning one "pickup"), that I (or rather Ruth, who was employed at the time and extraordinarily supportive) could afford. I always had a love-hate relationship with that bass; the neck was like a telephone pole, the strings weren't individually adjustable for height, and the one pickup seemed to be in the wrong place. On the other hand, it was a short-scale instrument, easy to play, and when I later replaced the Gibson pickup with a pair of Guild Humbuckers, the little guy developed a rich pear-shaped tone that really worked well in recording.[1]

Now that I had an instrument, we went back to the rehearsal room, where all the gear was set up. Old equipment boxes were stacked along the walls, leaving just enough space for the drums, organ, and four amps. A modicum of daylight filtered in through the high windows as

---

[1] I play this instrument on David Crosby's album *If I Could Only Remember My Name.*

Jerry turned on the lights and we crowded into the center of the room. Pig stomped out his cigarette and ran some scales on his organ as Bob, with a distant look in his eyes, tuned up his guitar, and Billy, nattily dressed as always, sat ramrod straight at his drums and rattled off a few warm-up flourishes. I plugged in my bass, for the first time, and tentatively plucked a few notes. *Hmm, doesn't sound quite right. Time to see what these knobs actually do. Let's see — more bass, less treble, more mid — there, that's better.* My mental image of the bass sound was mainly conditioned by the sound of the acoustic bass, as it was played both in jazz and in symphony orchestras: a deep, fundamental tone, colored by upper harmonics. I started playing with a pick at first, as that's how I'd been practicing on guitar. I later tried playing with my fingers but reverted to the pick most of the time.

We were all playing on borrowed amps at the time, and it would be several months and a few gigs until we would score some of our own, thanks to the generosity of Jerry's mom. I wasn't particularly nervous, just excited and eager to experience this music myself, mainly because everyone in the band was still learning his instrument. For example, even though Jerry was a banjo and acoustic guitar virtuoso, he was a relative newcomer to the electric guitar.

I had some experience with small groups from high school and college — Dixieland quintets, fraternity dance bands playing fifties hits, bop combos — but always as a trumpeter, the lead voice. Now I needed to become the foundation, along with the drummer, of the unfolding of time through which music manifests out of silence. In some ways, that role is more interesting than the lead voice, because the bassist cogenerates not only rhythm, but the nature and the rate of harmonic motion,[2] so that the archetypal character of the music is clearly defined.

---

[2] This can be done not only by playing the root note, but also by changing the root in context, and also by playing scales, modes, or other melodic patterns.

I hadn't been paying close attention to the bass when listening to jazz, although I was familiar with heroes like Scott LaFaro and Charlie Mingus — but upon reflection, their playing styles didn't seem appropriate for this music. At the time, there weren't really any rock bass players as such. Any models in popular music came from Motown, whose house bassist, James Jamerson, influenced *everybody,* or from James Brown's band. The Beatles were sui generis — no one could channel McCartney without sounding like a copycat, so I didn't even try. The Stones as a band were influential, but I could never make out from the records what Wyman was doing, so I was essentially left to my own devices. When I heard Jack Casady with Jefferson Airplane the next year, playing lead and bass at the same time, it confirmed my instinct: Play what's right for the context.

Curiously enough, I had once asked my college friend Lenny Lasher, himself an inspiring bassist, to teach me a little bass "as a second instrument." He gave me an owlish glance and calmly replied, "I would never teach anyone the bass as a second instrument." Now, as a bassist myself, I had to learn a new skill: to hear the whole, not just my part. As a lead voice, my concern had always been for my own part to be as interesting and well played as possible; on top of that sacred duty there was now the responsibility of providing a framework for others to build on, a support network for synergy.

I asked to start with "I Know You Rider," a traditional song I'd loved when I heard Jerry do it as a folkie, because I knew I could remember the chords (only five) and I wanted to try singing three-part harmonies. Jerry and Bob ran me through the form (twenty-four bars repeated ad infinitum), while Pig wrote out the words. We all tuned up, Jerry counted off the intro, and away we went. It turned out that the rest of the band hadn't been playing the song that long themselves, so even though I missed a few chord changes, I didn't feel too badly — after all, I had fewer notes to play per bar than either of the guitarists, and everyone was very tolerant of my mistakes. The hardest part was singing and playing at the same time. To sing accurately, expressively, and in tune while complementing the vocal line with rhythmic accents *and* keeping the groove flowing is truly a black art.

The next tune was easier for me, since I didn't have to sing — Pigpen looked out at me from under his battered old cowboy hat and called "I'm a King Bee," the snaky old Muddy Waters blues I'd heard him sing at Magoo's. This particular blues is based on three chords and a major scale with flattened third, fifth, and seventh notes — a scale familiar to me from some of the jazz charts I'd played in college. The tricky part was learning the harmonic implications of the "turn-arounds" — the altered cadences that take place over a nominal tonic chord. I started out just playing the root notes, but as we went through the tune, Pig would emphasize the upcoming deviations with a look or a nod, and soon I was able to figure them out. The best part was hearing Pig's addition to the lyrics — there were only three original verses, all of which were fairly similar, starting with "Well, I'm a king bee, baby." We used Pig's new verse as the grand climax of the song, after some blistering solos by Jerry and Pig (on harp). It cracked me up the first time I heard it: "Pull my car up in yo' drive-way, turn my lights *waaaayyy* down low/Pull my car up in yo' drive-way, turn my lights waaaayy down low/I'm gonna wind up yo' transmission, *'till yo' motor won't run no more!*"

We played for about seven hours that first day. I was so excited about playing an electric instrument, and with this band, that I didn't sleep at all that night; it felt as though the electricity flowing through the instrument had permanently amped up my aura to a new intensity.

The next day, we went at it again, going over and over the fairly small number of tunes the band had already learned. I found myself looking forward intensely to each day's work, knowing that I could always make my part better, or more interesting, or more expressive of the tune itself.

So I settled into a routine of playing music with the band — all day, every day. I mean, what better did I have to do? Besides, it was the most exciting musical challenge I'd ever faced, including composing for orchestras — I had to play new ideas without thinking, based solely upon context and expressive intent, and there was no space for reflection or revision. Except, of course, when I made a mistake: After playing a wrong note, for instance, I would quickly resolve it to a proper note — but then I took to repeating my mistakes (a simple matter, since the music was built out of repeating modules, or strophes) in order to resolve them differently each time. I soon began to see the dissonances caused by wrong notes, or right notes in the wrong place, as opportunities rather than liabilities — new ways to create tension and release, the lifeblood of music. This approach was to bear strange and wonderful fruit over the next five years of the band's development.

In my role as the new guy, it became my duty to get Pigpen out of bed for rehearsal every day. He still slept at his parents' house in Palo Alto (he actually lived at St. Mike's or the blues clubs in East Paly); we would drive by every afternoon in one of our two cars (Jerry's Corvair or Billy's station wagon). Pig was always asleep when we got there, no matter what time it was. His bedroom window was on the ground floor by the driveway, and on a typical morning the procedure was: Knock on the window. Wait. Knock again. Wait. Start talking. "Hey, Pig. Come on, man. Wake up now." Knock again. Wait. The curtain is pulled back just enough for an *eye* to peer around it. The curtain drops back. Shuffling and snuffling from within. The window slides open and Pig crawls out fully dressed, hat and all; we pile into the car, cruise for burgers, and head to the rehearsal room. This is what went down most days; every so often I would have to crawl in after him just to make sure he was awake.

Pig was born Ronald Charles McKernan in 1945 to Phil McKernan, a boogie-woogie piano player, and his wife, Esther. Phil went into radio after his son was born, working into the fifties as a rhythm-and-blues DJ named "Cool Breeze." He later became an engineer at Stanford Research Institute (SRI), now a freelance think tank operating out of Stanford University.

Ron soon followed his dad into the world of Afro-American music and culture; after the age of twelve or so, he could nearly always be found in East Palo Alto at one of the blues clubs — Popeye's, the Anchor — where he was not only accepted, but well-regarded. One night I went with a friend down to the Anchor to hear a local blues artist; a couple of white kids, we didn't dare go in unless Pig, our sponsor, was with us. But Pig never got there, and eventually we just chickened out and went home.

He cultivated a biker image, but he was more the Marlon Brando–*Wild Ones* sensitive, brooding type. But funkier, way funkier — for example, he had a leather shirt that I saw him wear every day I knew him; if it had ever left his side, it could have outrun a small horse. This was "Blue Ron": picking up some licks from Garcia here, playing in a band with Kreutzmann there, learning guitar, organ, and harmonica, or mouth harp.

Never was Pigpen more at home than with a bottle of wine and a guitar, at home or at some party, improvising epic blues rant lyrics, playing Lightnin' Hopkins songs, and doing Lord Buckley routines like "The Nazz" and my personal favorite, "God's Own Drunk." For him, joining the Mother McKree jug band with Bob and Jerry was just a small step away from what he did anyway, and a pleasantly anarchic environment for mindless fun to boot.

Some say that it was Garcia's idea to turn Mother McChree's into an electric blues band, but Garcia told me it was Pigpen's idea. At first he wanted to electrify the jug band, but then changed his mind, saying, "No, let's get a drummer and make it a blues band." When the band turned into the Grateful Dead, Pig became our keel, our roots, our fundamental tone; even in the midst of the most free-flying storm-racked howling madness no-mind improvisational waveforms, Pig had but to step to the mike and sing — "I went down . . . to see the gypsy woman . . . one day, oh, no . . ." or — "without a warnin, you broke my heart" — and the whole band would *snap* into the groove like the crack of a whip, and we'd be Back Home, rolling like "Otis on a Shakedown Cruise." Pig was the perfect front man for the band: intense, commanding, comforting; but I don't think he enjoyed doing that quite as much as sitting on a couch with a guitar and a jug.

After about two weeks of rehearsal, we somehow managed to land a gig for two nights at a place in Hayward, California, called Frenchy's Bikini-A-Go-Go. Magoo's, unfortunately, had discontinued live music because people just wouldn't stop dancing! So we packed all the gear into Bill's station wagon and drove over there on a Friday night for our first performance as a band.

If I remember correctly, there were about three people there that first night, two of whom were Sue Swanson and Connie Bonner, our faithful friends and first fans. The performance was a little stilted. At least I remember thinking: It feels so wooden, as if we were puppets being controlled by different people instead of manifesting the singular group mind that we later became. Aside from that, the music itself was unmemorable — we probably played the same set twice, as our repertoire at the time was severely limited.

The best part of the story, however, came the following night when we returned for (so we thought) our second show. We discovered that not only had our gear been moved offstage, but we had been replaced without notice by three elderly men — playing clarinet, upright bass, and accordion! ("Shades of the Nairobi Trio," whispered Jerry.) We were so humiliated that we just loaded up our stuff and left — without even asking for the first night's pay.

After that debacle, we threw ourselves into rehearsals with a vengeance, feeling, not without some justification, that we hadn't been *that* bad at Frenchy's — we just hadn't been what the management wanted. Although we did ask ourselves, What kind of place would replace *anything* with three wizened clowns playing clarinet, upright bass, and accordion? Who would pay to listen to that? Dance to it? Right?

So, back to the woodshed (the back of the music store; this was before garages) to learn more tunes, to learn our instruments better, and to learn, above all, how to play together, to entrain, to become, as we described it then, "fingers on a hand."

For more than two months we played together every day, and I can't exaggerate the importance of this experience. The unique organicity of our music reflects the fact that each of us consciously personalized his playing: to fit with what others were playing and to fit with who each man was as an individual, allowing us to meld our consciousnesses together in the unity of a group mind.[3] After rehearsal Jerry and Billy, who were both married with children, would go home to their families. Pig would head out to the blues clubs, and Bobby would go home to sleep before another day of high school.

One morning, Jerry and I were paid a visit by Bob's mother. Mrs. Weir, a gray-blond, slender woman with patrician features, was concerned about her son's education. It turned out that Bobby wasn't going back to Menlo-Atherton High School for his senior year. He had been asked to leave the public school system for having an "irreverent attitude." His parents, bowing to the inevitable, had enrolled him at Drew High School in San Francisco. The long and short of it was that if Jerry and I promised to make *sure* that Bob got to school *every day,* and that he got home all right after the gigs, she would allow him to remain in the band.

---

[3]For us, the philosophical basis of this concept was articulated by the science-fiction writer Theodore Sturgeon in his novel *More Than Human,* wherein the protagonists each have a single paranormal talent — telepathy, psychokinesis, teleportation — and are joined by a quadruple paraplegic who acts as a central processing unit. The process by which they become one is called "bleshing," from a combination of *mesh* and *blend.* (Today's archetype would be the X-Men.)

We promised. We swore mighty oaths. We somehow convinced her that we would indeed see that he got to school every day. In San Francisco. At 8:00 a.m.

Almost as soon as Mrs. Weir closed the door, Bobby himself knocked and entered, asking, "So, what did my mom want?" We sat him down in Jerry's big easy chair, perched ourselves on the arms, and, waving our hands in an incantatory manner, chanted, "Finish school, Bob! Finish school!" For the first few months of the school year, thanks to First Fan Sue Swanson and her '63 Pontiac "George," he actually got to school (if only to catch up on sleep) and did fairly well — for someone who was playing in clubs until 3:00 a.m.

We played three forgettable gigs in our local area, at clubs called the Fireside, Big Al's, and the Cinnamon-A-Go-Go. Things looked up a little when we scored a "house band" gig at a place called the In Room, across the tracks in Belmont, where we could play five nights a week. This sounded ideal to us because we had been slowly evolving a style of playing that was more extended than what was then, and now, considered by some musicians and all industry types to be the norm in rock music, even though the music that now defines that term was just then being born.

My approach to the bass had solidified fairly quickly. I soon reached a saturation point with the prevalent style of bass playing, which was to stick to the root and always play on the downbeat. (The old joke goes: What's the bass player thinking? EEEE, DDDD, AAAAAAAA, repeated ad infinitum.) I wanted to play in a way that heightened the beats by omission, as it were, by playing around them, in a way that added harmonic motion to the somewhat static chord progressions of the songs we were playing then. I wanted to play in a way that moved melodically but much more slowly than the lead melodies sung by the vocalists or played on guitar or keyboard. Contrast and complement: Each of us approached the music from a different direction, at angles to one another, like the spokes of a wheel.

I didn't have a practice amp at home, so I really was learning on the job, and we spent so much time playing together, in rehearsal and at gigs, that there wasn't time to practice by myself. When we weren't rehearsing, we'd drop acid and frolic around the woods behind Stanford, coming down just enough by gig time to play.

We had also started to collaborate on some original material, since the general consensus was that we'd never evolve very far if we just kept covering other people's stuff. We had learned a lot from listening to the Rolling Stones, going so far as to cover some of their covers, and Bob Dylan's songs were a major source of inspiration, as well as material for our sets. Songs like "Mindbender," "The Only Time Is Now," and "I Can't Come Down" were our first essays in collective originality. Alas, all of them were embarrassingly amateurish, so they didn't last long in the repertoire.

The gig at the In Room (don't you just *love* these names?) took place during the band's most intense and rapid development to date. We started off with a two-week run, which was later extended to six weeks total. Playing five nights straight, five sets a night, we continued our explorations in scaling up our material in order to, to paraphrase Coltrane,[4] "get it all in." We started to feel like a band, as opposed to a collection of individuals, as if we were onto something unique, something that hadn't existed previously in music. The band became more confident — and played louder. We learned to trust each other — and played longer. We learned to make music out of feedback, out of noise, if you will — and the walls melted (or so it seemed).

Our performances, however, became more coherent and focused, even as we expanded our musical time-scale. It was at the In Room that we first played one song for an entire forty-five-minute set — in

---

[4] A possibly apocryphal anecdote — Miles to 'Trane: "How come you play so long?" 'Trane replies: "Takes that long to get it all in."

this case "In the Midnight Hour," the Wilson Pickett R & B classic. We had started out by expanding tunes through extended solos, mainly to make them last longer since there were so few of them. However, the longer the solo, the less interesting it became to play the same material as background, so those of us who weren't soloing began to vary and differentiate our "background" material, almost as if we were also soloists, in a manner similar to jazz musicians. A good example of this technique is our version of the old Noah Lewis jug band tune "Viola Lee Blues," a traditional prison song. We electrified the song with a boogaloo beat and an intro lick borrowed from R & B artist Lee Dorsey's "Get Out of My Life Woman," and after each of the three verses, we tried to take the music *out* further — first expanding on the groove, then on the tonality, and then both, finally pulling out all the stops in a giant accelerando, culminating in a whirlwind of dissonance that, out of nowhere, would slam back into the original groove for a repetition of the final verse. It was after a run-through of this song that I turned to Jerry and remarked ingenuously, "Man — this could be *art!*"

In pursuit of this ideal, I urged the other band members to listen closely to the music of John Coltrane, especially his classic quartet, in which the band would take fairly simple structures (the show tune "My Favorite Things," for example) and extend them far beyond their original length with fantastical variations, frequently based on only one chord.

During this period I got to know Billy Kreutzmann a little better. When we were first learning tunes right and left, both Pig and Billy always knew where to find the coolest black music on the radio. Billy's dad, Bill Senior, had been an avid listener to KDIA, an R & B station in Oakland, even before Bill Jr. was born in 1946. Billy's mom was a dance teacher at Stanford. Early on she enlisted Billy as her drummer, counting the beats on an old drum while she created choreography for her students.

Drum lessons began at around age twelve, but Billy didn't really start *learning* the instrument until he began private study with Lee Anderson, a graduate physicist and jazz drummer. Lee also introduced him to a different level of aesthetic awareness, living as he did on Perry Lane, across the street from Kesey and Vic Lovell. I often wonder if Billy and I ever crossed paths there without knowing it.

During periods of parental disharmony, the drums gave Billy an outlet for some very strong feelings. When relations became too tense at home, Billy was shipped away to school in Arizona. His drums arrived just in time to save his sanity; daily practice gave him perhaps his only sense of stability.

Back at Palo Alto High School, Billy was recruited to play in bands such as the Legends (R & B, with uniforms) and the Zodiacs (rock 'n' roll/blues, with Garcia on bass and Pigpen). He married his girlfriend, Brenda, and fathered a child, Stacey, while still in high school; he supported them by selling wigs by day and teaching drums at night at Dana Morgan's Music. It was only natural for Jerry and Pig to tap Billy for the drum chair in the Warlocks — his fluid and open sense of time made him the perfect candidate for an electrified jug/ blues band, and he *swung like crazy,* even when playing old folk songs, in the new band.

When we started the band, Billy seemed really straight, locked in to the family-provider role. As we played more together, and as acid and music did their work, we all began to see another Billy emerge: the prankster leprechaun of the drums. He would drum irrepressibly on my shoulder as he sat behind me in Jerry's car, while chanting "Red Rab-bit! Red Rab-bit!" the name of the twenty-four-hour Automat-style fast-food kiosk we'd always hit on the way back from the In Room, all of us nearly fainting from the munchies.

His first love was jazz, though; and the unique flexibility of his time and the looseness of his swing made it a sheer delight to play with him from the very first bar. In fact, it became clear almost from the beginning that what we were doing wasn't rock music (even if we could have defined that) *or* jazz *or* blues — it was some kinda genre-busting rainbow polka-dot hybrid mutation.

At the end of our tenure at the In Room, we were more than ready to move on. The music had developed, some promoters had come to see us, and the management there in Belmont had had just about enough of our aesthetic delinquency. As we were loading out the morning after the last show, Dale, the club manager, remarked, "You guys will never make it. You're too weird." We laughed insanely: You're right, we are too weird. What of it? Living in the moment as we did, we weren't even sure we *wanted* to make it in the world of pop music as it was then.

Our last club gig (courtesy of my college chum Hank Harrison, infamous in the '90s as the father of Courtney Love) was a two- or three-night stand on Broadway in a San Francisco strip club called Pierre's, playing backup for the strippers. I think that's where the über-backbeat first lodged in our consciousness: Bump! Grind! It was actually pretty straight, except when the strippers began to fight over who would take Bobby home. The winner was "the plump one with the bite like a bulldog." Much later, she turned up at a gig in L.A., in a new incarnation as a Playboy Bunny and accompanied by her friend Miss September, who wound up going home with Bobby.

Right after that gig, I was browsing in a record store and found a single by a band called the Warlocks, on Columbia. I brought the bad news to the guys, and we started to bandy new names about — Mythical Ethical Icicle Tricycle was one of my favorites — but nothing really sounded right, and we just couldn't decide. Meanwhile, we were recording some demo songs for a local record label, and we needed not to be the Warlocks anymore. So, we agreed on a temporary name — the Emergency Crew — for our first recording sessions.

What on earth to call ourselves? The dam finally broke when one day Jerry danced in my door all asparkle. We pored over all the reference books in the house, including *Bartlett's Familiar Quotations,* coming up empty until Jer picked up an old *Britannica World Language Dictionary* that Ruth had in the house. In that silvery elf-voice he said to me, "Hey, man, how about the Grateful Dead?" It hit me like a hammer — it seemed to describe us so perfectly. I started jumping up and down, shouting, "That's it! That's it!" Our suggestion didn't immediately warm the hearts of all the other guys; Pig and Bob, I know, thought it was too weird. Jerry and I pushed it tirelessly, though, and used it for the first big gig we played in San Francisco, a Mime Troupe benefit.

In retrospect, it seems that we were extremely fortunate to have been starting out at this time; within six months the ballrooms were jumping five nights a week and a whole culture erupted full-blown from the City by the Bay.

Weave a circle round him thrice,
And close your eyes with holy dread,
For he on honey-dew hath fed,
And drunk the milk of Paradise.

— Samuel Taylor Coleridge, "Kubla Khan"

In late '65 strange posters began to appear on telephone poles and in bookstores around the South Bay: CAN YOU PASS THE ACID TEST? A tall, narrow, off-yellow strip of paper promised attendance by the Beats! Neal Cassady! Freaks! the Merry Pranksters! and by implication, had one eyes to see and ears to hear, something perhaps more intangible. Since we were constantly ready to drop a little acid at a moment's notice, I wangled invitations for the band to the first Test through my good friend Page Browning.

The event was held in Ken Babbs's living room at his home in the small town of Soquel, near Santa Cruz. Babbs, a former marine helicopter pilot known as "Intrepid Traveler," was by then Kesey's lieutenant and chief co-conspirator among the Merry Pranksters. The Pranksters were a diverse group of freaks clustered around Kesey, some from the Perry Lane days, some drawn to Kesey by his books. Their first rite of passage as a group mind came in the summer of '64, when they took an old school bus, tricked it out with all manner of audio-visual gear, and drove across the country to the New York World's Fair — with the aim of staying high all the way — and recording it on film and tape. Unfortunately, stoned people don't make very good camera operators (it's difficult to actually record the hallucinations), but some of the audio recordings of Neal Cassady really capture his rap.

True to traditional practice, some of our apprentice shamans took or were given Acid Test names: "Chief" (Kesey), "Speed Limit" (Neal), "Gretchen Fetchin the Slime Queen" (a cool blond lady who became Mrs. Babbs); when we started coming around, Jerry became "Captain Trips" because he was continually marveling "What a trip!" or shouting "More trips!" I became "Reddy Kilowatt," or sometimes "Flash," as Jerry named me after a particularly wild gig. Pig already had his name; Billy became (lucky man!) "Bill the Drummer."

We were at the first Test not to play, but just to feel it out, and we hadn't brought any instruments or gear. The equipment there — some audio, some visual — was brought in by the Pranksters from Kesey's compound in La Honda. It, being the Pranksters' stuff, naturally had all kinds of colorful collages pasted all over it, and also was kinda beat-up, in a way that suggested it had just returned from a circumnavigation of the globe on Kesey's bus, *Furthur*. I remember *wanting* the only electric guitar in the place, though — I vibed poor Kesey so hard he just thrust it at me, grumbling, "OK, OK" — but then I discovered I couldn't make any sense out of it after all. Ah, well, the night sky was ever so much more fascinating. . . .

Although it was considered the seed experience out of which the whole ballroom, psychedelic-light-show, multimedia phenomenon would grow, that first iteration of the Test was a curiously subdued occasion. It ended up being just like every other acid party — people getting high and doing pretty much what they wanted. There were a few sporadic attempts at getting a collective experience going, but the energy was too spread out. It seemed as though some kind of focus was needed to transform diffuse individual energies into coherent collectives. Clearly, music was the answer, even if it meant turning the event into a performance of sorts. Everybody in the band except Pig, who at the time preferred Southern Comfort, was taking acid on a regular basis, and we were ready to take the next step: actually performing while high, in a setting with similarly enhanced participants. Several days after the Soquel Test, Jerry picked Bobby and me up in his old Corvair, and we drove up to La Honda to meet with Kesey. We all agreed that the band would play at the next Test.

The next Test was in San Jose, at a house occupied by a friend of Kesey's known as "Big Nig." It was located down the street from the old San Jose Coliseum, where the Rolling Stones were playing that night. We set up our equipment on the other side of the room from the Pranksters, an orientation that would later prove very productive. Kesey's avowed goal was to "defuse the pyramid of attention" so that people weren't focused solely on the stage; we were after a more *rounded* experience, where many types of stimuli were occurring simultaneously.

Unfortunately the room was very small, so all the attendees were crammed into the same space as the band, and the crush of bodies together with the wind-tunnel sound and flashing projections turned the Test into a mind-numbing blur of noise, light, and heat. There was no way any one individual could be aware of everything going on in the place. It was a free-for-all, with untold amounts of input quanta streaming into one's sensory cortex all at the same time. The band was set up in one corner, with speaker columns so large one could crawl into the subwoofers and lie there. Across the room was Prankster Central, where the supplemental sound and some lights resided. The tape-loop master control was in Prankster hands; this ran a series of very long delays through a Möbius-strip speaker setup, with speakers in all corners of the room, receiving input from microphones and other mixers scattered everywhere.[1]

---

[1] I've often wondered how the great modernist composer Karlheinz Stockhausen, a profound influence on our multimedia approach and the high priest of German *Ordnung* in music, felt when he came to teach at UC Davis in '68 and discovered all these shaggy hippies doing all the things he'd advocated in Europe for years — only *funky,* loose, sloppy, the very antithesis of high modernism, and for thousands of people at once!

Occasionally, the Thunder Machine — Ron Boise's tuned metal sculpture bristling with contact microphones and festooned with areas marked HIT ME!, STROKE ME, SCRAPE ME, and other tender endearments designed to encourage participation — would make an appearance. The output of this was also plugged into Prankster Central. And then there were the strobe lights: intensely powerful flashes of pure white light, which could be pulsed quickly or slowly, or anything in between. With several of these light sources operating at different speeds throughout the whole darkened space, the experience could be intensely disorienting, even phantasmagorical. The finest exemplar of strobe-light art was, of course, Neal Cassady. Even in broad daylight, his every move was part of a sacred dance of life — under a strobe, the line was split up and reassembled in time, leaving me wondering: How on earth can he catch that hammer in the dark, or in between those flashes? Neal was the closest thing to poetry in motion I've ever seen.

The chaos at the San Jose Test didn't stop us from playing as long and as loud as we could, and we found that while high we were able to go very far out musically but still come back to some kind of recognizable space or song structure. I knew instantly that this combination — acid and music — was the tool I'd been looking for. After the cops closed the party down, it was low comedy at its finest to watch Kesey, Babbs, and Billy divvy up the take (one dollar at the door) at the end of the evening.

Between San Jose and the next Test, in Palo Alto, the band landed a slot in the lineup for the most coveted gig of the year: the Mime Troupe benefit produced by Bill Graham at the Fillmore Auditorium. My earlier association with the Troupe made this gig pleasing for me, but also for all of us, as a previous benefit had been a breakout event for the nascent subculture. Bill had been very reluctant to bill us as the Grateful Dead, but I managed to persuade him to use the name by suggesting that instead of a picture (which we didn't have anyway), he could put "formerly the Warlocks" under our name on the event's poster.[2]

A week or so later, we all gathered at the Big Beat nightclub in Palo Alto for the first full-scale Acid Test. People from outside the local area had heard about the events, and a lot of folks had come down from the city. The highlight of the Big Beat Test was unquestionably the performance of a multimedia extravaganza called "America Needs Indians," created by Stewart Brand, later to become famous for the *Whole Earth Catalog.* This audiovisual presentation of Native American myths and spiritual thinking revealed Native Americans to us as a people with a great depth of culture and a natural philosophy unsurpassed in the traditional world. To many of us — white kids who had grown up watching Westerns in the fifties — these revelations struck like lightning bolts. Also that evening, Ken Babbs showed us what may have been the world's first music "video" — his smokin' little three-minute film inspired by and illustrating a pop hit by Del Shannon called "Keep Searchin' (We'll Follow the Sun)." The later Tests and Trips Festival would see the evolution of these "compositional" audiovisual works into a fully improvisational art form: the rock 'n' roll light show.

Our next outing, held at Muir Beach, was interesting chiefly because of the appearance of Owsley Stanley. Scion of a great Kentucky family, he'd applied his formidable will and intelligence to science, engineering, and dance. During his first experience with acid, he had found his calling: to be the Johnny Appleseed of LSD. At that time he thought of himself as an alchemist, one who takes base metal and transmutes it into gold. We would later learn, through reading Jung and others, that alchemical terms were often metaphors for spiritual states.

---

[2]There's some confusion over whether this poster referred to the second or third Mime Troupe benefit.

Owsley had just begun his brief career as the King of Acid, but his product was already considered the gold standard. He first showed up on our screens pushing a chair around the floor, in love with the screeching sound of plastic on linoleum, reminding me how I had once felt that the sound of an unlubricated truck transmission was singing to me. I didn't meet him that night; after the Test was over, he crashed his car on the way home up Mt. Tam. As he related it to us later, he'd spun off the road and *seen* his whole life — all the incidents of a crowded lifetime in seconds — as a tape loop. Where the splice is, "That's birth and death," he swore.

Although we played most of our standard repertoire at the Tests — usually featuring Pigpen as the lead vocalist, since he wasn't too stoned to sing — our best music that night was "Death Don't Have No Mercy." Seeing Kesey and Babbs, sweat pouring off them, gyrating and undulating and screaming, "Yes!" "Righteous!" and similar ecstatic exhortations of approval, I thought that if we could grab those guys like that, we might just have something going.

You'll be forgiven for concluding from much of the foregoing that the Acid Test was a celebration of barely controlled anarchy. Not so. It was in fact totally uncontrolled anarchy, ordered only by those same mysterious laws that govern the evolution of weather patterns, or the turbulence in a rising column of smoke.

Let's walk (or should I say dance? crawl?) through a "typical" Acid Test layout. Entering, we find ourselves in darkness, relieved only by the blinding flashes of strobe lights (carefully timed to be out of sync with one another *and* the music). What seems like several hundred people are variously milling about, dancing strenuously, or puddled in the corners, against the walls, and on the floor, all clad in colorful and exotic clothing. (My favorite costume has always been Prankster Paul Foster's outfit at Palo Alto: swathed in bandages like a mummy, wearing a World War II vintage gas mask and a sign around his neck that read I'M IN THE PEPSI GENERATION AND YOU'RE A PIMPLY FREAK.)

Several projection screens are showing vastly different sequences of images, film clips, or full-color quasi-protoplasmic blobs moving in time (or not) to the music. The music itself is manifesting not from silence, but from a bed of ambient sound created by the aforementioned Möbius loops of microphones and speakers, and is enhanced by interjections of what we called "Prankster music" — loud, incomprehensible, jagged, and not exactly lyrical — and punctuated by shrieks, moans, expostulations, cries, murmurs, and laughter emitted spontaneously by the assembled freaks.

When a large crowd is present, as at the Fillmore or the Trips Festival, the experience of the group mind becomes much more intense, and much larger-scale; see how the entire wildly dancing audience behaves like waves in the ocean: whole groups of dancers rising and falling, lifting their arms or spinning rapidly in synchronized movement, darting swiftly through the crowd or languidly undulating in place — manifesting the same sort of spontaneous consensus seen in flocks of birds, schools of fish, or clusters of galaxies.

To make music for dancers like these is the rarest honor — to be coresponsible for what really is the dance of the cosmos. If, as some savants of consciousness suggest, we are actually agreeing to create, from moment to moment, everything we perceive as real, then it stands to reason that we're also responsible for keeping it going in some harmonious manner. The fervent belief we shared then, and that perseveres today, is that the energy liberated by this combination of music and ecstatic dancing is somehow making the world *better,* or at least holding the line against the depredations of entropy and ignorance.

After Palo Alto, the Test was ready for the big time — the Fillmore Auditorium. Much has been written about the role of the Fillmore in the then emerging countercultural groundswell, but at that moment it was simply the best possible venue for our trip: a huge (for us) audience space; a wide, low stage; and, best of all, balconies on three sides so that the light show and Prankster Central could spread out and be able to throw light on anything occurring in the hall. This Test also marked the emergence of Mountain Girl (aka Carolyn Adams, a Stanford student from Poughkeepsie, New York, who had been introduced to the Prankster scene by Neal Cassady; later to become one of the great loves of Jerry's life) as the Prankster Queen — at least in my eyes. She ended up being responsible (if that concept is even thinkable in this context) for mixing the multiple mutable audio loops connecting every part of the space with every other. Occasionally, her voice could be heard floating — the sound actually *moving* through the hall — with a loving and humorous commentary on some piece of the action.

We've loaded our gear into the Fillmore, we're all set up, the people are arriving, the Pranksters are firing up the Möbius loops, and, like a conquering hero or some Robin Hood figure out of swashbuckling antiquity, in comes Owsley, wearing an Aussie digger hat and a leather cape. Every inch the figure of the psychedelic warrior, here's a man who knows that he's *on to something,* something cosmic and eternal. It's hard to reconcile this vision with the freaked-out dude from Muir Beach. I walk up and shake his hand. "So you're Owsley," I say. "I feel as if I've known you through many lifetimes." "You have," he replies, "and you will through many more to come." Indeed, I felt as if I'd been living inside his head; maybe that was the result of all the trips I'd taken using his product.

During the Test itself, the acoustic space of the hall was finely sculptured and very dense — it was very much a sonic "landscape,"[3] with solid objects here, open spaces there, paths of least resistance (for sound). One could wander from an area dominated by the Thunder Machine, traversing a space populated by disembodied voices carrying

---

[3]As conceptualized by the European avant-garde in the early sixties; the music of the postserialists, including that of my teacher Luciano Berio (see his *Sinfonia* or *Formazioni*), manifested this method of structural organization as opposed to the motivic development that characterized earlier music.

on many simultaneous conversations (almost like being in Neal's head) to a space in front of the stage where the music was pretty obviously being played by the band. However, the so-called nonmusical sounds from the other regions would come stealing in, sometimes masking the music being played. These experiences set off some interesting trains of thought for me: Why couldn't noise, or speech, or sounds that weren't made up of a series of harmonics be part of musical thought, musical discourse,[4] especially if used rhythmically? We had already begun experimenting with feedback (extremely loud distorted tones wrenched from the speakers by electromagnetic interaction between the musical notes perceived by the pickups and the magnetic fields of the pickup, speaker, and amplifier), and one of our favorite tricks became fading down to sixty-cycle hum (normally the bane of a musician's existence) and using that as our fundamental tone to generate harmonic music.[5]

The main event at the Fillmore, however, was the manifestation of the group mind in a large crowd. For the first time, the physical, luminous, and sonic spaces were unified — the dancers moving, the musical sound breathing, the lights pulsing — as one being, limited only by the inscrutable laws of probability. At the end, after eternities of ecstatic ego loss, a voice was heard, asking, "Who's in charge here?" The depth of existential thought revealed in that question dropped us all right into the theater of the absurd. The voice belonged, of course, to a San Francisco police officer, whose duty it was to see that all events involving alcohol were shut down at 2:00 a.m., according to state law. After being shown the dearth of alcohol on the premises, but still highly suspicious of the general hilarity still resounding around

---

[4]We later learned that this approach was a fundamental tenet of John Cage's work — see his Imaginary Landscape no. 4 or Aria with Fontana Mix; also the electronic works of Stockhausen *Kontakte* or *Hymnen*.
[5]A wonderful example of this is at the very end of "Caution (Do Not Stop on Tracks)," from *Anthem of the Sun*.

the original question, a decision was reached: "Ya gotta shut it down." So, OK, we'll shut it down; but in our own inimitable manner, we just couldn't let it go without a last gasp: Bob Weir climbing a very tall ladder in the middle of the floor, shrieking the "Star-Spangled Banner" at the top of his voice, accompanied by myself and others, for all the world like some demented fundamentalist pirate TV network ending its broadcast day with a bang.

There was one more out-of-town tryout for us, the Beaver Hall Test in Portland. The Test itself has receded into the mists of antiquity, except for the vague memory of playing in an upstairs warehouse with concrete pillars everywhere and bare lath and wiring on the walls. What mattered about the Portland Acid Test was the journey toward it.

It began as our first trip together on *Furthur,* Kesey's fabled bus. Bobby and I had day-tripped on the bus to see the Beatles at the Cow Palace earlier that year, but for the majority of the band it was a first. Leaving Palo Alto as early as possible, by midafternoon or so we were halfway up the Central Valley bound for Shasta and points north, and then: catastrophe! The bus breaks down! Never let it be said that the show did not go on! What to do?

We rent a U-Haul truck; we strip the bus and cram all of us — the band, the Pranksters — and everything else into the truck. I jump into the shotgun seat up front, and we cruise off into the darkening storm of the worst blizzard in years: over the Siskiyou Mountains in the dead of night, Neal pressing ever onward, the rhythm of the falling snow sweeping through the headlights, sliding in and out of sync with the music piped into the cockpit by means of our patented two-way distort-o-phonic communication system, set up so that those in the back could also hear Neal's multiple personalities conversing with one another. If ever the magic of the open road was distilled into a single experience, it was, for me, that night sitting next to Neal, hurtling into the dazzling play of light and shade on the whirling snow with his voice turning every sentence into a poem, all sensory input synced up (or sometimes not, and that's good too) with the rhythm of the wipers and whatever music happened to randomly penetrate our awareness.

Upon our return from Portland, all the scuttlebutt was ablaze with the plans for the "Big One"; the Trips Festival, to take place in San Francisco's Longshoreman's Hall. It was to be a three-day multimedia festival planned by several of the countercultural artistic entities that were beginning to surface. The Tape Music Center on Divisadero Street was loosely associated with both the Mime Troupe and Mills College; one of its founders, Ramon Sender, together with Stewart Brand and some Pranksters, formed the steering committee. The event featured participants from the Open Theater; Dancers' Workshop; and the Congress of Wonders, an improvisatory acid-comedy troupe; Michael McClure read; Bruce Conner showed films; and countless unsung freaks added their costumes, movements, and general good vibes to the mix.

We play our set on Saturday, the second night. Big Brother and the Holding Company is playing a short set — their first gig? I'm not certain. Janis Joplin hasn't yet arrived on the scene. I'm puddled on the floor with my new girlfriend, Rosie, tripping out behind all the sound and color. After Big Brother leaves the stage, quantum probability takes full control, and about time, too. Babbs's voice, looped like a hundred snakes: "OK, the Acid Test is takin' over now." Mountain Girl ascends the platform; no, the scaffolding; no, the *tower* that has suddenly sprouted Pranksters from its every point. I crawl over to my instrument and haul myself shakily to my feet. The Ouroboros of sound has manifested onstage in the form of hundreds of wires and cables presumably connecting every electronic entity in known space. The energy generated by three to five thousand linked and synced minds is playing havoc with our conventional electronic gear; the amps are fizzing and frying, sometimes emitting piercing ultrasonic shrieks like the beacon in *2001: A Space Odyssey*. But curiously, it's almost benign; no one is being shocked. The stage is very high; I can see all around the hall, which is literally filled from floor to roof's peak with light, color, and movement. At first, my mind attempts to find patterns — am I *seeing* this or looking through it? But then shapes emerge, always in motion, extending further through time than normally, motions leaving rainbow trails. "So, cool, let's play." "What a trip, huh?" "Wait a minute, my amp stopped working" — and I turn around just in time to see a plug leap out of its socket and scurry across the stage like an arachnoid rubber band. And then another! And another! "It's a conspiracy! The electrons are freaked out in the presence of the higher energy — that's like God to them." "We must propitiate the local hierarchy. Let us pray." "Oh Mighty Electron, hear our vow; we will entrain our Metatronic essences in purest eleven-tenths harmony. Let us commingle together." Ahem. The amps are working now; no one knows why. I look out over the people, and they are an ocean, oily swells moving on the vast deep; even though we're not playing yet, there's plenty of rhythm — audible, tactile, visible, with waves of light connecting the dancers as they move. We play — what else? "In the Midnight Hour," our signature rave-up jam-out lost-in-the-stars tune; and just how did that R & B standard love-call turn into some kind of cosmic anthem, anyhow? Pigpen is in as fine form as I've ever seen him — cajoling, exhorting, crooooning, rapping (in the sense of laying down a rap);[6] the band is howling around him, now flashing a shy grin, now tiptoeing carefully past the window of the father of the girl Pig's rappin' his story about. And then Pig's finished his story for a while, and we go off on those two chords as if they are Jacob's ladder, with souls rising up on one side and drifting down on the other. We are showing serious respect to the power of these relationships: D–G–D–G–D–G. Hang on! The only pattern better for playing than two chords is one

---

[6]As in "When the Nazz laid it down, it *stayed* there" (Lord Buckley).

chord! So away we charge to wring the neck of some poor hapless tonic (D, in this case) and ravage all its sniveling overtones until the very air screams for mercy — it feels so good, why should we stop, or even slow up? But wait! The skies are opening! The Old Ones are returning! No, we've merely reached the eye of the storm, and suddenly the music broadens out into an almost hymnlike character; we're back to the two chords now, rich and glowing as they march endlessly into infinity, mirroring the waves of dancers. The form moves on, the particles remain.

On a more mundane level, Kesey had been busted twice in the weeks before the Trips Festival and had been forced to attend incognito, in a silver space suit complete with mirror-visored helmet. Therefore, the very next weekend we held the last Acid Test in San Francisco, at the Sound City Recording Studio, just before Ken split for Mexico. A greater contrast to the cosmic imagasm of the previous week can't be imagined. This was really Pig's night at the Test; usually, when he wasn't onstage, he would retire to a cool place with a bottle, and from there observe the craziness passing by. But tonight, even though he wasn't partaking of the Sacrament, he was holding court in his finest manner, playing acoustic guitar and singing songs with Jerry and other assorted folks. It was the neatest psychedelic jug band scene imaginable, and very warm and inclusive as an environment.

For my part, I was *hung! up!* outside in the lobby raving with Owsley, or should I say listening to Owsley rave at me. Fortunately, he was a very compelling advocate of his own views, as well as those of the authorities he cited to support his premises. Other than Jerry, I'd not known anyone with as great a breadth of interests before, and it seemed that he was actually articulating some of the fuzzy visions we'd had regarding the Meaning Of It All.[7] In any case, I was fascinated, and since he knew he was preaching to the choir, we had a great

---

[7] We referred to these nebulous concepts as the "science-fiction movie."

time roaming the universe of science and theology, ethics and technology, and on and on.

By this time, everyone in the band, except for Pigpen, had been taking acid at least once a week for more than six months. It's safe to say that in the ninety days or so that the Acid Tests existed, our band took more and longer strides into another realm of musical consciousness, not to mention pure awareness, than ever before or since. At the beginning, we were a band playing a gig. At the end, we had become shamans helping to channel the transcendent into our mundane lives and those of our listeners. We felt, all of us — band, Pranksters, participants — privileged to be at the arrow's point of human evolution; and from that standpoint, everything was possible.

In all honesty, I don't really remember why we felt it was necessary to move our whole scene to L.A. in February '66; maybe we felt that after the Trips Festival, club gigs and the like would be distinctly anticlimactic, or maybe we still considered ourselves the Pranksters' house band. In any case, since the whole Prankster scene was moving south (to meet up eventually with Kesey in Mexico), we decided to follow the Pranksters to L.A., where they planned to host more Tests.

Our decision to go south evolved, as many others would, casually over time. But being closer to record labels wasn't a big factor: not even the Airplane, the best known of the San Francisco bands, had signed a record contract at that time. We certainly weren't looking to — we had very few original songs at that point.

We were cautiously delighted when Bear (as Owsley now wished to be known) became interested in applying his alchemical focus to our sound, a development that turned out to be a mixed blessing in many ways. Bear wanted to develop a sound system for us commensurate with the vision we were beginning to share of music and dancing as an ecstatic release and a sacred rite. His ideal was musical sound undistorted by the artifacts present in the sound-reproduction system — the entire signal path from pickup through preamp through power amp to speaker. Only the vibrating string and the vibrating air had purity (forget about keyboards — equal temperament is so *rigid*); everything else was compromised and must be made transparent. A noble goal, and one we endorsed gladly, even if we didn't want to give up the keyboards just yet.

The main purpose of our stay in Watts (for that's where we ended up) is a bit hazy at this remove, but the result was a lot of rehearsal, a few great trips, three or four Acid Tests, a few poorly attended gigs, and not so much as a dent in the so-called consciousness of the music industry meat market.

Before we settled down at the big pink house in Watts, however, we made our L.A. performance debut at the Watts [sic] Acid Test, actually held in a warehouse in the central L.A. County city of Compton ("the Hub City," proclaimed the seal on all the cop cars). This warehouse was probably the scuzziest place I ever had to play. There was all kinds of description-defying debris lying about (mostly in the corners, thank goodness). High windows let through brown light, even in the middle of the day. The concrete floors, walls, ceiling, and pillars were all painted with a faded hepatitis yellow, which reminded me of descriptions I'd read of the color of mustard gas. All in all, a rather poisonous atmosphere in which to attempt the transcendent, and it became apparent early on that this would not be an ecstatic experience.

It began for me at the moment we were supposed to start playing; Bear and his tech wizard Tim Scully had laboriously converted the guitars to a low-impedance output mode so that they could be played through the "hi-fi" rig that was now our amp line. My instrument was the last to be so altered, and in our shortsighted excitement at the thought of being able to play through the new system, we had left all our other amps behind in San Francisco. The conversion mainly involved an external transformer box plugged between the instrument and the preamp-amp stages. It was this box, resting on the floor by the amp line, that Bear and Tim were attempting to build as we waited to play. As I watched them struggle with wires the size of a thread and a soldering iron like a Polish sausage, colors dripping off of them like big drops of sweat, it slowly dawned on me that my bass wasn't going to work and that we had no other way to amplify it. No sooner had I drawn breath to let forth a screech of dismay than Bear had screwed the cover back on the box, and we were ready to go. We may have played one, maybe two tunes, when Jerry decided he didn't feel like playing anymore, spending the rest of the night in an animated philosophical discussion with George Walker, one of the Pranksters. My disappointment must have been palpable. I'd wanted to play so badly, and it had actually sounded good in that awful place. I guess I must have felt that if we'd continued, the downward spiral would have been halted, or at least slowed down. Given the nature of the Test, there was no contractual requirement for us to play, nor were we paid. The take, such as it was, was divided evenly among us all. It didn't matter much, in theory, whether we played or not, since there was always plenty going on to occupy one's awareness.

And so it came to pass, after a formless period of pyschedelic glossolalia, that a new voice was heard in the land: "Ray! Who Cares?" The Who Cares Lady was lamenting the tragedy of existence, loud and long. At first just a sound source among many — grain for the Möbius mill — her voice came to dominate the whole experience, essentially taking over the function of music as the thread or carrier wave to *blesh* the assembled minds into a gestalt totality. At one point, Pigpen, the only band member left onstage, began to sing and chant in response to her wailing, occasionally singing in harmony with or in counterpoint to her cries; his theme, as always, was the infinite glory and variety of love. Gradually, the oppressive atmosphere began to lift and dissipate through the magical warmth of his voice. After that, I started to feel that we would survive the rest of the night with a modicum of hope for the future.

In the raucous light of morning, the Hub City revealed its true nature: industrial wasteland, populated only by machines — and cops. Lots of cops — in cars, behind sawhorses, standing around, staring at us as we straggled out of the warehouse and onto the bus. Since there had been no complaint (no one lived anywhere nearby) and we weren't obviously intoxicated (read: *drunk*), the only casualty was Prankster Paul Foster — arrested mostly because he was just *too weird* to be allowed on the streets. This is almost understandable, since his face was painted white on one side and black on the other. While Beautiful Downtown Compton was thus preserving its domestic tranquillity, Neal blithely poured the remains of the electric Kool-Aid down the nearest drain. Not that it was illegal, then, but it would have been hard to explain to the cops why they shouldn't drink any.

I've heard it said that at Watts Neal was actually *too high* at the end to drive the bus, but I saw him drive smoothly away, followed by various cars (Bear's truck, the *Dread Dormammu,* and Billy's station wagon, with Brenda and Stacey aboard, among them). The bus was en route to Hugh Romney's place (Hugh later became Wavy Gravy, in a transformation hailed by all and predicted by none) for some R & R, while Jerry and I, in another car, turned aside to see the famous Watts Towers.

The towers, built by Simon Rodia, on his own property, in the fifties, are a classic example of outsider art. Constructed from found objects — car parts, old bottles, concrete — and rising more than a hundred feet in places, the structure stands as testimony to the determination of an Everyman to create something unique and lasting. What impressed me most (aside from the sheer whimsy and exuberance of the place) was the bewildering variety of shapes and colors used in the service of a single vision, as if the walls and roof had been removed from a cathedral and only the bare bones had been left in place to define the shape of the space.

Later that morning we met up with everybody at Romney's just in time to see Neal back the bus into a wooden NO PARKING sign, bending it back at about a sixty-degree angle and shredding the pole somewhat. (To the best of my knowledge, that's the only accident Neal ever had while driving. Maybe he *was* pretty high.) One of the finest and most indelible memories of my life comes from Neal's expression as he stood, his back to the sign, propping it upright, as two elderly churchgoers shuffled by. Imagine how it must have looked, on an otherwise ordinary Sunday morning. One huge weirdly painted school bus parked illegally. Across the street, lounging on the lawn, twenty to thirty strangely clad individuals frolicking and yukking it up. One more or less regular-looking guy — leaning on a sign, but *swaying* a little, as if on a boat — beads of sweat popping out on his forehead, the goofiest grin on his face, managing to appear reasonably casual as he tips an imaginary hat and remarks, "Good morning, ladies," in such a respectful tone that they actually titter in response.

In retrospect, the Watts Test resounds in my memory as the last manifestation of the incestuo-subjective Prankster-Dead combine; the Tests that followed — Pico, Sunset, the Trips '66 attempt at recapturing the January magic — were more about putting on a *show* than creating a gestalt, or group mind.

Soon after, we moved into a three-story pink house, second from the corner, on a street west of Adams Boulevard, two blocks from the Santa Monica freeway. The idea was, I guess, to rehearse, write new material, develop the sound system, and play some gigs; although at that time, without a record deal and the associated promotional machinery, we couldn't even get an audition at the Whisky A Go-Go, the only place in town for rock music. (It's a misnomer to refer to L.A. as a "town"; it's really hundreds of neighborhoods, some incorporated as discrete entities, isolated from one another in some fundamental and mysterious way.) This meant that we (or rather, Bear) had to pay to put on our own gigs — rent the hall, provide refreshments, put up posters in however many of those hundreds of neighborhoods — small wonder the largest crowd we had was about twenty people.

Despite all these hassles, I was having the time of my life. My girlfriend, Rosie, had quit her job and come down to stay with me, while the band had quickly settled into a routine of practice, eat, sleep, trip on the weekends, and play the occasional gig or Acid Test. It didn't matter at all that we weren't working and earning money: Bear was taking care of us, and for the time being, all we had to do was play.

The equipment was set up in the living room: the "lead sled" of Mac amps (four McIntosh 240 stereo tube amps running mono, one for each electric instrument — two guitars, bass, and keyboard — bolted onto a single sheet of two-inch plywood), the Altec "Voice of the Theater" speakers (huge woofer and horn combo speakers, four in all, one for each amp), and all the drums and instruments. The volume level of this gear was enough to bulge out the sides of the house when we cranked it. Of course, several noise complaints ensued (although some neighbors were reluctant to involve the authorities, considering that their nocturnal activities involved tumbling dice and, some said, prostitution).

Bear had some friends who had a house on the beach in Venice, and one fine Saturday night we all decided to visit there, with a little present to cushion the shock. About halfway to the peak of the experience, Jerry and I wandered out to the water, watching the rising moon turn the local oil derricks into strangely animated tyrannosauro-mantises. *Weird enough!* thought I, just before we turned around and saw the entire house pulsing rhythmically, emitting beams of varicolored light at odd intervals, both floors ablaze with energy, with every window thrown wide open and filled with a milling vortex of — *freaks!* Freaks hanging out the windows! Freaks going in and out of the doors! Freaks draped along and over the low adobe wall fronting the sidewalk! It turned out that, once again, the Rolling Stones were playing somewhere in "town," and their fans were having parties all over. One of those had melded with our little séance, and we had now achieved liftoff.

One of Billy's high-school buddies happened to be passing

through that night on his way to service in Vietnam, thinking he'd fall by and party with his old pal Bill. Just about then, he came streaking through my field of vision, screaming "In hell! Climbing mountains! Mother!" clearly having second thoughts about some of his decisions. Close behind, however, was Danny Rifkin, an old acquaintance from the San Francisco Post Office and Haight Street, having come down to join his partner, Rock Scully, in the management of this new entity the Grateful Dead. Danny took it upon himself to shepherd this young man through what was obviously a really rough experience — holding his hand, reassuring him, eventually coaxing him inside to the "freak-out room" — a serene, candlelit space where Jean, the owner of the house, then read to him from *The Psychedelic Experience* (Tim Leary's version of the Tibetan Book of the Dead), an "operating manual" for accessing the realms of the collective unconscious. After several hours, Danny and Jean brought our traveler home safely.

Most of my other memories of this period have to do with experiences of altered awareness — with the exception of the Great Food Schism. Would our heroes be forced to follow the precepts of the Bear Diet and eat nothing but meat? Bear's childhood experience with what he called "rabbit food" had indeed scarred him for life — either that or, as he claimed, his intestines were configured at birth in such a way that eating fruits, vegetables, and other nonbleeding food groups made him sick. So, since he was supporting us, we ate meat. And drank milk. For three solid months. This in itself was enough to sow the seeds of dissent among us. Sara had taken Heather and left Jerry, moving in with the Pranksters. Bobby's underage girlfriend, Barbara, had reluctantly returned to her home in the Bay Area. Everybody was getting tired of Bear's controlling ways. It wasn't worth arguing with him because he could always outtalk you with a long-winded blast of tortuous reasoning. As Jerry once said, "There's nothing wrong with Bear that a few billion less brain cells wouldn't cure."

We needed to return to San Francisco and catch a ride on the new ballroom scene that was opening up there. We had watched with some dismay as the energy and methodology of the Trips Festival was, as we saw it, co-opted by commercialism. When we left in February, the Fillmore had been taken over by Bill Graham, and the first events there were billed as "Sights and Sounds of the Trips Festival"; the era of the multimedia light-and-sound dance concert had begun. We knew that what we wanted to do most was to play our music live in front of dancers, since that provided the biggest payoff punch aesthetically for us and for the community — and the ballrooms were made to order: liquid projection light shows, stable sound systems, congenial environments, and, best of all, places where we could play three or four nights a week as late as we liked.

The Grateful Dead have always had a special relationship with Bill Graham, who with the help of Ralph Gleason, the jazz, and later pop-music, critic for the *San Francisco Chronicle,* paved the way for public acceptance of the whole phenomenon, and who is responsible for the flowering of the San Francisco music scene in all its diversity. It was Bill who went in front of the Board of Supes in '66 and persuaded them to revoke the ridiculous statute (probably on the books since the gold rush) that required a separate permit for each and every dance held in the city. Whether you were a church, a neighborhood community center, a theater, or the Avalon Ballroom: one dance, one permit. Bill led the charge to make nightly dance concerts legal in San Francisco, and for that we all owe him an immense debt of gratitude.

During the last weeks of our stay at Big Pink, our weekend excursions became much more intense, and the group-mind phenomenon began manifesting in clear examples of telepathy (defined by me as the transmission of information or thought-forms directly from mind to mind, without being transposed into material modes, that is: words, spoken or on paper, drawings, etc.).

Freeze-frame:

Bear's attic room in Big Pink, hung with patterned cloth hangings, candles flickering, mattresses scattered about, a dozen or so sapient humans literally puddled *together — draped over and around one another in a completely nonsensuous and inclusive bond, seemingly as natural as breathing. (The amazing thing was that all of us were so comfortable being in everyone else's head; what if this* were *our natural state, and we've let it slip away over time as we sink deeper into the material realm?)*

Action:

"I" become aware that "my" right hand is rolling dice in a brightly lit room, while "my" left hand is picking up a phone in a booth on the street; at the same time "I" am holding a nonverbal dialogue with "Jerry" about the nature of the Demiurge: "Whose attributes are unmentionable!" "Whose name is unpronounceable!" punctuated sporadically by raucous laughter.

Freeze-frame:

The slopes of a canyon on Mount Wilson, home of the Palomar astronomical telescope; all of us are separated physically, wandering the trails among the shrubs and dust.

Action:

Enter the Tight and Curlies: an entire family (two parents, two kids) of porcine persons making their way down the canyon, possibly heading for a picnic site, accompanied by their two piggy little dogs, the curl of whose tails perfectly matched the curls in the hair of the humans, and each individual followed down the trail by a wave of tightly curled color. Just the rhythm *of their progress elicits paroxysms of giggling from the assembled freaks.*

Action:

We sit on rocks and on tree branches, playing a ball game with no ball and no hands: spheres of light, trailing clouds of glory, soar back and forth between us, weaving a glowing web of joy and exaltation.

Action:

I'm wandering on a trail, and suddenly onto my astral screen flies an icon *— a pattern of paisley and peacock feathers that I instantly recognize as "JerryandDiane." Sure enough, within seconds, around the corner amble — Jerry and Diane! For me, those two had special "astral signatures" that preceded them wherever they went. Pigpen also had one; strangely enough, it was more abstract-looking than I would have predicted.*

Action:

All of us together at the top of the canyon; a sound *like the hammers of hell rises from the earth, vibrating up from our feet, and completely obliterates all the wonderful telepathy flourishing just a split second ago — is it an earthquake? Have we finally called down the saucers? Over here! Over here! Eventually it diminishes, sinks back into the earth, and leaves us completely straight and sober — as if it had* erased *the visions from our minds. (Bear later told us that the Rocketdyne Aerospace Company, by whom he'd once been employed, had a rocket engine testing facility in the desert on the other side of the mountain and that they'd been testing an engine for the Saturn V moon rocket that day. Worked great. All the way through the mountain, on an expressway to my skull.)*

(Note: All these visions were confirmed later by the others involved.)

These experiences helped to confirm for me the existence of a reality beyond the physical, to know that all is not always as it seems; that there's more to reality than what can be seen, tasted, or touched; that there's more to heaven and earth than dreamed of in materialist science and philosophy. But hey, any musician should know this —

music is a perfect metaphor for the manifestation of reality, being ephemeral and mimetic. Right?

In the final analysis, we didn't really get much *done* in L.A., but we sure had some barn-burning trips. Man cannot live on hallucinations alone, however, so at the end of April '66, we skulked back into San Francisco just in time to play the latest Trips Fest clone — Trips '66.

Soon after our return to the Bay Area in spring '66, the band, together with Bear and our new management team, Danny Rifkin and Rock Scully, moved into a rental that was to become the finest venue for our ongoing communal-living experiment: Rancho Olompali, in Novato, about thirty minutes north of San Francisco. Formerly a feasting and gathering site for the Miwok tribe and situated among rolling hills just across the highway from the site of the battle of the Bear Flag Rebellion,[1] it has since become, in its own right, a state historical landmark. With its huge adobe mansion, several large outbuildings, a swimming pool, and acres of grounds, including a classic fountain and reflecting pool in the front yard (stained, crumbling, and choked with weeds in the timeless tradition of romantic ruins), it still retained much of the flavor of the culture that flourished there before the gold rush. In the back, near the largest outbuilding, a grove of trees marked the feasting place of old; the largest, central tree was hollowed out and had clearly been used for cooking fires over many years. Almost every morning, jet fighters from Hamilton Air Force Base, which was just down the road, would fly over our swim-

---

[1] This battle effectively ended Mexican rule in "Alta California," and set the stage for the admission of California into the United States in 1850.

Playing violin (the serious-looking boy with glasses on the right) in the
Young People's Symphony Orchestra in Berkeley, 1951 (courtesy of Phil Lesh)

Phil, his parents, Frank and Barbara, and dog Lady in 1956
(courtesy of Phil Lesh)

Phil playing trumpet on one of his first gigs with high school friends in 1957 (courtesy of Phil Lesh)

Phil and Bobby in 1965 (© Jim Marshall)

The band in 1966, clockwise from top left: Bill Kreutzmann, Bob Weir, Phil Lesh, Jerry Garcia, Pigpen (© Jim Marshall)

The band on TV, 1966 (© Jim Marshall)

Haight-Ashbury in
1966 (© Herb Greene)

Pigpen and Phil on Haight
Street, 1966 (© Herb Greene)

Jerry and Phil at 710
Ashbury, 1966 (© Herb Greene)

Bob and Phil at the Heliport in Sausalito, 1966
(©Wolfgangsvault.com/photo by Gene Anthony)

Olompali party in 1966 (© Herb Greene)

Golden Gate
Park Panhandle
in 1967 (© Jim
Marshall)

Phil in San Francisco, 1967 (© Jim Marshall)

Phil in 1968 (© Tom Copi)

Playing for free on Haight Street,
1968 (© Jim Marshall)

Phil on Haight Street, 1968
(© Jim Marshall)

Feedback, 1969 (© Jim Marshall)

Jack Casady, David Crosby, and Phil in 1969 (© Jim Marshall)

In the studio in 1970 (© Jim Marshall)

Bobby Petersen (courtesy of Phil Lesh)

The band in 1970: Bill, Keith Godchaux, Jerry, Pigpen, Bob, Phil
(© Mary Ann Mayer/GDP)

En route to Denmark: Keith, Donna Godchaux, Jerry, Phil, Pigpen, Bill, Bob, 1972 (© Mary Ann Mayer/GDP)

Bozos in Copenhagen, 1972 (© Mary Ann Mayer/GDP)

Jerry, Bob, Bill, Phil in 1972 (© Mary Ann Mayer/GDP)

Wall of Sound, Santa Barbara,
California, 1974 (© Ed Perlstein)

Winterland, 1974 (© Larry Hulst)

Golden Gate Park in 1975 (© Jim Marshall)

Golden Gate Park in 1975
(© Jim Marshall)

Kezar Stadium in 1975
(© Peter Simon)

Onstage with Bill Graham, 1976 (© Richard McCaffrey)

San Francisco, 1976 (© Ed Perlstein)

Not enough sleep: Mickey Hart, Phil, Donna, Jerry, Bob, Bill, Keith in front, 1976 (© Jim Marshall)

Phil in 1977

(© Chris Nelson)

Winterland, 1977 (© Bob Minkin)

Bay Area Music Awards, 1978 (© Richard McCaffrey)

Closing of Winterland, December 31, 1978 (© Ed Perlstein)

Rochester, New York, September 1, 1979 (© Jay Blakesberg)

The band in 1979 (© Herb Greene)

New Year's Eve in Oakland, 1979 (© Jay Blakesberg)

ming pool, lighting their afterburners and punching through the sound barrier directly above our heads. We took to lounging there waiting for these flights — environmentally incorrect (but still legal) even then, but . . . the *sound!*

The surrounding fields were leased by some kind of rancher, who took an immediate dislike to our presence; we were informed that trespassing on his land would not be tolerated for any reason. He was so serious about this that during our parties he would station himself in a tree line above the house (with binoculars, no doubt) and would ride down any transgressors, herding them back down the hill as if they were cattle. Just like John Wayne.

Mostly, though, life was pretty good there at Olompali; Bear was still paying the rent, and we would go into town, play our gigs, and then repair to our paradisiacal retreat and continue the explorations of consciousness and inspiration that had come to define our lives. We continued, of course, to trip every weekend, whether we were playing a gig or not.

That summer, we invited pretty much everybody in the local music scene (the bands, the promoters, the poster artists) out to Olompali to celebrate "mostly ourselves," as the flyer put it. All the local musicians came and played (or not). Bear and some of the Pranksters (who had just returned from Mexico) set up the Möbius microphone / speaker loop in the living room and all over the grounds; there was food and drink for all, and the pool was wall to wall with mostly nude people.

Under a perfect blue sky, I wandered over the grounds, greeting every familiar face with a smile and directions to the Kool-Aid barrel. Over by the main front porch, a short, chubby, shirtless person was performing an odd ritual involving Tai Chi poses and a yo-yo. The smell of barbecue tingled in my nostrils from the old cooking tree. An old friend from the Palo Alto scene sat poolside in his wheelchair with a movie camera, capturing for posterity every jiggle of breast and buttock. I suddenly felt an uncontrollable urge to lie down on the grass and look at the passing clouds, so I just crumpled where I stood, narrowly missing Bobby Petersen and Dusty, one of the KMPX djs, on the way down. From the makeshift bandstand by the kitchen terrace, an ad hoc band composed of members of the Dead, Quicksilver, and the Airplane played some of the most startling music I'd ever heard, a new kind of music no one had ever made before, a true synergy of spontaneity and structure, created on the spot. Not a bad way to spend a Sunday, I thought, as I spread myself out on the grass.

Just as all good things must pass, our lease ran out; we decided to stay in Marin County, finding another, smaller place in the West Marin town of Lagunitas. A former kids' summer camp, it was a little strange from the git-go: We had drawn straws to determine who would get first pick of the available rooms, and I drew the short straw. After some debate as to whether short or long was the winner, I emerged triumphant and chose the largest room, on the lower floor of the building. Right away a sewer line broke, spilling effluent out under the house just in back of my closet. Talk about the luck of the draw. To top it off, we discovered that a former owner had hanged himself in the garage — suspicions confirmed! I *knew* this place was weird!

We weren't the only San Francisco band living in Marin at that time — Quicksilver Messenger Service was out in Olema, by the coast, and Big Brother was living just down Arroyo Road from us in Lagunitas. Pigpen struck up an acquaintance with Janis Joplin, Big Brother's new singer, who had just hit town from Texas. Both blues people, and sharing a fondness for booze, their friendship soon ripened into something more. On many a night, they would kill off a couple of bottles of Southern Comfort, play and sing themselves into a romantic mood, and retire to Pig's room, which was situated just above mine. I could hear them grunting and screeching ecstatically very clearly, and I often wonder if the line "Did you ever waken to the sound/of street cats making love" from Bob's song "Looks Like Rain" was inspired by the music Pig and Janis made in the dead of night.

Soon after our move, we received an offer to play three days of a "Trips Festival," in Vancouver, British Columbia. It seemed like a good opportunity to bring our music to a new audience, since we'd been preaching to the choir, so to speak, for a while now. Since we couldn't afford to fly, the band took the train, leaving Oakland one morning and arriving the next day, while the gear drove up in a truck. While on the train, we took smoke breaks in the only place where we could have a little privacy: the open vestibule between the cars. At one point, we were standing out there entranced by the rhythm of the wheels clickety-clacking over the welds in the rails; Billy and I looked at each other and just *knew* — we simultaneously burst out, "We can *play* this!"

"This" later turned into "Caution (Do Not Stop On Tracks)," one of our simplest, yet farthest-reaching musical explorations. Based on the train rhythm, it had only one chord and was played at a blistering tempo; the music ranged from bluesy ("I went down . . . to see the gypsy woman one day . . . tryin' ta find out — what's wrong — with me an' my baby") to mind-shattering feedback ("Just a touch . . . of *mojo hand*"), the lyrics delivered by Pigpen with all the spooky, snaky, insinuating delivery he could summon.

At the next moment, the train lurched, and Jerry, who was standing near the exit, lost his footing and started to fall! Outward! Quick as a mongoose, Bobby reached out and grabbed his shirt, pulling him back into the car just as another train roared past in the opposite direction at a closing speed of what seemed like two hundred miles per hour. Whew!

Tragedy narrowly averted, we made it to Vancouver without any further incidents, and the gigs came off as planned, with a few minor glitches: When we got there, we discovered that the stage was so high as to cause nosebleeds, and the acoustics, of course, were bloody awful. We played one of the worst performances I can remember, and after finishing up the festival and a couple of perfunctory club gigs in Vancouver (they just didn't seem to *get it* up there yet), we returned home, not particularly wiser for our experience.

Back at home in Lagunitas, everyone was grumbling about the sound problems we'd had, and about the fact that Bear was still on a control trip. We were all getting a little tired of meat and milk, not to mention muddy sound compounded by interminable delays while Bear tuned the system to be *just exactly perfect.* Bear, for his part, was reaching his limit with our constant grousing; he was ready to cut us loose and return to his alchemical work, which was already earning him legendary status on the streets of the Haight. Since we were now earning just enough to survive without a patron, we talked it over and agreed to part amicably, but not before Bear, in an unexpected act of generosity, offered to buy us all new stage equipment.

We played a bunch of gigs that summer and fall, none of which are singularly memorable, except for one Sunday afternoon at a high school gym in Walnut Creek, across the bay and over the hills. We're in the middle of the show (this was before we started playing multiple sets), and I look up and out into the audience — everybody's smiling, kind of grooving in their folding chairs — except for two unsmiling faces on the aisle in about the tenth row. What's with these folks? Omigod! No, it can't be! Dad? Mom? Sure enough — the only people in the place not enjoying themselves: my parents. They had sour pusses on, that's for sure. After the show, my dad asks, "Couldn't wave hello, huh?" and Mom says, "Isn't it awfully loud, dear?" I think maybe they were a little shocked by their first sight of Pig and Jerry, who didn't *look* like the kind of guys they'd want their only child to hang out with. They later reconciled themselves to everyone, especially Jerry and Mountain Girl,[2] who bonded with them endearingly on a visit the next year.

---

[2] My dad would ask, "How's that 'Mountain Dew'?" Mountain Girl referred to him as "that great old coot."

Sometime in the fall of '66, we moved from Lagunitas into 710 Ashbury Street in San Francisco, a house where Danny Rifkin had an apartment and was the building manager. As rooms became available, we slowly insinuated ourselves until we'd basically taken over. Pig, with his new girlfriend, Veronica, and Danny had separate rooms in the basement; Bobby had the attic room, where Neal would crash when he came to town. Billy (who had split from Brenda and Stacey when we moved back from L.A.) and Rock had the second floor; Rosie and I shared the living room, which also served as an office, with Jerry and his current girlfriend. I was in hog heaven; all I had to do was hang out, get high, and play music, while Danny and Rock took care of bookings and finances, and all the women cooked and cleaned.

By this time, the Haight community had reached its full flowering. On any afternoon, I could walk down from 710, turn left on Haight, and find myself in the midst of a sea of brightly clad humanity, each and every one glowing with delight at the sheer joy of being alive. There was truly magic in the air in those days; everyone seemed to know and love one another, and spontaneous gatherings would occur on the sidewalk — small and large clumps of people, seated or sprawling out, sharing a toke or some food, with foot traffic funneling carefully around them. I would walk down Haight, past the Psychedelic Shop — run by Ron Thelin, who with Allan Cohen had just recently begun to publish the *San Francisco Oracle,* a weekly newspaper devoted to the psychedelic worldview — and on into the park, eventually ending up at Hippie Hill, a broad expanse of grass gently rising to a rounded peak. There I could find anyone that I hadn't already greeted on the street — other musicians, someone to share a joint with, someone to argue philosophy with; there was always a crowd of people there on any clear day, and even sometimes when it was cold and rainy. Banners and balloons were flying, Frisbees soaring, dogs playing, children giggling with glee. Life in the Haight was one great celebration — all day, every day.

We had just scored a rehearsal room at the Sausalito Heliport, and started working there most days, and playing gigs at night. Pig brought in a whole bunch of songs to work on: "Big Boss Man," a new Jimmy Reed tune; "Good Morning Little Schoolgirl," a nasty, snaky song from a Junior Wells/Buddy Guy album; and "Turn on Your Love-light," a showstopper that we all jumped on when we heard James Cotton do it when he opened one of our shows at the Fillmore. Pig was still the major front man in the band; Jerry and Bob were each singing a few songs, but the show really belonged to Pig, whose soulful voice and warmhearted presence belied his rough-hewn appearance.

The excitement of being a full-time musician was simply intoxicating to me; every day it seemed as if I discovered something new and profound about what we could do together. My progress on the bass had been rapid, almost as rapid as with the trumpet, and I was delighting in those aspects of our music that allowed me the most freedom. Playing on one chord, or root note, might seem restrictive, but I found it empowering. The possibilities engendered from playing any other interval against the tonic note are virtually infinite (to say nothing of the potential when a third, or fourth, note is added), and I began to think of those infinities as my personal playground.

On those nights when we weren't gigging, we would hang in the kitchen or the office at 710, snacking and goofing while KMPX, the original free-form radio station, streamed from the stereo. We looted an awful lot of ideas from the music we heard; sometimes we could recognize the artists, sometimes not, but there was always something provocative being played.

As Jerry's roommate, I was reintroduced every night to one of the great stentorian snores of our time: immense, turbulent, Druidic; rising to a climax, subsiding; then, one last huge percussive *gahznrmpf!* and a whistling diminuendo. Over and over again. All Night Long. After several sleepless weeks, I was ready to throw in the towel. Hell, I was ready to throw in the whole bathtub.

Finally, Billy, who was also feeling cramped, and I moved out to a place in Diamond Heights, and from there to a first-floor flat on Belvedere Street, down the block from an old church rented by one of our friends. Bobby, and later T.C., moved in with us there; when Mickey joined the band in late '67, he came to live under our stairs with his mattress and sleeping bag, his stereo, and some flashlights.

On the last night of the year, together with the Airplane and Quicksilver, we played the first of what seems now to be an infinite number of New Year's Eve shows. This began Bill Graham's tradition of kick-out-the-jams New Year's Eve events that over the years would include the closing of Winterland and the "breakfast" shows, where we played all night and then Bill served breakfast to all surviving audience members. On this occasion, however, we went right out the next day to the Panhandle in Golden Gate Park and played a New Year's Day festival for the Diggers.

In the next few months, we would see the flowering of our community at the Human Be-In, and its collapse in the disastrous aftermath of the Summer of Love, but in that brief shining moment a spirit was alive in the land: a spirit that blazed like a flaming heart, that could have (and should have) lit up the world. Fear not — that light still lives, peeking out through the cracks in the wall of our materialistic civilization.

Put on your colors and run come see
Everybody's saying that music's for free
Take off your clothes and lie in the sun
Everybody's saying that music's for fun

— David Crosby, "Music Is Love"

ight after New Year's Day '67, Allan Cohen and Michael Bowen, from the *Oracle,* began gathering members of the community to plan a large outdoor event — the Gathering of the Tribes. Almost one year to the day after the original Trips Festival, this "Human Be-in" was planned to introduce the community to itself and the members of the community to each other, taking it to the next level of self-awareness. In January '66, the Trips Festival may have processed perhaps five or six thousand people through the stargate over three nights; this time we were hoping for tens of thousands at an outdoor all-day festival. The organizers consulted astrologers Ambrose Hollingsworth (Quicksilver's former manager) and Gavin Arthur (the dean of local astrologers and the grandson of Chester A. Arthur, vice president under Andrew Johnson) to determine the most cosmically exalted date for the occasion, and the location was to be the Polo Fields in Golden Gate Park, a warm, sheltering earthwork enclosure (much like the ancient temple of Avebury in Somerset, England, only surrounded by trees instead of stones) already sanctified by many a good trip. The date chosen was January 14; the Airplane, Quicksilver, Charlatans, Country Joe and the Fish, and the Dead would play, and Tim Leary, Allen Ginsberg, Gary Snyder, Lenore Kandel, Michael Mc-Clure, and others would speak or read poetry.

The big day dawned bright and crisp, and as I made my way to the park, together with our band and family, I found myself in company with thousands of colorfully clad freaks: playing flutes, banging tambourines, waving banners, dancing ecstatically — and we weren't even there yet. It was as if I'd been swept back in time to some medieval festival — a gathering to give thanks for the harvest, or the investiture of an archbishop, or the dedication of a great cathedral. I was carried along, as if by a flood, as everyone surged into the Polo Fields like a river of color. The atmosphere was crackling with excitement and anticipation.

The stage was, following Panhandle tradition, two flatbed trucks strapped together; taking up most of the available room was a hodgepodge of gear from all the bands, leaving a narrow strip of space in front for the various chanters and speakers. In keeping with the almost religious feeling of the moment, the ceremonies were initiated with a Buddhist chant led by Allen Ginsberg; after that, poets read, bands played, people danced. We even had some leftist politicos from Berkeley ranting, the only bring-down of the day.

The sense of timelessness was even stronger for me as we kicked into our opener, "Dancing in the Streets." The crowd scrambled to its feet, and all I could see from the stage was brightly woven waves of dancing movement, punctuated by swaying banners and an occasional conga line. At the end of "Morning Dew," a new song that we'd just learned, the power suddenly failed (apparently someone had kicked a cord loose near the generator), and everyone was compelled to relax a little and enjoy one another and the day without the benefit of music or oratory. When the power came back on, with the generators now guarded by the Hells Angels, flutist Charles Lloyd joined us for Pig's tour de force "Good Morning Little Schoolgirl." Charles really lit a fire under me with his ecstatic chanting and the rippling sound of his flute, and after he left the stage, we charged into "Viola Lee Blues," our closer, with a vengeance. The music that day was unusually concise and pithy, and we rounded off the tune, and the set, with a furious jam, dropping back into the final verse with a most satisfying chunky groove. *Chronicle* columnist Ralph Gleason was to tell me later that he'd been hanging that day with Dizzy Gillespie, the great bebop trumpeter and godfather of modern jazz. We must have played pretty well, because Dizzy asked Ralph during our set, "Who are those guys? They sure can swing."

At the end of the day, as Ginsberg led the clean-up chant, I felt as if I'd been privileged to be part of something that was bigger and more important even than music: a community of loving, peaceful people gathered together to celebrate a new form of consciousness — one that I hoped would expand to embrace the whole world. Like a Native American powwow, or the opening of some cosmic Olympiad, the Be-In created a sense of unity that was solid enough to walk on. It was the first time that the community gazed upon itself and experienced the glow of recognition.

The next week, we were off to L.A. to start work on our first album. The record companies had been sniffing around San Francisco for a while, and we had landed a contract with Warner Brothers Records the previous fall — a really good contract, we were told. We had artistic control and unlimited studio time, but it turned out later that the single most important point had been overlooked: The record company would own our masters in perpetuity. Blissfully ignorant of that, we rumbled into the RCA studio complex and set up our gear under the watchful eye of our new producer, Dave Hassinger.

The material for the album was fairly representative of our repertoire — blues, jug-band tunes, traditional ballads, and one current folk song ("Morning Dew") — rearranged, electrified, and amped up — and two originals: "Cream Puff War" (one of only two Garcia lyrics ever recorded) and our first collaborative composition, "The Golden Road (to Unlimited Devotion)." "McGannahan Skjellyfetti," to whom some of the publishing is credited, was Pigpen's whimsical moniker for the five of us writing together. We cut tracks on a couple of other tunes, too, but they were never used. To my ear, the only track on the record that sounds at all like we did at the time is "Viola Lee Blues." The recording *almost* captures in ten minutes what used to take thirty or more — especially the last big craze-out buildup to the verse recap.

I was nervous coming into that kind of high-pressure scene, so on the first day I huddled together with the other guys in the center of Studio A at RCA, which is about the size of the Vehicle Assembly Building at Cape Canaveral, and went to work. None of us had any experience with performing for recording, so we tended to accept the judgment of the production team, although the whole process felt a bit rushed. In fact, the resultant album sounds rushed, even hyper: sound and fury buried in a cavern. All in all, it was a learning experience. The main thing I took away was the knowledge that the next time I wanted to do it very differently. I didn't know exactly how, but I knew for sure that we'd take more time. The record, when released that summer, was called *San Francisco's Grateful Dead.*

After the sessions were over, we went right back to work at the Sausalito Heliport. Every day around noon Billy and I would cruise over to 710. Jerry would be ready and waiting; he would come right out, lumber down the stairs, and jump into the car. Then the three of us would wait for Pig and Bobby to straggle out and cram into the backseat with Jerry. I always rode shotgun, because I could call it when Billy and I left our place. I had to be careful though; more than once I forgot to call "spot back" when I got out to let Pig in, and he grabbed the seat from me. You always had to watch out for Pig when riding in a car: As our foremost authority on the "Shotgun Papers," his was the final word on seating priorities.

Our rehearsal room had a homey kind of atmosphere, even though the place was a concrete blockhouse. We would play for a while, and then send out for burgers and Coke (Coca-Cola, at this stage). M.G., who was now living with Jerry, and her daughter, Sunshine, would visit and hang out; Danny and Rock would fall by to see how we were doing, or to tell us about upcoming gigs. At this point, we were mostly working on new covers and jamming, because we all felt that our first batch of original material had basically failed the test of time.

In May of '67, we decided to take up an offer made to us by John Warnecke, a friend of Billy's from high school, who had invited us to his dad's summer place up on the Russian River to hang out. We accepted gladly, with the caveat that we'd be bringing our gear; it seemed a wonderful opportunity to keep playing every day in a new setting, and to try again to work up some new material. It was a beautiful spring day when we crammed into Billy's car and, with an equipment truck following behind, drove out of San Francisco across the Golden Gate Bridge, north on Highway 101 through Marin and into Sonoma. We finally found the place after some detours involving John's directions and a gas station map. The house was a long, low structure built on a bluff about twenty feet above the river, with lots of parking space and several outbuildings, including a sauna.

We set up our gear outside on a covered deck next to the river, and when unsuspecting boaters would float by, we would confuse them with low-level feedback — just subliminal enough to catch their attention — while Pig and Bobby muttered strange imprecations into the mikes. Most of the time, though, we just jammed, searching for ideas we could incorporate into tunes.

It was at this time that we received our first lyrics from Bob Hunter, Jerry's old carmate from the Château days. Hunter was born to be a poet: His birth name was Robert Burns. Like both Jerry and I, he was a voracious reader from early childhood, and he began writing while still in grade school. Bob's stepfather was a prominent literary editor and gave him his first grounding in literate thinking.

Hunter had been moving around quite a bit since the closing of the Château. He was currently living in Taos, and out of the blue he mailed Jerry a lyric at 710, which was promptly forgotten until Jer found it in his guitar case — something about a "sleepy alligator in the noonday sun/lying by the river just like he usually done." This was meat and mead to Pigpen, who immediately added some lyrics to what Hunter had sent, and he and I came up with some music for them the same day. The whole band goofed up some chorus lyrics to add to the mix: "Turn on the hippies, leave the heat alone"; "Bird shit over on the avenues"; "Hung up waitin' on a windy day"; "Burn down the Fillmore, gas the Avalon" (all of which we sang simultaneously, one man to a part), and we had our first Hunter song. It was tremendous fun working with his lyrics, and I realized right away that here was the poetic sensibility we'd been lacking (our own lyrics, except for Pig's, were decidedly lame). Immediately I hit on Jerry to get right back to Bob and ask for more lyrics. Anything — just get us more!

At the same time, we were jamming on a one-chord riff in a fast ⁶⁄₈ time. This, with lyrics written by Bobby celebrating (1) his bust for throwing a water balloon at a cop, and (2) the bus and Neal, became one of our all-time bomb-dropping barn burners. At the time, we couldn't think of a name for it, so we called it "The Other One" (as opposed to this or that one).

The most exciting development, though, was a little two-chord theme that Jer had been noodling on. As we played around with it, it started expanding itself into a flood of endless melody, and from there into some scarifying, chaotic feedback, and back to the original theme, almost of its own accord — as if the music wanted to be expanded far beyond any concept of "song." Some months later, when Hunter arrived in San Francisco and heard us jamming on this theme, he sat right down and ripped off some words that still resonate poetically and scientifically: "Dark star crashes/pouring its light into ashes" — and this was *before* the discovery that black holes, or singularities, actually existed in nature! This theme, because of its infinite mutability, became our signature space-out tune, consciously designed to be opened up into alternate universes — a tone poem reflecting the possibility that the collapse of a star into a singularity in our universe could be the birth of another complete universe. This little acorn of a song was never released on an album in a studio version. We released a two-minute single of it the next year, with Bob's tune "Born Cross-eyed" as the B side, complete with the only recorded example to date of Jerry's banjo playing on the out chorus. Naturally, it sank like a stone.

All in all, this short sojourn allowed us to initiate a process of collective creation that became the main paradigm for our "experimental" period, during which we also developed a methodology that would serve us well over the years: allowing the music to evolve to maturity in live performance before attempting to record it. We were able to develop our music to such a level of sophistication so quickly because since the beginning we had done our best to play together every day, no matter for how long; by this time, almost two years on, it was starting to pay off.

And our live performances were about to begin occurring in a lot of new places. Danny and Rock decided that we were finally ready to go national and persuaded Warner Brothers to pay for a trip to New York for some club gigs. Even then, New York was seen by many as the cultural capital of the country, if not the world. To me, it was a fantasyland, full of fascinating characters and exciting places — the Museum of Modern Art, Carnegie Hall, the Empire State Building (at that time still the tallest building in the world), Fifty-second Street, the birthplace of bebop, and on and on. Indeed, when I actually arrived there, it was as if I'd been transported into a full-color version of all the black-and-white images I carried in my head from movies and TV shows. Just walking down Fifth Avenue toward Washington Square became a mythic adventure, especially when I was accosted by a street freak and told to get a haircut (this, in New York? Maybe this place ain't so cutting-edge after all).

Our first show in town was a free concert in Tompkins Square Park. There'd been some tension between the local Hispanic community and New York's version of "hippies," and our promoter felt that perhaps the gesture of free music would defuse the situation somewhat. For us, it was the perfect way to introduce ourselves to the Big Apple: a San Francisco–style park scene. At the event, the vibe turned out just a little differently than what we'd been used to back home. That is to say, it was wound tightly and decidedly off-balance. Some would attribute the difference to different drugs (crank versus pot, say). Coming from the West Coast as I did, I had an image of the city as the ultimate sci-fi hive-mind/rats-in-the-maze environment, and I wasn't disappointed. At least, not at first . . .

Our first night in New York: I drag Bobby, Jerry, and Billy (Pig was already out at some blues club) over to the gig, the Café A Go-Go, to check it out (we don't start until tomorrow); then, I tell them, let's catch Zappa upstairs at the Garrick. The Café is downstairs on Bleecker Street in the heart of Greenwich Village, a rectangular brick room with a bar and the stage on one long wall, with tables scattered about between the stage and the opposite wall, about thirty feet away. I shudder, knowing that it will be painfully loud for everyone, especially us, but — so what? We're playing in New York!

Up and out on the street, up the stairs next door, here's the Garrick: a small theater with rows of seats and a real proscenium. Real nice place — too bad we couldn't play here. The Mothers of Invention, Zappa's band, comes on and dives into an insane torrent of sound. We listen, jaws on the floor. Zappa's music is brilliantly composed and precisely played — hey, he won't let his band smoke pot — but short on any kind of improvised epiphanies. I've always seen Zappa as part of a long line of true composers, whose individual visions are so powerful that they must be manifested as purely as possible, a true successor to his hero, Edgar Varèse.

After the show we say hey to the band and cruise off to our lodgings in a building called One Fifth Avenue. Number One Fifth Avenue! How that phrase resonates in my imagination. I visualize some elegant Attic facade with cars and people coming and going. Sorry, no. It's an old seedy apartment building right off Washington Square that has been converted halfheartedly to a hotel with rooms by the week. This will be our home for the next five days. "Hey, the air conditioning doesn't work!" "That's right, we couldn't afford to pay extra for it. Open the windows already." And so began one of the most extraordinary nights of my life. Trying to sleep your first night in New York ain't easy anytime, but having the windows open to the music of the city made it impossible. Layer upon layer of sound — cars, horns, shouts, rumbles, sirens, cries, laughter, gunshots, screams, sirens, bells, impacts, screeches, sirens — the whole urban symphony of Industrial Man, coming from near and far, high and low, finally weaving a shimmering web of discontinuous rhythm, and in the longest slow fade ever, subsiding over hours to a dull roar, felt rather than heard, only to rouse itself anew as the sky brightened with the light of another day. If I slept at all that night, I must have dreamed it.

We showed up for our afternoon sound check at the Café, and my worst fears about the sound were confirmed immediately. The band was playing directly into a brick wall at point-blank range, and the ambient noise and bounce back were deafening. We didn't really need a PA; the stage monitors would have done the job just fine. The gig went off pretty smoothly, even with the god-awful sound. We played stuff from our regular repertoire — Pig's blues and R & B, arrangements of traditional songs, a Dylan tune, etc. — until I called for a tuning break. In those days, before electronic tuning machines, all the guitars were tuned by ear, and it took time, to say the least. During the lull, a voice yelled from the audience: "Hey, Jerry, how about something new?" Jerry and I looked at each other, and I turned to Billy and whispered, "Alligator! One, two, three . . . ," and we kicked into the new tune at full tilt. Forty-five minutes later, as we slowly let the feedback fade down, Jerry stepped to the mike and said, "That's all we got that's new for now, but we'll be back with more."

The next day, we played for free in Central Park to an audience of about three hundred, at the band shell by the Great Meadow. Once again, the audience vibe was jacked tight. No one danced — they just stood, watching expectantly. I realized then that these folks were demanding that we give them our best, and that the payoff in feedback would be worthy of our efforts. That has turned out to be the gospel truth. There's something *extra* that New York always pulled out of us, as if the audience were more a member of the band than elsewhere. It always seems as if there's more at stake in a New York performance, not just in terms of success but that the possibility exists for transformation on a grand scale, rippling like waves out through the collective consciousness.

After our performance, one of our promoters came up, saying breathlessly, "Phil, come on down and meet Charles Mingus!" The great jazz bassist and composer had materialized by the side of the crowd during the set; I recognized his imposing figure immediately from a dozen record jackets. I walked down from the stage and hung out with him for a while, just shootin' the breeze. We didn't talk about music, but mostly about the crowd — he hadn't seen that many people show up for a show at the band shell before. I was way too intimidated to ask what he thought about our sound.

After one more gig in New York, at a place called the Cheetah, which I've totally blanked out, we went home briefly to inaugurate the Straight Theater on Haight Street and then presto! off to the now-infamous Monterey Pop Festival. Monterey Pop was the brainchild of two L.A. industry types: Lou Adler and John Phillips. The goal of the whole project seemed to be: "We'll throw this festival, invite all of the top acts, and then we'll *make a movie* of the whole thing! That's where the money is." Not that we would have refused the offer — we existed to play for people — but we did refuse to be filmed, mainly because we couldn't get straight answers about where the festival profit would go and who was going to own the film.

We were scheduled to go on after the Who, a band that was known over here only from the one record "My Generation," and from news reports of their, shall we say, destructive tendencies. I should have known something was up when I wandered into their dressing room by accident and found them all red-faced and raving — in a completely incomprehensible dialect, unrecognizable as English. I thought at first they'd been dosed, but later found out they were all blind drunk. That didn't stop them from going out and blowing the roof off the Monterey arena; they rocked the house down and ripped their gear to shreds. The crowd went nuts.

So then it was our turn. I don't think we played very well that night, but then I don't really remember much except a couple of incidents during our set: Lou Adler personally trying to prevent my girl-friend, Rosie, from dancing on stage, and Peter Tork from the Monkees coming on to exhort the kids to "stop trying to get in, the Beatles aren't here."

This was the inauguration of the Grateful Dead tradition of always blowing the Big Ones. I convinced myself that it really didn't matter, who would remember what we sounded like anyway, sandwiched between the Who and — what's his name? Hendrix? The guy who lit his guitar on fire?

On the way out of town, Danny and Rock decided to "liberate" some gear from the clutches of Hollywood, planning to let some of the new bands use it at the solstice celebration back in San Francisco. (Being the good, honest hippies they were, they later returned everything.)

The Solstice Festival was planned to be the official kickoff for the "Summer of Love" in the city of St. Francis — a three-month festival of "free celebrations, happenings, events, and ideas." The quote on the poster read:

> *Lord, make me an instrument of thy peace.*
> *Where there is hatred, let me sow love;*
> *where there is injury, pardon;*
> *where there is doubt, faith;*
> *where there is darkness, light;*
> *and where there is sadness, joy.*
> *O divine Master, grant that I may not so*
> *much seek to be consoled as to console;*
> *to be understood as to understand;*
> *to be loved as to love.*
> *For it is in giving that we receive;*
> *it is in pardoning that we are pardoned;*
> *and it is in dying that we are born to eternal life.*

— St. Francis of Assisi

Armed with about a dozen brand-new Fender amps, we arrived at the Polo Fields on June 21 to find two stages, one at either end of the field. Theoretically, the distance between them was great enough to make moot any sonic conflict, as the setup was designed to allow two bands to play at once. However, once we got started, the extra power of the "donated" gear made the situation a little lopsided. Escalation soon followed, and for those lucky few in the center of the field it must have been a metamusical moment: two bands, each trying to play loud enough to drown out the other. If only they could have marched around the field . . .

Everyone in the Haight knew that there were some serious problems looming with the expected influx of thousands of seekers. The massive media coverage of the scene had generated widespread interest in what was increasingly seen as an alternative lifestyle. The general vibe on the street had degenerated badly from its peak six months

earlier. The city wasn't much help — the Board of Supes passed a resolution deeming the expected visitors "unwelcome."[1] When the summer came, tens of thousands of young people thronged the streets of
the Haight, in what I saw as a throwback to the medieval Children's
Crusade, coming from all over the country to seek whatever it was the
media had told them to expect — free love, enlightenment, like-
minded companionship, the freedom to just be themselves — and instead finding hard drugs, rip-offs, rapes, and murders. It seemed that
the "love generation" was seen by many to be an easy mark, a passive
target for exploitation. The Diggers, an offshoot of the Mime Troupe
dedicated to radicalizing the culture by giving away free food, and
other groups such as the recently formed Haight-Ashbury Free Clinic,
a medical collective, tried valiantly to provide some modicum of assistance to the mostly cash-strapped pilgrims. Alas, it was like trying
to hold back the tide with beach toys — there were just too many, and
the indifference or outright hostility evinced by the city establish-
ment virtually sealed the fate of the Haight-Ashbury communal experiment. If we'd only had eyes to see, the whole Summer of Love
catastrophe could have been read as a metaphor for the Grateful
Dead's future: the influx of hard drugs, the increasing isolation from
and indifference to one another, the resultant failure of communication and shared responsibility.

We couldn't stay around to watch. We had gigs all over the place
that summer of '67. First a quick Northwest run (Seattle, Portland),
two gigs in Santa Clara, and a super-fun evening at the Straight when

---

[1]Prompting this response from Willie Brown, then state legislator for the Haight-
Ashbury and later three-term mayor of San Francisco: "the issue is whether you can
by fiat declare a minority 'unwelcome' in our community. . . . I suggest instead that
you direct the city agencies to a positive effort of cooperation with those organiza-
tions trying to deal with the problems rather than to suppress them. . . . We can
have a summer of peace or of dreadful discord. . . ." *San Francisco Oracle* 8 (June
1967).

Neal sat in and rapped with us for a long jam. Then, we joined up with the Airplane for a big "Bill Graham Presents the San Francisco Scene" run to Canada — Toronto, and two free gigs in Montreal. That's when the fun began.

We rolled into Toronto to perform at the O'Keefe Center (considered by the locals to be the Carnegie Hall of Canada) and immediately hit snags. The sound system had a buzzsaw noise in it, probably caused by one of the stage-light dimmers. Also, for the first time, Jerry and I started grumbling to each other about the music. With too many shows and not enough rehearsal, the music wasn't moving forward to our satisfaction; Bobby, being years younger and a bit spaced, became our target. We confronted him after the show about working harder to keep up. The end result, whether because of the confrontation or not: We all played better the next night. As we later learned, it's never that bad two nights in a row. Still, this was the first sign of dissatisfaction among us, and it wouldn't be the last.

The review of our first night still cracks me up: "five simian men, presumably reeking with San Francisco authenticity . . . not volume, but noise . . . a jet taking off in your inner ear, while the mad doctor is perversely scraping your nerves to shreds." Wow, we got his attention, huh? At least we now know what we are — we're *Musimians!*

After six days in Toronto, we moved on to Montreal, where we were set to play two free shows. The first was downtown at the city center, in a plaza (Place Ville-Marie) surrounded on three sides by immense highrise buildings. The sound had an amazingly tactile quality as it bounced from the walls. The crowd had been invited to a "love-in," and about twenty-five thousand showed up, including (in a first for us, but probably not for the Airplane) a disproportionate number of stunning young women. Go figure. That was at about 11:00 a.m.; by 1:00 p.m. we had moved over to the grounds of Expo '67, the Montreal World's Fair. It's true that the expo had a lot of monorail tracks, but there was actually only one geodesic dome: one of Buckminster

Fuller's first large-scale projects, so large that the monorail tracks went through it in three or four places. One could ride through the whole dome in an open car, thus discovering that it was a huge arboretum, full of green growing things — the "Flora of North America" exhibit, perhaps. When the light struck the dome at a certain angle, the windows became opaque and golden, turning them into facets of a gigantic jewel.

We're set to play at the "Youth Pavilion," a tiny structure with a low-walled courtyard that could hold about fifty people, and that's before we set up the stage. We're opening for the Airplane, so we warm up with a couple of quickies — "Cold Rain and Snow," maybe, or "Sittin' on Top of the World," and then slope right into "Viola Lee Blues." As we sail out of the first verse into the jam, I notice that the entire area is suddenly full of people — and more are jamming in with every bar we play. The cops appear and join arms to keep the surging people off the stage (which is at ground level). All the while Bill Graham is standing behind the amps, screaming, "Don't play so good!" and "Calm it down!" We play on, exhilarated by the knowledge that the music is literally pulling people in off the street but oblivious to the fact that those same people are slowly being squeezed into paste. Finally, Bill runs onto the stage between Pig and Jerry, just as we're beginning our last big leap into orbit, waving his arms and screaming, "Stop! Stop playing!" We grudgingly acquiesce. As the music dribbles to a stop, I look up from my instrument and see: at least two little old ladies being slowly *extruded* by the crowd; the sorely overburdened line of blue-shirted police standing nose to nose with those of us in the front line of the band; and behind them, the distended faces of the public crushed up against one another. We lower our instruments and leave the stage, still living in the music: "Whoa, that woulda been the greatest Viola Lee ever!" "Yeah, too bad." But the crisis is over, and no one is hurt. We don't get to finish our set, even, much less "Viola Lee"; but the Airplane goes on (after the crowd has dispersed somewhat and the place has been made a little more secure), and they play one of the best shows I ever heard from them: tight and powerful, closing with an explosive "White Rabbit."

There we were — suffering "blue brains" from "musicus interruptus" — with nowhere to go. The Airplane was returning to the West Coast, and we had nothing for the next four days, so we got off the bus in downtown Montreal and sat down on the street with our gear and luggage. Without missing a beat, Ron Rakow, generalissimo in chief of the Pleasure Crew (a rotating lineup of loosely affiliated friends, who seemed to be present backstage at every gig we played — and no one knew how they got there), and his lady friend Peggy rode to the rescue: her brother Billy had invited Tim Leary, Dick Alpert, and their whole International Foundation for Internal Freedom crew to a residency at the family summer cottage (twenty-five rooms or so) in Millbrook, New York. All were living in luxury, with each pursuing his or her researches into the permeability of consciousness, so let's visit for a couple of days: hang with Leary, have a "psychedelic summit meeting," or some such? Why not indeed? Off to the rental car agency — thank goodness someone (Peggy? Rifkin?) possessed a credit card so we could at least rent a truck for our gear. Our group (band and crew) arrived at Millbrook early the next evening, only to find that the whole bunch had gone off to get high in the woods and weren't expected back for two days. We ended up spending the night, taking a swim in the charming old pond, and piling back into the rentals for the drive to our next gig — at the Chelsea Hotel in New York City.

The Diggers had decided to export their trip to swinging London but didn't have the wherewithal to get there. Their chief honcho, Emmett Grogan, knew some people in New York and set up a sort of benefit on the roof of the Chelsea attended by such luminaries as Shirley Clarke, the theatrical director, and artist Andy Warhol, who entered looking like an ambulatory black hole. The idea was to hustle ticket money for Grogan and a couple of the other Diggers; hence the name "Trip Without a Ticket." We played a few tunes, and even did a little vocal rap — "it's the money, honey" — to this day I don't know if they ever got their tickets covered, or even got to London at all. It was kind of cool, playing on a rooftop in New York, but whatever energy we could muster fell flat on the floor, oozing over to Warhol's feet where it disappeared into the singularity. Not a fun event; the New York vibe was asserting its darker side that night.

On a lighter note, I did find time to enjoy a very pleasant dinner date with a young woman whom I'd met when she came to 710 Ashbury to take pictures of the band. Her name was Linda Eastman, and she too was on her way to London, where she would eventually meet and marry Paul McCartney. Oh well, at least she married another bass player.

It was a relief to get out of town, until we arrived at our next destination — Detroit. There had been riots the previous week that had left the town with an atmosphere that tasted of metallic rage; we were perfectly happy to just play our gigs and move on to Ann Arbor, where we played a free show in the park. The feeling there was a complete antithesis of the uptight urban chew-nails-and-spit-out-tacks vibe we'd experienced so far. Everywhere but Montreal.

It's a shame that the institution of the spontaneous free concert has fallen prey to economic realities; it was one of the most satisfying manifestations of our collective transformation program. We'd show up at the park, or the local band shell, wherever, set up our gear, and play to whoever was there. As we brought the phenomenon from San Francisco out to the rest of the country, we would plan announcements with the local college radio stations (not to be broadcast until the day of the show), and there would usually be a very enthusiastic and receptive, if not large, audience.

The day after we got back home, Bill Graham put on one of the finest of his double bills at the Fillmore: Chuck Berry and Count

Basie's big band. Everybody in the band loved Chuck (naturally, we were doing some of his tunes), and Basie was a must-see for us all — partly for the great drummer, Sonny Payne (Basie's drummers were always world-class), but also for the band's almost telepathic communication and supernatural swing. It was the habit of audiences in San Francisco at that time, when they were presented with unfamiliar music, to sit down on the floor at first, and then stand up and move as the spirit suggested. On this night, we arrived just in time and joined the crowd, weaseling our way right to dead center (no pun intended). The band came on, settled in, and started with the patented Basie opening: quiet, intense swinging from the drums, bass, and guitar, with Basie punctuating puckishly on piano. Without warning, the sky cracked open and lightning struck, in the form of a *fff* band riff from eight brass and five saxophones, kicked back into the stratosphere by suddenly dominant drums. I was literally moved backward by the sound, my ass sliding at least six inches on the highly polished floor. That was the last time anybody's butt touched the floor that night; with a roar, the entire crowd leaped to its feet, and what a sight to see — one of the most surreally dissonant I can remember — hippies doing free-form dances to swing music. If I closed my eyes, jitterbugging patterns played on my eyelids.

Meanwhile, a cosmic event was taking place elsewhere in the Fillmore; Mickey Hart, a drummer from Brooklyn via the Air Force Band, was in the crowd to see his friend and colleague Sonny Payne play with Basie. After the set, a total stranger approached him: "That guy over there? Bill Kreutzmann, drummer for the Grateful Dead. You should meet him." So this stranger introduces Mick to Billy, and then disappears into the mists of prehistory, and the best part is, he was a total stranger to Billy also. Anyway, the two of them hit it off pretty well, and they spent the rest of the night drumming through the city (on light poles, fences, cars) until the break of day — Mickey showing Billy some rhythm tricks that Billy knew he had to have.

They stopped over at the Matrix to hear Big Brother (Billy says to Mickey: "You ever hear Janis Joplin?" "Nope." "She's fire, and Grace [Slick] is ice."), and it was there that Mickey encountered true intensity of volume for the first time; he would later make loudness his spiritual home.

With the rest of us more or less unaware of this latest development, the band continued its string of summer gigs, including two nights at Lake Tahoe and a free memorial in Golden Gate Park for Chocolate George, a Hells Angel who had died in a car wreck. The highlight was two nights at the dance hall at Rio Nido, a resort on the Russian River, on Labor Day weekend. The place has a curious history for me; as a student at the College of San Mateo, I'd lobbied furiously for a seat in the big band that Dick Crest, our band director, had put together to work the whole summer at that very venue. I lost out to the first-chair trumpet, Buddy Powers, which was only righteous; he was a better man for the job — but here I am, seven years later. The big bands are gone, and the place only has live music on the weekends. We play two nights, one of which features perhaps the finest "In the Midnight Hour" we ever played.[2] This version sounds just like electric chamber music, the intricacy and sensitivity of the interaction startlingly reminiscent of that friendliest of all musical genres. A sure way to tell if you're listening to collective improvisation is if the music is so jaw-droppingly intricate and flexible that no single mind could think it all up in such detail.

Even more significantly, this was the moment when Bob Hunter caught up with us — and began a serious collaboration that was to last for almost forty years. The very first fruit of this, and a sign of things to come, was the lyric for "Dark Star." We'd been working up the form of it since May, and when Hunter heard us noodling on it up at the river, he immediately fired off the lyrics for the first verse and

---

[2]Preserved on *Fallout from the Phil Zone,* a compilation I did in '97 or so.

chorus, which really set us free to create the "final" version of the song. The images in the lyrics insist that we pass "through the transitive nightfall" into as many new universes as imagination could conjure.

After a quick run to L.A. to play the Hollywood Bowl, another "Bill Graham Presents San Francisco" gig, we returned to open the Straight Theater on Haight Street with a series of Dance Lessons, so-called because the permit hassle still made it very difficult to hold a "dance." Everybody paid a fee and filled out registration cards, and the lobby was crowded with attorneys, cops, and TV cameras, all hoping for a bust. The cops decided not to make the permit an issue this time; even so, the Board of Supes briefly entertained the idea of requiring all dance schools to buy permits — until Arthur Murray, the king of ballroom dance classes, weighed in against it.

On the second night, Billy's new pal Mickey Hart was in the audience; he hadn't been able to find our rehearsal hall, and Billy had stopped in to his drum store to invite him to the show and maybe to sit in. Mick remembers the sound of the first set: "Oceanic, with waves crashing and currents flowing — all I could really hear was the guitar and bass — and loud!" During the break he met up with Billy, and with a second drum set being found, joined us for "Alligator/Caution/Feedback," a charming little chunk of extended mayhem that we'd been doing for a while. Mickey recalls it being like "jumping into the jet stream; I didn't know any of the songs, so I just put my head down and played." That was one of the highest-energy sets ever; at the end, there was a very long silence while people put their minds back together; right then Jerry goes over to Mickey and hugs him, saying: "*This* is the Grateful Dead; we can take *this* all over the world!"

Another piece of the puzzle falls into place; we can now embark upon an ambitious program of polyrhythmic development, which will lead us to the creation of our most innovative album — and to the birth of experimental improvisation in rock 'n' roll.

Perhaps we'd been a little too high-profile in our outrageousness, especially after tweaking the powers-that-be over the dance permit issue: On October 2, 1967, the house at 710 Ashbury was raided by state narcotics officers and city police, tipped off to our nefarious activities by an informant, who snitched on us to avoid a prison term for child molestation. I was living up the hill near Twin Peaks with Billy; the first I heard of it was a phone call: "Phil?" "Yeah?" "Whatever you do, don't come over to 710." "What? Why?" Click. Uh-oh, what's happening? What to do. Stay here and panic, or go over and get busted, or worse? I decide to call 710; at least I'll be able to glean *something* out of that. I dial. *Ring, ring* — "Hello?" — a very serious, masculine, *unknown* voice. "Yeah, lemme speak to Danny." "Who's calling, please?" "Who wants to know?" "Danny's busy right now, can I tell him who's calling?" "Not a chance!" I yell into the phone as I slam it down. That settles it; I'm just going to cower mindlessly here until they — what? Come for me? Not smart. OK. I'll sneak down there and check it out from a distance. They won't know I'm part of the band. After all, how many hippies on Haight Street are wearing pegged black-and-white checkerboard pants, an eye-attacking Day-Glo persistence-of-vision sweater, zip-up boots, and Ben Franklin shades? I'll just blend right in. . . .

I'm skulking down Ashbury Street, trying to blend into the background (it's *hard* to merge with a streetlight pole, especially dressed like a neon sign) when I hear my name: "Pssstt! Phil!" I look around — I'm alone on the street. So much for swimming in the sea of the people. "Pssstt! Hey, Phil! Up here!" I look up — and there's M.G. and Jerry, grinning like thieves, in the second-floor window of the HALO (Haight-Ashbury Legal Organization) building. If you're gonna get busted, better to have a rabid bunch of civil-liberties lawyers right across the street, no? I climb the stairs to discover that the fun was over and everyone in the house had been hauled off to the pokey. Jerry and M.G. were lured out of the house by the informer (who had developed a soft spot for M.G.) but avoided arrest when returning because of the quick thinking of a neighbor, who got them off the street before they were spotted.

The funniest part of the whole charade: After Pigpen, Bobby, Rosie, Rock, and several others were handcuffed and loaded into the paddy wagon, the whole caravan peeled off for the downtown Hall of Justice, leaving an empty house with *a beautiful fresh kilo of Acapulco gold on a shelf in the pantry!* I have to wonder — what evidence did they actually take with them? Later, a grand jury indicted the unlucky few on charges of possession. The charges, of course, were soon dropped. The other hilarious aspect of the bust was the *Chronicle*'s coverage: a huge headline, *GRATEFUL DEAD BUSTED* (at least they spelled it right), and a photo of Pigpen, who didn't even smoke weed, with the caption "Source of Supply."

An experience like that is enough to make a band feel unwanted, and since it was about time to make another record, we packed it up and headed for Hollywood — specifically a studio in North Hollywood called "American Studios," which was as tiny as RCA had been huge. Because we were going to be working there for a month, we rented a house up above Sunset, a three-story villa with a tower and grounds. The Castle, as we called it, was situated just down the street from a home designed by Frank Lloyd Wright for Bela Lugosi; from the outside, Lugosi's house looked just like the kind of prison a lonely man would build for himself, if he could afford it: low ceilings, arrow-slit windows, huge oak door, only enough parking space for one car. Pig and I spent hours watching the place and conjecturing (not without a few delicious chills) — what must it have been like in there when the old boy was alive? Creeeepy, you bet.

We actually spent most of our time working in the studio; this time, though, we were determined to do it *our* way. This meant changing arrangements, extending songs, and composing on the spot in the studio — not a popular approach with our producer and the suits at Warner Brothers. The right to unlimited studio time and artistic control were written into our contract, however; no matter how many phone calls and nasty letters we received, nothing was going to make us move any faster than was necessary to understand and control how our music was manipulated in the studio.

Recording was interrupted by some gigs on the East Coast, notably at the old Village Theater on Second Avenue in New York. Just as we were leaving for the gigs, we got some bad news — the feds had busted Bear and some colleagues at a house in Orinda. They were caught with a large amount of acid and were charged with conspiracy, manufacturing, and possession. Bear got out on bail and returned to work, but he couldn't travel with us anymore.

It was bone-marrow-chillingly cold that December, and just our luck, the theater wasn't heated; either that or no one felt like paying to warm the place up. If a good friend, Paul Kantner of the Airplane, hadn't happened by with some "Icebag" (bright-green Michoacán weed), our brains would have been too sluggish from the cold to play. The crew built a fire backstage so they could keep *their* hands warm, and while we played, snow actually fell on us from a hole in the roof directly above the stage. Thankfully, by late spring the place would be taken over and renovated by Bill Graham, renamed the Fillmore

East, and emerge as the most prestigious rock music venue on the East Coast.

The next day, I was wandering around town before our session, and I happened to walk down Fifty-seventh Street past Carnegie Hall, where I saw a poster for the weekend's concerts. Among them were two performances by the American Symphony Orchestra of Charles Ives's Fourth Symphony, conducted by that old sorcerer Leopold Stokowski. I must have stood rooted to the spot for several minutes absorbing the magnitude of this news. Ives's Fourth had only been premiered two years before, in 1965, more than forty years after its completion — and the recording had only been out for a year; here was a chance to hear the entire symphony twice, performed by the same forces as at the premiere, and *we didn't have any gigs or sessions scheduled!*

Now, this particular piece of music was welded into my DNA, ever since I'd heard the record mysteriously appear as background music for one of my finest trips: After a glorious afternoon in Berkeley's Tilden Park, we piled giggling into the car and I punched up the radio. Slithering out of the speakers: the hallucinatory second movement, "Commedia," one of Ives's most radical works. The piece is made from simultaneously sounding layers of different musics — hymn tunes, marches, popular songs of Ives's day — all woven together within a fantastical flux of sound.

I get to the studio as fast as I can; I can't wait to give the guys this piece of news. We hustle tickets for both nights and turn up at Carnegie on the first night. I'd managed to persuade the entire band (including Pigpen) to come; the sight of us as we all walked in is enough to energize a Deadhead concertgoer, whose shocked query was: "What are *you guys* doing here?" After all, we couldn't be considered dressed for the occasion. My rejoinder: "We might well ask you the same question, *hippie.*" Yuks all around. We take our seats; the music begins. The sense of space (height, width, and depth) is palpable: the music reaches out to embrace us; withdraws into the distance; then, like a steam locomotive, comes suddenly roaring back. Invisible bands march across the soundstage in two different directions at different speeds; a solo viola mutters an occult hymn-tune as the rest of the orchestra sprays fireworks in all directions; the chorus intones wordless transcendental benedictions as the music fades away into silence. We all were blown completely away. None of us could even speak for the longest time. Mickey was so amazed ("Holographic! Life-transforming!") at the cross-rhythmic marching bands, he had to hear it again, so he and I went back for the second night. The fact that that particular passage required three conductors made it even more fascinating. Right then and there, Mick and I began trying to figure a way to do something similar with our music.

We had a two-week tour of the Northwest (with Quicksilver) coming right up. Dan Healy, one of our sound crew, would be recording us on a variety of tape media — two-track, hybrid two/four track, full four-track — and at three different speeds: 7½, 15, and 30 inches per second (ips) (clearly the problem of assemblage would have to be addressed before mix-down).

Before the tour, though, we played our first gig at a place called the Carousel Ballroom in San Francisco. Located on the second floor above a Ford dealership at Van Ness and Market, the Carousel had lived through several incarnations as a dance palace, most recently as an Irish dance hall. The Carousel was about the same size as the Fillmore, but with a more rectangular room and a lower ceiling. It had a welcoming feeling to it, an intimate, almost nurturing atmosphere. With the stage repositioned, and light show screens and gear, it was a perfect venue for the cosmic dance. Over the next three years, we played some of our most visionary and exploratory music there, along with some that was completely incomprehensible and some that was just plain pitiful, as when we had to follow Miles Davis on that stage in 1970. Hey, we never claimed to be consistent — just persistent.

The great Northwest tour of '68 got moving right thereafter; we had put together a tight little self-contained module consisting of the Grateful Dead, Quicksilver, and Jerry Abrams's Head Lights light show. This was our first real tour, and it was a flaming success from the git-go, in terms of bringing "The Quick and the Dead" to college gyms and city dance halls up and down the coast. I saw us as the Psychedelic Pony Express, bringing the news over the mountains. We weren't yet sure whether the trip would "travel," as they say, but as the cities flew by, we had to admit that yes, the people were coming out in droves, and they were *digging* it. The high point was two nights at the Crystal Ballroom in Portland, a venue that had been built in the twenties for big-band dancing. It came complete with a flexible, spring-loaded, ball-bearing dance floor. What a blast to dance on that floor, as I did to Quicksilver's music on the first night — one couldn't put a foot wrong.

Throughout the next few weeks we filled reel upon reel of tape with live performances of the new material — mostly at the Carousel, but also at King's Beach, Lake Tahoe, and other local venues. A "consortium" of San Francisco bands had leased the Carousel under the general management of one Ron Rakow, who had been hanging around the Pleasure Crew for a while, even taking some (pretty good) photos of us on our first trip to New York. Ron wasn't a very good businessman, however; he negotiated a deal that made it impossible to pay the lease and keep running the business.

We opened the Carousel on St. Valentine's Day 1968, an event that was clouded for us by the loss, ten days earlier, of Neal Cassady. Neal, apparently in response to a wager about the number of railroad ties on the track between Nogales and San Miguel, had died of exposure while walking the tracks and counting. It hardly seemed credible that a life force like his, so generously endowed with the *rhythm* of motion through time, could be smothered and shut down at such an early age (he was forty-two). When I told a friend we'd lit a candle for Neal, his response was, "Did you light it at both ends?" My reply: "No, in the middle; it gives off more light that way." *That's* how Neal lived: giving off more light than heat, ceaselessly interacting with the multitudinous cast of characters (including everyone he'd ever met and some he hadn't) living inside his head, infinite waves of probability dancing around him like a cloud of cherubs — "Over here, Neal!" "Me!" "No, me!" — or snuggling up to him as if they were warm puppies. On opening night at the Carousel, we dedicated the second set to Neal's memory and played the full sequence of new music we'd been working on. That performance led us to settle on the particular sequence of songs that would appear on the album. I truly believe we were channeling Neal that night. The music was such a living thing: growing and changing from bar to bar, with his turn-on-a-dime responsiveness to context and novelty. More than once I thought I saw, out of the corner of my eye, a nine-pound sledgehammer describing a graceful arc through my field of vision. When we listened back to the show, it was spectacular — vivid, protean, and relentless.

The contrast couldn't have been greater between that performance and a show one month later, on the weekend of my twenty-eighth birthday. Neal's death had hit me harder than I knew; I'd been obsessing on the loss of one of the most inspiring people I'd ever known personally. At one point in the show, I entered a state of total brain-sag — frighteningly, nothing that was being played made any *sense* to me. I was so panicked that I stopped playing to try to figure it out. Even worse, I suddenly noticed that Jerry was *glaring* at me from across the stage — something that had never happened before. I was so distressed that I stared blankly back at him. After the show, as I was trying to slink out without anyone noticing, I encountered Jerry at the top of the stairs leading to the dressing room. He grabbed me by the collar, and snarled, "You play, motherfucker!" and shoved me aside. I tripped over my own feet and fell down the stairs right on my ass. Jerry was normally such a sweetheart that I was shocked beyond belief at being physically manhandled by him. I must have provoked him beyond reason, something I promised myself I would avoid assiduously in the future. To top it all off, as I was leaving the Carousel and walking along Market Street to the car, a San Francisco police car deliberately drove into the trolley lane, which was filled with standing water from a recent storm, and sped past — drenching me from head to toe with scummy rainwater. All in all, not a good night for me. But Jerry's vehement response shook me out of my lethargy, and I vowed to myself that in the future I would live up to Neal's inspirational example.

At the gig the following evening, Jerry was apologetic: "Sorry, man — I don't know what came over me." Typically, we never discussed exactly what had triggered his anger. It was a relief that we were back on good terms, but my feeling was that he had been upset because I let my ongoing distraction over Neal's death get in the way of the music. Even without the influence of drugs, one's sense of elapsed time expands and contracts when playing music. I had thought I'd stopped playing that night for several minutes, an eternity in musical time. Listening back, I found that it had only been eight bars, about twenty seconds. Moreover, the rest of the show was spectacular, teeming brilliantly with ideas and contrasts. So good, in fact, that we ended up featuring it on our album.

Meanwhile, over in the Haight, the locals, after a long, rainy winter, had thronged the streets on the first sunny Sunday they'd seen in living memory. With cars still cruising Haight Street, a minor incident occurred involving pedestrians and a car; the resultant overreaction by the police led to a full-scale riot, with bottle-chucking hippies, fully-equipped tactical squads, and seventy-five arrests. In order to back off from their confrontational stance, the authorities decreed that Sunday, March 3, 1968, would be a day of reconciliation and peace. And, by the way, Haight Street will be closed to traffic until 6:00 p.m. Whacko! What an opportunity! The conspiracy began to gather momentum: Why don't we go down there and play for free?

All we need is two flatbeds ("Check"), some electricity ("Run a line from the Straight Theater. Check"), and a scam to get past the block-ade. ("Check. We'll go in by Sergeant Sunshine's[1] spot — he's right there by the Straight. There's supposed to be music — we'll tell them we're it.") Our managers, Rock Scully and Danny Rifkin, put it all to-gether in a matter of hours. I remained blissfully unaware of this par-ticular spasm of frenzied activity until the day itself dawned, and the call came: Come down and bring your instrument, we're gonna play on Haight Street. Hot-diggety-damn! Let's ramble!

To minimize hassle, the band rides in on the trucks; all except Jerry, who walks down Haight carrying his guitar, just another hippie on his way to play music in the park. It's easy, almost as if we'd paid somebody off. We drive down Stanyan Street, turn right on Haight, and see the other truck waiting a block up, at the corner of Cole. Our truck approaches the barricade; sure enough, there's Sergeant Sun-shine. Rock leans out, shouting something about we're the music, they told us to set up here, yadda yadda; the barricade *melts* away and we swing smoothly into position. The Cole Street truck pulls up tight and close, and a roadie slaps some plywood down to bridge the two truck beds; the drums come out and are nailed down. A bright-orange electrical extension cord, then two more, then another three, sail through the air from a window in the Straight Theater. We plug in our power strips. We power up the amps. We tune our instruments. Jerry arrives and climbs on the truck. He plugs in. We rip off our standard warm-up licks, set volumes (loud!), and launch into "Viola Lee Blues" with a chord (played in four keys at once) like the impact of a planet-killer asteroid. Out of the shock waves comes Bobby's gui-tar with the song hook, and we're into it — our favorite launchpad.

We play on through that sparkling spring afternoon, and it's as if we've moved into a timeless realm where only the music and the

---

[1]A simpatico San Francisco police officer.

people listening exist, the whole world of confrontation and conflict seems to have faded away. Of all the free shows we played during the time we lived in the Haight — the Panhandle, in the park itself, the Be-In — this is the Grateful Dead's finest hour. Sidewalk-to-sidewalk people, people hanging out of windows, clutching fire escape railings, crowding onto apartment rooftops, all grooving impossibly hard, as if they know that this is a swan song, a farewell to the spirit that brought us all together at that time and place. And so it was; within three months the entire band would leave San Francisco for Marin County, just across the Golden Gate.

For our second album, *Anthem of the Sun,* we started out working on our songs "Dark Star," "The Other One," "Alice D. Millionaire," "Alligator/Caution," "Born Cross-eyed," and a little thing I had pecked out on the studio harpsichord back when we were at RCA for our first album — which later, with some lyrics from my mad beatnik college buddy, Bobby Petersen, became "New Potato Caboose." It's interesting to consider the evolution of this particular song: It didn't spring into being all at once, but rather amalgamated itself over time, with small but crucial contributions from the whole band. Pig added a celesta part to the intro, Jerry a melodic phrase for the verse, and Mickey a glockenspiel riff and a very important gong roll. Bob sang lead on the song, since I wasn't ready to try singing leads yet.

After a month in the studio, however, we didn't have even one song complete, just a bunch of fragments, and this was already twice as long as we'd taken to record the entire first album. We instinctively realized that none of the songs would really be ready for prime time until we had played them live for a while. We didn't care; we were going to do this one *right,* and it was going to reflect the real Grateful Dead experience.

Since we were going to New York for some gigs over Christmas, we booked some studio time in Manhattan. Century Studios had a nice medium-sized recording room, and the control room was located up two flights of stairs, looking out over the room like the command tower on an aircraft carrier. They also had a great-sounding grand piano, a colossal gong, and a pair of timpani, which I pounced on immediately, using them to quote Beethoven's Ninth Symphony in the chorus of "Born Cross-eyed."

This was also the venue for the Prepared Piano Incident — a landmark moment for our determination to work in an oppression-free environment. My old friend T.C. flew in to add some keyboard texture to the transition from the "Cryptical" reprise into "New Potato Caboose"; later in the week he also played a few licks on "Alligator" and "Born Cross-eyed." To prepare a piano, one inserts objects between the strings of a given note, causing the pitch and timbre to be changed radically; the resultant sound depends heavily on the location of the object in relation to the harmonic nodes of the strings. T.C. had set this one up so that it sounded as if three gamelan orchestras were playing at once, each about a quarter-tone out of tune with the others. It sounded eerily beautiful, surging and swelling like an ocean of bells — just what the transition wanted; we then overdubbed part of a tape piece that T.C. had done while studying in Europe. Almost there; it needs — something, right about . . . here? "OK," said Tom. "I got just what you need — roll it one more time." We chugged back up to the control room. The tape rolled, and the sequence played. At just the right moment, like an axe and a chainsaw combined, the most glorious glissando poured ripping and tearing out of the speakers, sounding just like a portcullis being lowered at a medieval castle. Our producer came halfway out of his chair, staring white-faced at us as we, giggling inanely, luxuriated in the sheer noise of it. I've rarely seen such shock on a human face. He must have thought that we'd actually destroyed something — if not the piano, then the speakers, or the mikes . . . *something!* He ran down to the main room, followed by all of us, only to discover T.C. standing by the piano with a goofy smile on his face, holding — a top. That's right: a child's toy gyroscope, which he had set spinning and then applied, none too gently, to the piano soundboard at the crucial moment. "Wow," he said sheepishly. "I heard that all the way down here" — through the walls, floor, and two panes of vacuum-sealed glass.

We might still have had a producer even after that if Bob, on the same night (always ahead of his time), hadn't asked for the sound of "thick air" (actually a perfectly reasonable request, a concept later to be legitimized by Stockhausen as "colored silence": silence that's sculpted through equalized reverberation, delay, or some other electronic trick). For Dave Hassinger it was the final indignity. Convinced that he'd finally been locked up with the inmates at the asylum, he threw up his hands and stalked out, muttering, "Thick air — he wants the sound of *thick air!*"

The first few days after our producer's exit frequently found all of us in the main room playing, with no one behind the board in the control room. We didn't get a lot done that way, so in time-honored Grateful Dead tradition we turned frantically to the nearest possible help, inviting Dan Healy (our live sound mixer and bull-goose electrical troubleshooter) to join us in the hunt. Dan eagerly took up the challenge and instantly became the core of the tech team: from running the board and the tape machines, to soldering forbidden connections in the guts of the various rented tape machines, to *performing* a transfer of live tracks by controlling the speed of the machine with his thumb on the tape reel — his expertise, flexibility, imaginative approach, and can-do spirit validated the concept, giving us the confidence that we needed in order to "mix it for the hallucinations," as Jerry described it.

We had been recording live performances of all the material we thought we wanted to use: "Cryptical Envelopment," "The Other One," "New Potato Caboose," "Born Cross-eyed," "Alligator," and "Caution." We also had complete studio tracks of most of the songs (all except "Caution" and "The Other One"). Why not grow a hybrid using both? The Grateful Dead have always primarily been a live band; we've never quite managed to capture on record just exactly what it is that we do so well. *Anthem of the Sun* comes closest, but that work is a paraphrase — an attempt to convey the experience of consciousness itself, in a manner that fully articulates its simultaneous, layered, multifarious, dimension-hopping nature. Musically, it takes the form of two extended *compositions* (the two sides of the original album), using the songs as material to be developed, rather than as ends in themselves.

In order to finish *Anthem,* we had to find a way to organize the formidable body of material we'd amassed over the last three months. After agonizing over this problem for weeks, an epiphany flashed into my mind: the sound of a thousand-petal lotus, unfolding in constant renewal. To realize this concept, we had to find identical thematic statements and play several back simultaneously, in order to bifurcate the material into many layers of the same music, all derived from different performances. For example, for "The Other One," we took recordings of performances from the Carousel Ballroom, the King's Beach Bowl, and the Shrine Auditorium in L.A. and blended them with our core performance from St. Valentine's Day. All four performances start together at the same point in the music but almost immediately begin to diverge from one another ever so slowly; suddenly we can see all the possibilities at once, and hear time from the standpoint of eternity, as if the music had *broken through* into a higher dimension of awareness. This lasts just long enough to engender a feeling of disorientation; it's then faded down, allowing the core performance (now expanded from two to four tracks) to emerge, as if this *one,* this particular musical universe, had evolved inevitably out of the probabilities generated by the *many* (the others heard previously). We then play through the song in a live performance, cutting back to the studio at the beginning of the next vocal segment (the reprise of "Cryptical Envelopment").

This technique provided us with both a means of extending the material through thematic improvisation, and a means of transition between live and studio recording; we wanted to take a larger view of the recording art, feeling as we did that "live" and "studio" were faces of a coin: aspects of something bigger than their differences.

There was a basic problem built into the mix of side 2: the first section (about two thirds of the total length) had been recorded at fifteen ips, the final third, at thirty ips. The splice between the two came at a very inconvenient point in the composition (right after Pigpen sings "just a touch . . . of mojo hand," the sparsest and quietest part of the side), right in the middle of a buildup and crescendo where a simple splice would be much too obvious. We elected to perform the mix "live" as it was going down to the two-track master: as we approached the critical point, Healy would ramp up the oscillator he'd illegally attached to the main motor of the eight track (thereby providing a continuum of tape speeds between fifteen and thirty ips). This meant that everything would be getting faster and higher — the old tracks from "normal" pitch and speed, and the new tracks from subharmonic realms to "normal." At the same time Jerry and I were frantically fading out the old tracks and bringing in the new, trying desperately to avoid any taint of the dreaded Chipmunk syndrome.

Primarily, though, we had to make it *musical:* to lead the ear, and through it the mind, from one sonic reality to another without stumbling over non sequiturs. It did help that the tempos were the same on either side of the splice, but the sounds of all the different performances we were using were so different from one another that we couldn't really find a common sonic denominator for the whole album. We decided to celebrate those differences by editing them cinematically, sometimes jump-cutting instantaneously between soundworlds, or, as in this case, cross-fading from one to the other as delicately as we could. I lost track of the number of times we performed this mix, trying to achieve just the right timing and balance;

it never occurred to us that the continual playing and rewinding was taking a toll on the high frequencies, especially on the outer tracks. This is one reason *Anthem* came out sounding a bit distant, a bit veiled. Personally, I always liked that aspect aesthetically; it helped give it a mythic, "once upon a time" flavor.

The creative experience of assembling this album — combing fragments of studio work with full-blown live performances — served to further solidify the artistic and personal bond between Jerry and me. Both of us were seekers, brimming with intellectual and spiritual curiosity; both of us were always actively searching for the next wave, or what was around the next corner, or what was hidden behind the surface of appearances. To be sure, this obsession sometimes drove the other members of the band crazy, but boy, did Jerry and I have fun. During the many hours we spent performing the mix, it became clear that we were improvising with the studio in much the same way we did with our instruments. From absolute neophytes in the studio, we had grown in our understanding of what could be done there and were applying that understanding to our shared vision.

I've always felt that as an artistic statement *Anthem of the Sun* was our most innovative and far-reaching achievement on record: as a metaphor for the manifestations in our live performances, as a temporal collage, as a summation of our musical direction to date. The problem is, once you've delivered yourself of that radical a rethinking, it's just not workable to keep repeating yourself in the same vein; for continued growth, it's necessary to take an almost dialectical approach: to consider the polar opposite. Our live performances, then, would build upon the discoveries of *Anthem* and result in a double live album (*Live/ Dead*), while in the studio, the creative pendulum would swing from organized chaos to a far simpler, more "focused" approach: songs, songs, and more songs.

All during this period we were working on new material in our rehearsal hall at the old Potrero Theater in San Francisco. A windy, cavernous, *funky* old place (we more than once blew insulating material off the ceiling with low-frequency feedback), its only virtue was that we could play loud and long there during the day. Mickey had been obsessed by the polyrhythmic virtuosity of North Indian classical music since hearing a drum record by Alla Rakha, Ravi Shankar's tabla player (he had literally worn a hole through the vinyl disc, promptly initiating a frantic search for another copy). This particular obsession culminated in a meeting with the master; the subsequent colloquy (at the far end of darkest Long Island one cold and wintry night) left Mickey with his mind reeling: Everything we know is wrong! Well, maybe not *everything,* but we sure can have fun trying out all kinds of new combinations: You play *that* pattern in seven for four bars, while at the same time I play *this* pattern in four for seven bars; we should come out together, right?

At this point we began working with exotic time signatures: seven, ten, eleven beats to a bar. In some instances, we could take phrases that were in normal meters, such as four or three, and simply extend one segment, arriving at irregular pulses in that way. In other instances, we could be working on a pattern in, say, eight beats, and someone would mistakenly play it a beat, or half-beat, shorter or longer: "Hold it! Do that again!" "What?" "What you just did!" "What? You mean this?" "No! You know [hands waving descriptively] . . . the other thing!" "Oh! This?" "Yeah! Let's all try that!" Our improvisational philosophies such as "There are no mistakes, only opportunities" and "The one [downbeat] is always where it seems to be" began with this type of discovery.

The major themes that came out of these sessions were a seven-beat jam in G^7 that we used as a destination in "Viola Lee Blues"; a seven-beat riff in D minor that when extended to ten beats became "Playin' in the Band," a Hunter/Hart/Weir collaboration; and a deeply demented waltz-groove of twelve beats and three chords in A, which when shortened by one beat became — you guessed it — "The Eleven," a song I cowrote with Hunter. I was so excited by these developments that I instantly wanted to take it further: Let's play in and out of these meters and weave them into the flow of the improv (for example, when half the band plays twelve bars of eleven and the other half plays eleven bars of twelve, all with accents), instead of just playing riffs that we work out on and then move on to some other box. "Why, we can shift rhythmic gears seamlessly if we play on the pulse! Let's try it. Five, six, seven . . ." I was so driven by this vision that I became somewhat, shall we say, insistent about going *over* and *over* these transitions — in short, pulling a Toscanini on my brothers. Sometimes these very intense rehearsal sessions would tip me over the edge and I'd start yelling at the drummers: "Let's do it again — right this time."

The inevitable result of this behavior was that it was my turn to be on the receiving end of an intervention-type meeting with the band and management. Led by the drummers, the agenda was to persuade Phil to "back off with the pressure, all right?" I capitulated, albeit rather grumpily. The payoff, though, was that the playing we did at the Potrero welded us more deeply together as a musical unit.

In the real world of 1968, the social fabric of the whole country was being stretched and battered almost beyond repair by opposing forces of dissent and repression; the Vietnam War was coming to be seen by many as more of a threat to our country than the Commies in Hanoi. The Tet Offensive in March '68 had led to widespread disenchantment with the progress of the military option, and an election-year challenge arose to President Johnson from within his own party (led at first by Eugene McCarthy and then by Robert Kennedy). The vehemence of this reaction caused LBJ to withdraw his candidacy, throwing the race for the presidency wide open. (Me: "Do you know what this means?" Jer: "Yeah, it means Bobby Kennedy's gonna be the president.") Four days after Johnson's announcement, Martin Luther King Jr. was assassinated in Memphis; riots broke out in more than one hundred U.S. cities.

Amid this chaotic flux of energy, our April tour of the East Coast began in Miami at a club called Thee Image; after three days in Philly, we moved out to Stony Brook, Long Island, for one show, then back to the city for seven more. Meantime, protests and sit-ins were occurring all over the country, chiefly at universities and other academic institutions. The most high-profile of these student insurrections was the takeover at Columbia University in late April '68. The students had taken over the administration offices, protesting, among other grievances, the university's business ties to the "military-industrial complex." The powers-that-be unleashed the police, ejecting the students from the offices and locking down the campus. All classes were canceled, and the university, one of the pearls of the Ivy League, was virtually shut down except for two camps: students and security, both nervously waiting for the inevitable spark that would blow the whole place up.

Enter the wild card: into this face-off blithely trip the Grateful Dead, smuggled onto the campus disguised as loaves of bread like a parody of Robin Hood and his Merry Men entering the sheriff's archery contest at Nottingham. Shedding our plastic disguises, we pile out of the bread truck and run the fastest setup ever: faster even than Haight Street (where most of the amps were already set up on the truck, and all we had to do was bring out the drums and mikes). We play a short set, pack up, and split — the whole operation taking less than two hours.

Ultimately, the event left us with a less than satisfying feeling; the band and the students weren't on the same wavelength. We all thought of this as a prank, the ultimate guerrilla music mission — while the students were in a much more serious frame of mind. Two days later we joined the Airplane and Paul Butterfield at the Central Park band shell for a free gig, and that afternoon in the park felt as if, for the first time, we had been able to invoke the spirit of the Haight in New York, if only for four hours.

Back home in San Francisco, the Carousel era was rapidly drawing to a close. The lease made it impossible to make money, and some of the performers didn't draw, as hip as they were (a weekend with Thelonius Monk? I was there every night). The bands (Grateful Dead, Airplane, and Quicksilver, with Big Brother as a silent partner), who had formed an umbrella organization to run the place, lacked the desire and the business sense to be hands-on daily-detail managers. They were too busy making music, playing gigs, etc. The place really was, during those four months, a kind of clubhouse for everyone in the scene. My social life at the time was severely constricted, consisting mostly of the Grateful Dead, and the Carousel was a place where I could hang out when I wasn't working, or fall by after the gig was over. Light-show artists would have their own "jam" going on, and personnel and staff from the Fillmore and Avalon could be found there almost any night. All in all, a very loose, welcoming, and inclusive scene — I should have known it couldn't last. Indeed, even as the Carousel became submerged in the rising tide of demands from special interests in the community, Bill Graham was looking for an exit from the Fillmore, which had become too small and expensive to operate. Through a combination of mismanagement and social provocation on our side, shrewd thinking and quick action on Bill's part, and with a huge sigh of relief from the owners, Bill negotiated a deal that gave him control and allowed him to close the Fillmore Auditorium one day and open the Fillmore West (formerly the Carousel) the next. It was a relief to discover that under Bill's management the scene itself didn't change much — just that it was now a fully functional business.

While the Carousel was going through the throes of rebirth, the Grateful Dead band members (with the exception of Pigpen) were leaving the Haight (and the city) to take up residence in verdant, bucolic Marin County. Jerry moved to Larkspur, where Hunter later joined him; Bobby and Mickey to Novato; Billy to Lucas Valley, San

Rafael. My girlfriend, Rosie, found a house for us in Fairfax, a small town on the edge of wild-and-woolly West Marin (today the last bastion of hippiedom in the Bay Area, for those who can afford it). I moved into my new home the morning after the '68 California primary election. After unloading my stuff, I turned on the TV, and as soon as I saw Walter Cronkite's face, even before the sound came up, I knew. Oh no, not again. Yep. Again. Walter's voice faded in, saying, "And if you've just joined us, Senator Kennedy was shot in the kitchen of the Ambassador Hotel. . . ." The Martin Luther King and RFK assassinations seemed to tip the whole precarious top-heavy scaffolding of society over a cliff; the resulting chaos in the streets and at the conventions made it feel as if there might be a revolution going on.

There certainly was a revolution going on in our band: Jerry was definitely emerging as the undeclared leader. As much as we all loved playing with one another, everyone's primary musical bond was with Jerry. Musically, we had come so far so fast that Jerry and I were trying to expand our musical language into new rhythmic and harmonic realms. Elsewhere in the band, the texture of Bobby's rhythm playing was showing signs of his innate whimsical originality; unfortunately, neither Jerry nor I recognized this development for what it would become. Pig had always been the drinker of the bunch (he had only tried acid once — involuntarily), while Jerry and I were operating in an acid-fueled collective mind field. We were so excited by this that we were ignoring the fact that Pig didn't seem to be connecting with us on a musical level. As Jerry and I spun further and further out, we began to see Pig's contribution more as an anchor than as a balance or a ground.

It seemed to be time for another confrontation, so Jerry suggested to me that we ask Rock to help us communicate our frustrations to the rest of the band. Rock's solution: call a meeting of the band and lay everything out on the table. Despite Rock's efforts to help us verbalize our feelings, neither Jerry nor I was very eloquent, and the meeting ended with everyone feeling bad — and with no resolution.

Mickey formed a side group (Mickey Hart and the Hartbeats) to play the kind of free-rave stuff we were trying to develop. I felt confused and depressed by what had happened at the meeting, and I only came out a couple of times to play with the Hartbeats. That depressed me even further: the music didn't feel right to me. I especially missed Pigpen's warmth and organic *greasiness.* Eventually realizing our mistake, and thankful that we hadn't yet burned our bridges behind us, we quietly left the Hartbeats behind.

Even though we knew that the band worked best with all of us playing, Jerry and I thought it would be a good idea to add another element. We decided to ask T.C. to come in and augment the keyboard slot, thus freeing up Pig to concentrate more on singing and the harp. T.C. joined us on our next tour, and he and Pig shared the organ seat, giving the band a rich, strange sound. It was very stimulating to have a new voice providing a running commentary on the music from such oblique and wonderful perspectives.

As we realized the importance of Bobby's and Pig's contributions, it became increasingly clear that we needed to turn away from balls-against-the-wall psychedelia toward a different mode of expression. It seems that music needs to periodically return to basics and build itself up again. Luckily, Jerry and Hunter had been writing songs, one of which, "St. Stephen," had already made its way into our set list as part of a major sequence: "Dark Star"> "St. Stephen"> "The Eleven"> "Lovelight." This would become the most played sequence of '69 and appear on record as the heart of our album *Live/Dead.*"

Hunter had sent the lyrics of "St. Stephen" to Jerry back in the previous year, along with another lyric, "China Cat Sunflower." Maybe Jerry had stuffed them in a drawer and forgotten them — at any rate, these lyrics suddenly surfaced in late spring '68, when Hunter and Jerry moved to Larkspur in Marin County, sharing a house with M.G.

and her daughter, Sunshine. Jerry invited me over one day to fool around with some tunes, and we settled down to work outside on the porch as he played and sang the verses to "St. Stephen." He had some verses, but the song needed an intro and a bridge section. Jerry played me a little melodic phrase he was considering for the intro; I could hear harmonies under it, so I played triple-stop bass chords under the first phrase. That worked, so we extended the whole phrase through three more patterns, coming up with a structure that was both sequential and circular: repeating itself just enough to be comprehensible, but still leading strongly into the first verse. I then suggested that we use a variation of the intro chords for the unset bridge; Jerry sang a rough vocal line, and everything fit just right. Jerry was never happy, though, with the fact that the bridge had to be played and sung in a slower tempo than the rest of the song: He felt that it lost momentum, and that's probably true. Be that as it may, that's the aspect of the song that I liked best; we had to slow down for the bridge, and then accelerate back to the original tempo for the next verse. If done well, it could be very exciting.

Hunter and Jerry's other songs — "Cosmic Charley," "Mountains of the Moon," "Dupree's Diamond Blues," "Rosemary," "What's Become of the Baby," "Doin' That Rag" — were very different in their scope and ambition. Even as we were reaching the culmination of our first "experimental" period, the seeds of the future were being sown. These were the first rivulets of what would become a flood of wonderful songs, with which we would make our most popular records — and create the backbone of our repertoire.

The new songs were so well suited for recording — full of character and incident; short, yet with lots of diversity in the settings — that we wanted to start making a new studio record. This project would eventually be released as *Aoxomoxoa*. We decided to collaborate with Bobby's friend Bob Matthews, who was working as an engineer at Pacific Recording in San Mateo. The studio had a new Ampex eight-track machine and a state-of-the-art board, so we started work there in the fall of '68 recording almost all the songs that would eventually appear on the record. A harbinger of things to come was our first extensive use of acoustic guitars on record. I also played acoustic bass for the first time on a couple of songs ("Dupree's" and "Mountains of the Moon"). The fun part of that was trying to play in tune with no frets to guide my fingers, just like on a violin. I eventually put little skinny masking-tape markers on the neck of the bass where the fret markers would have been. That helped a lot.

Just as we were finishing the tracks, it was time to pay the rent with another two-week tour of (mostly) the Midwest — in the dead of winter. We start off at the Veteran's Hall in Columbus, Ohio, pulling up to the hall in our rented cars. We pile out of the cars and head in to check out the venue. The hall is huge, cold, and hollow-sounding. We run through a couple of tunes for a sound check and retire quickly to the warm dressing room. Always glad when it's time to play, we head for the stage. I look out into the hall and see — no one. Oh, wait, there are some people right down in front of the stage, cheering us on gamely. About three hundred souls in a hall built for six thousand.

We tune up the guitars, the drummers rattle off paradiddles, and Jerry counts into "Morning Dew." I know from the first chord that it's going to be a good night, in spite of the feedback from the PA. Jerry is on fire, his guitar snarling and caressing at the same time. The drummers are crunching out the groove as if their lives depend on it — Mickey gesturing grandly after each backbeat, and Billy grimly holding the groove close to home. The tune builds to its harrowing climax; Jerry screams out the final line — "I guess it doesn't matter anyway" — and we hammer home the final chords.

Jerry looks over at me, and I gave him a "way to go, man" grin. Most of the time, we don't use a set list — usually whoever wants to sing a song will call it — so Pig calls "Schoolgirl" and we go from there. Jerry lays down the intro lick, and Pig insinuates his way into the song. His harp break fires the band up; Jerry counters with a ferocious lead, and we slide into the rave section, where Pig prowls the stage and really lays down all the reasons why this little schoolgirl should bring him home with her — and there are many. We cap the rave with an instrumental and drop the dynamics back down for Pig to bring it home. He closes it off with a big ritard and a final line — "Hey, I don't care if you're only seventeen years of age" — which brings a jovial response from the crowd.

We finish up and cram into the cars, bubbling over with glee at the quality of the show, knowing that if need be, we can play our best music for small crowds in big halls. "Great set, Pig," I say. "'Tain't nothing, man," he replies. "All I need is one lil' schoolgirl down in front to give me some inspiration."

When we returned to the studio, we discovered that while we were gone, Pacific Recording had replaced their nice eight-track machine with one of the two sixteen-track tape machines in the whole world — just in time for us to record the whole album again. See the Grateful Dead throw away months of work and start recording from the beginning, in order to load up these simple songs with all the extra tracks we can think of. Our rationalization: We'll perform the songs so much better now that we've played them on the road; and besides, now we can add a whole bunch of keyboard, guitar, and percussion tracks! The gnashing of teeth from Warner Brothers corporate headquarters could be heard the length and breadth of the land. It's also curious how this particular recording project (*Aoxomoxoa*) had so many incarnations — two complete recorded versions and two complete mixes. Perhaps the reason was the inexplicable decision to mix by committee. At several points, there were at least eight hands on the mix faders. The original mix sounded as if the songs themselves were almost inaudible; two years later Jerry remixed the album, stripping the dross from the songs and restoring them to life. At that point the original mix disappeared into the vaults at Warner Brothers and was never heard again.

At this time (early '69), we were basically moving in two directions at once: At the same time we were in the studio working on focusing the flow of our music into rigorously delineated song forms, we were also recording live performances of extended sequences in order to capture the group mind in full flight. These tendencies were destined to fuse during the next decade. In the short term, we would reintroduce older material that had been sidelined during our most exploratory period and continue to introduce new songs into the live repertoire practically as soon as they were written, and often before they'd been fully rehearsed.

There's one misconception about the Grateful Dead that I'd like to clear up once and for all: the legend of the master plan. When I say "our goal was" or "we decided," it's not as if I'm describing conscious decisions made in the *now*. From the beginning, every one of our moves was powered by deep waves in the group unconscious.

These mighty currents were now moving us in a singular direction, toward a musical polar opposite: from the big bang of the Acid Tests and the inflation of the first touring and ballroom period to a trajectory of cooling and stratification. Songs from the past that had been dropped as we ignited our experimental stage began returning, slipping into the sequences at odd moments; new material that was being recorded in the studio also made its appearance onstage. The intensity of the peaks and valleys in the sets would begin to smooth out a bit, and the smaller climaxes would be closer together.

None of this was particularly obvious to us as we brought "our" sixteen-track machine to the Avalon Ballroom in January '69. Our immediate concern was to record a live album and get it out as fast as we could, to help pay off the debts we had incurred in the studio. We might have had unlimited studio time, but we were beginning to understand that it wasn't free. Every dime had to be earned back in sales before we made any royalties.

Bob Matthews and Betty Cantor were the recording team. Bear also encouraged Ron Wickersham (a former Ampex engineer co-opted by the Grateful Dead) to invent the key piece of new technology we needed to make high-quality live recordings: a mike splitter, which delivered the signal from each microphone or instrument to both the PA and the record inputs without any loss of quality. It's easy to forget, at this remove, that many of the tools we take for granted today in electric music didn't exist in 1969. Back then, they occasionally had to be cobbled together on the spot.

We started off the three-night Avalon gig with a "test run" of the setup, making sure everything worked OK. On the second night, we opened the show with our current major sequence: "Dark Star," "St. Stephen," "The Eleven," and "Lovelight," and played it for all it was worth; so much so that we came offstage saying things like "I don't believe it!" and "That was the one!" The one that got away, that is: at the same time we were happily playing along, Bear, who at this point was working on the recording team, was crouching under the board working on an input card, mumbling, "I can't seem to get anything from the number thirteen line driver" — the channel for Bob's guitar. When we came running up to the recording room demanding to hear the playback and discovered that not one note Bob had played had gone on tape, we turned on Bear like a pack of rabid wolves, reducing him nearly to tears within minutes. We all felt as if we'd played one of the finest sets ever, only to be betrayed by the very tools we'd just brought to life.

Well, just to show you never can tell, the very next night we went out and did it *again* — this time capturing the complete sequence in glorious multitrack Technicolor. Everyone in the band was ecstatic that we'd been able to play at all well, let alone at that level. It was as if the music itself was a living being once again: growing, experiencing, evolving. Sighs of relief all around — we had a major part of an album on tape. One month later, at the Carousel, we would record another version of the same sequence; that performance provided the album with an even finer "Dark Star" and "St. Stephen." Two nights later, we would nail down the final tracks, recording "Death Don't Have No Mercy," "Feedback," and "And We Bid You Goodnight"; all that would remain would be to mix, master, and deliver what was to be our first live album, aptly named *Live/Dead*.

But having two albums in the can didn't help us in the short term; we were suffering the consequences of bad business decisions. The huge debt for studio time could come out of the proceeds of the albums; the studio album ended up being amortized by the live one (it sold better and had been cheaper to make), but we were sorely in need of some help with our spending. The attitude of the Grateful Dead was always If it won't work, throw money at it, even if we were broke. Rock simply couldn't say no to himself or to anyone else. We'd even tried Bill Graham's management, but when Bill made us choose between Bear and him, it was all over.

It didn't seem too much of a reach, therefore, when Mickey introduced us to his father, Lenny Hart, to hire him as our manager; they'd been in business together just before Mick joined the band, partners in a drum store in San Carlos. If Lenny regretted the loss of his son and partner to rock 'n' roll, he didn't show it, and Mickey seemed genuinely glad to have him around, recommending him to us as someone who knew about business. When the drum store closed, he'd become a Bible-thumping evangelist preacher; he came on to us as if he were doing God a favor by helping us hapless hippies hang on to our ill-gotten gains, and that should have raised some hackles on our necks. Since Lenny was Mickey's father, and a religious man, we assumed he'd be honest — and hoped he could control our spending better than Rock had.

Since the previous fall, we'd been renting a warehouse in Novato as a rehearsal hall and equipment storage facility. Bear saw an opportunity there for further research into the perfect PA; he hoped to produce the most purely transparent musical sound yet by analyzing and tuning the sound as the band played (with the introduction of computers into the system, it's now possible to do this automatically in real time; Bear's basic concept has become the paradigm for modern sound reinforcement). He also wanted to purify the signal path, starting with the instruments themselves: "low impedance" was his mantra (lower impedance = less resistance to the flow of electrons, therefore less distortion). Low-impedance pickups would flow through special cables, carrying the signal into custom-built preamps and hi-fi power amps (all low impedance); we would also build our own speaker cabinets, each tuned to its own instrument.

At that point Bear, Ron Wickersham, and guitarmaker Rick Turner joined forces to create Alembic, named after the sealed vessel or retort within which alchemical processes take place. Their first project was to modify my Guild Starfire bass, known as "Big Red," into a new kind of super instrument: custom-made low-impedance pickups, the first active electronics ever installed in a string instrument, and, best of all, a quadraphonic pickup with which I could send the notes from each string to a separate set of speakers (sadly, this feature would remain unusable until we developed the Wall of Sound in 1974). This instrument had so many knobs on it that I could never have used them all — five for each pickup: direct volume, EQ volume, EQ frequency, bandwidth or "Q," and type of filter (low-pass, high-pass, band-pass), plus master volume, quad volume, pickup selector, and quad distribution (which string to which channel), all conveyed to the system by a cable the size of your thumb and a solid steel connector like a NASCAR fueling nozzle. Well, you get what you ask for; the instrument was very flexible, but ever so much heavier, and it never did feed back quite as well as the stock version did. Renamed "Big Brown," it remained my main instrument until '74, when I had another one built to almost the same specs — this time with TTL logic touch switches for pickup signal routing, and extras such as LED status lights and fret markers (on the side of the neck). Unfortunately, the switching logic boards were so sensitive to fluctuations in current and magnetic fields that the instrument spent most of its time in the shop — just like a couple of cars I've owned.

Also about this time, Jerry stumbled into a music store in Boulder on his way to the gig and tried out a pedal-steel guitar. The backbone of the contemporary country band, this ten-stringed instrument is capable of many different tunings and textures; the right hand picks the strings with a three-fingered banjo-style technique, and the pitches and voicings are controlled by six pedals, four knee levers, and a steel bar used like a guitar slide. It's a very complicated instrument to play, one that requires all four limbs (the player has to dance while sitting down, much as a trap drummer does). One has to pick with the right hand, slide the bar with the left, control both volume pedals and three to five string pedals with the right foot, control more string pedals with the left foot, and control different strings than those dedicated to the foot pedals by twitching both knees left and right. Try saying that fast, much less doing it. It's a wonder anyone can master it, but Jerry was determined to give it a try. And just as with any other instrument he picked up, he made it sing.

The main impetus for this development was the nature of the new songs Hunter and Jerry had been writing; many of them had a decided country flavor ("Dire Wolf," "Friend of the Devil," "High Time," "Casey Jones," "Ripple"), and Jerry began using the new axe on these as they were slotted into the set lists. Bobby also began bringing in covers of his favorite country tunes and some originals in that vein, so we were starting to see a trend developing. Personally, I was thrilled that the band could make such a complete musical about-face while still maintaining the flat-out weirdness that I'd come to know and love.

Meanwhile, our new manager Lenny hadn't been idle: He was trying to persuade us to star in a really bad movie as psychedelic cowboys (the only good thing that came out of that was learning to ride horses,

courtesy of Mickey) and, more distressing, extending our record contract with Warner Brothers without our knowledge. We later found
out there had been a (re-)signing bonus; although we never saw a
dime, it still came out of our royalties. How naive are these guys?
you're probably asking — and rightly so — but the truth is we didn't
really care about any of those details, partly out of laziness and partly
because deep down we all feared that delving too deeply into the business end might compromise the music somehow.

At this time, and indeed up until we finally had a big record, in
1987, none of the band members made anything above a cost-of-
living salary. In true communal fashion, everything went into the pot
and was immediately spent to further the trip: on equipment, mostly,
but also on overhead for our umbrella organization — salaries, expenses for advancing tours and gigs, office supplies, etc.

In late spring 1969 we played a series of four shows at our regular
hangout, the Fillmore West in San Francisco. I hadn't been taking acid
regularly for some time — only every so often, when the spirit moved
me. As the band moved from the flat-out psychedelic weirdness of our
experimental period into the song era, we all found ourselves tripping
less and less. One evening during this run may have been the first occasion since the Trips Festival in '66 that so many people were dosed so
hard for so long. It began more or less normally; we arrived at the gig
one by one (the days of communal living were by then long past), went
to the dressing room behind the stage to hang out and wait for the
opening band to finish and the set change to take place.

As always, the room was filled to bursting with the band, their
friends and families, and the Pleasure Crew, a group of loosely associated freaks who came to hang out. Among them were Rock's future
girlfriend, Nikki, and her husband, Ken, known to us all as "Goldfinger" for his striking resemblance to the villain in the eponymous
James Bond film from the early sixties. Ken was at the time a notorious
dope smuggler, later responsible for the first pharmaceutical cocaine to

reach San Francisco, and an inexhaustible supplier of Acapulco Gold, Michoacán Green (also known as "Icebag," from the containers used to smuggle it), and other gourmet weed of the day. Also present were Janis Joplin, with Snooky Flowers, her sax player; Bob Hunter and his lady, Christy; Bear; and many other psychedelic rangers.

While waiting for our set to begin, we were passed an innocuous-looking (except for the faint subliminal glow emanating from the liquid, and the barely noticeable sediment at the bottom) bottle of — apple juice! Without any hesitation, we each sampled the bottle and passed it on. As soon as that juice hit my taste buds, my entire consciousness went into "oh shit" mode — I had never experienced the *taste* of acid like that before. Normally one would ingest less than one hundred micrograms (ten thousandths of a gram), and it would be completely tasteless. For the taste to be perceptible, there must have been one hundred milligrams (one thousandth of a gram) in each mouthful. We later found out that not only had Goldfinger, with his usual Prankster attitude, hit the bottle, but that every other acid cowboy in town had added their gram or two's worth.

So there we were — everyone looking at each other thinking, *Are you as high as I am? I hope so, 'cause that's the only way we're going to get through this gig.* As for me, I was launched into outer space: worlds and universes orbiting past, time stretching into eternity, laughing archetypes manifesting cosmic jokes, and then some soft words in my ear — "Phil, it's time to play the set."

What? What set? Mickey was standing next to me with a most compassionate expression, saying, "Phil, come on, we gotta play now." Never had I imagined that I would find myself in a state of being where playing music would be a bring-down — but there I jolly well was. "Mick," sez I, "I wish you could be where I am right now — it's so beautiful; but I couldn't possibly play music now. I don't even know what music is." And I drifted away, back to the glory unfolding inside.

After aeons of time seemed to have passed, I became aware that I was, on some level, still in a room full of people; one of them, whom I recognized as "Mickey," was holding an obscure, elongated device with knobs on both ends and iridescent silver scaly strands holding it together. "Phil," he said, "this is your bass. You play this instrument in our band." Oh, yes, I remember now. How does it work? "Just put the strap over your head like this" — and Mickey took me by the hand and led me to some stairs and then up onto the stage. To this day, I don't really know whether or not Mick was as high as I was, but his tenderness and compassion toward me that night have never left me, and I've never loved him more than at that moment.

Once on stage, everything seemed somewhat more familiar, even though the instruments and amplifiers (not to mention the other musicians) were grinning at me with alien features superimposed on their own. Somehow, I don't know how, we managed to start playing: It was as if the music was being sung by gigantic dragons on the timescale of plate tectonics; each note seemed to take days to develop, every overtone sang its own song, each drumbeat generated a new heaven and a new earth. We were seeing and singing the quantum collapse of probability into actuality — it was frightening and exhilarating at the same time. At one point, I looked over at Jerry and saw a bridge of light like a rainbow of a thousand colors streaming between us; and flowing back and forth across that bridge: three-dimensional musical notes — some swirling like the planet Jupiter rotating at 100 times normal speed, some like fuzzy little tennis balls with dozens of legs and feet (each foot wearing a different sock!), some striped like zebras, some like pool balls, some even rectangular or hexagonal, all brilliantly colored and evolving as they flowed, not only the notes that were being played, but all the possible notes that could have been played. That moment may well have been the peak of psychedelic music for me — the combination of absolute inevitability and ecstatic freedom has never been equaled.

After that high point, things started to get a little weird — Jerry saw Elvin Bishop on the side of the stage and invited him to come up and play some blues. Maybe, just maybe, Jerry hadn't had any of the electric apple juice; he had come later to the hall than the rest of us — but I can still see the sly little grin on his face as he introduced Elvin. I don't remember what tune we tried to play, but it was obvious that Elvin had not partaken of the same libation we had; he was playing away at some twelve-bar blues for all he was worth, while the rest of us were playing the dragon's-breath version of the essence of three-chord polyphonic (in the literal sense of "many-voiced") madness. For example, at least one of us (perhaps even myself) was deliberately playing thirteen-bar patterns in a different key than the one in which we had started; even so, the myriad voices of the music were *fused* into an oblique, schizoid, undulating, seven-dimensional parallelogram. When I finally dredged up the nerve to look at Elvin, he had the most clearly delineated "deer in the headlights" expression that I've ever seen spread all over his face — and when I then glanced at Garcia, his sly little smirk had expanded into a demonic grimace, for all the world as if he'd planned the whole thing.

The rest of the set must have gone by without much incident; we managed to get back to Marin, to T.C. and Bobby's place — a guest-house on an estate in Ross. The dawn found me leaning against the outside wall of their house listening to Scriabin's "Poem of Ecstasy" playing from inside (T.C. at one time considered himself to be a reincarnation of Scriabin, and I must say, the physical resemblance was striking).

Over the next few days, the various adventures experienced by the members of our little tribe that night surfaced piece by piece: Bear, for example, who for once had nothing whatsoever to do with dosing the famous bottle, was accosted by Janis, who put him up against the wall, screaming, "You motherfucker! You killed my sax player!" In fact, Snooky (the sax player in question) had simply wandered out into the streets of the city, later ending up in the drunk tank. Next,

Hunter punched him out ("Owsleystein! Take that!"), blaming Bear for his beloved girlfriend Christy's disappearance (she later returned, unharmed, from the wilds of Daly City). I suppose we can only be thankful that our luck continued to hold and that no one suffered any lasting consequences — except for some great (and some not-so-great) memories.

During the spring and summer of '69, our music moved into a more balanced space; the "songs" were being given all due respect, and the "zones" were flowing freely from song to song. It was altogether revelatory to make a music so fluid that the band could slide from the swampiest blues feeling (with a quick detour through the free-fall zone) into a straight-ahead rock tune, a seventeenth-century border ballad, or some hybrid-groove Hunter/Garcia opus, all within sixteen bars.

Everyone was feeling really good about the way we were playing; the problems with Bob and Pig had melted away. Pig, in fact, was coming on strong as the show closer, the third leg of the tripod, if you will; the absolute master of the bring-the-house-down blockbuster, taking tunes like "Good Lovin'," "Lovelight," or "Midnight Hour" into new realms of outrageousness.

We would sail into the song out of some exploratory jam; Pig *materializes* at center stage: stocky, denim-clad, goateed, cowboy-hatted, snatching the mike (*Thhhwuck!* the band drops into a weed-choked and greasy Pig-space groove): "Without a warning, you took my heart" . . . and we're off; for the next thirty minutes Pig takes us into a world where love is standing right next to you, if you could just "take yo' *hands* outta yo' *pockets!*" — or a world where you've just bought the Brooklyn Bridge, "fo' a dolla and a quartuh."

When Pig's in charge, the grooves get fatter ("fur-lined" is the term we use), each beat has just a little more weight and the space around it is more vivid, the texture gets leaner, and the give-and-take between the individual band members (as well as the interplay between Pig and the band as a whole) becomes sharper, more pointed, and faster.

Now we had three main areas of attraction that we could dance around and between as we chose: mossy-tooth blues and flag-waving R & B ("King Bee," "Midnight Hour," "Caution"); mythical/legendary alternate-America ("Dire Wolf," "Dupree's," "Cosmic Charley"); and visionary/poetic ("Dark Star," "The Other One," "Morning Dew") — all woven together by flat-out free jamming, which could contain elements of all three simultaneously.

We all felt as if we were on a roll as we drove up to Bethel, New York, that August to play the Woodstock music and arts festival; we had been touring off and on for about six weeks, including a run at the Fillmore East and one last free gig in Central Park. The festival was originally planned to serve about 150,000 patrons; three times that many eventually showed up.

Our caravan of rented cars rolled in on Friday, the first day of the festival; luckily, the roads were still open to the site. Our first stop was at the Prankster camp, which was some distance from the stage, over a low hill. The fabled bus *Furthur* was making an appearance, having come out of retirement on Kesey's farm for the occasion. Next to the bus, a stage with open mikes was attracting a few ravers, but as yet nothing like the flood to come. Bob and Jer decided to stay over with the Pranksters, while the rest of us swung by the main stage on our way to that night's lodgings.

The natural amphitheater in front of the stage hadn't filled up yet, and folks in the crowd were calmly staking out their turf, hampered only by the most important single element of the festival — mud. The off-again, on-again upstate New York summer thundershowers and the sudden presence of thousands of humans combined to make the grounds one huge mud-puddle, veined by lines of trees and covered with tarps, tents, blankets, vehicles, and people, most of whose colorful clothing was already becoming a uniform shade of gray.

Backstage, I stopped long enough to greet the Airplane's road crew and join Janis for a paper cup of expensive champagne. After hanging in the dressing room for a while, I decided to check out the stage. I walked up from the dressing rooms to a narrow, tall footbridge that stretched over a hundred yards to the stage. Below, people were hurrying to their various tasks, while golf carts valiantly slogged along the muddy paths. The stage seemed normal enough, but very high, and larger than what I was used to — several turntables were set up to quickly move band gear on and off stage, and a large screen was set up behind the performers for visuals.

We left the site just as the first act, Richie Havens, was taking the stage and spent the night at our motel, a one-story building on a knoll (facing a level expanse of tall grass that would soon be pressed into service as a helipad). We awoke the next day to the news that the roads around the site had been completely choked off; people parked their cars first on the shoulder, then in the lanes, leaving only the centerline down which to trickle, two abreast, toward the festival. So many people had shown up that the organizers themselves had pulled the fences down and welcomed everyone — for free. We knew then that suddenly this gig was a *very* big deal indeed. This was confirmed by the sound of the first airlift arriving to pick up the Santana band guys, who were due to go on in early afternoon; we all stood waving as the chopper lifted off.

Everyone was just itching to get there and get it on, but as always, the operating mode at these festivals was "hurry up and wait" — so we waited. Waited at the motel for our turn on the chopper; waited backstage as the schedule was pushed back, and back, and back; waited onstage while the turntables collapsed under the weight of our gear.

At least our time backstage was punctuated by some fascinating incidents. My favorite: Paul Kantner and stage manager Bill Laudner of the Airplane trying to dose the main water supply (and the coffee urn) with some speckled-pink tablets of acid, and being busted by Bill

Graham, who excoriated them mercilessly until Laudner sought to trump him with "Bill! You don't understand! This is in solidarity with our brothers and sisters in Czechoslovakia! Prague Spring, man!" Bill was not impressed enough to acquiesce, however; it was agreed that the tablets would be given out by hand, individually.

The Woodstock Festival also marked the first appearance of a new countercultural subgroup: the Mud People. Rainwater had collected in a shallow depression near the right side of the stage, near the path from the stage itself to the lines of Portosan toilets that were so essential to the collective experience. The sheer volume of traffic forced pedestrians into the pool of water, and as the rain stopped and more people passed, it turned into a pool of mud. I don't know who it was that first threw propriety to the winds and plunged headlong into the center, emerging coated with mud from head to toe — perhaps figuring that it was better to be muddy than merely wet. At one point during Sly Stone's set I did see dozens of very stoned people dancing furiously, with mud flying off in all directions.

The Mud People took their role very seriously, going so far as to actively recruit new members. One poor girl was going to get some bottled water when she passed too close to the gravitational influence of the mudhole. A dripping form rose from the muck, a hand closed on her arm, and dragged her struggling into the center of the pool. Her protests were drowned out by the music, but I later saw her (or someone who seemed to be her — it was hard to tell under the mud, but I thought I recognized the hair) dancing ecstatically and celebrating her muddiness.

The Mud People continued to materialize at many more outdoor festivals and concerts on the East Coast and in the Midwest over the next few years; all it took was a little rain and enough acid.

I've always felt that different batches of acid had different personalities, alchemically fused into the experience by the consciousness of the person who made it. It's not possible to make the stuff and not be high all the time: molecules of acid are everywhere in the air one breathes. This batch (actually made in Czechoslovakia) was particularly mellow and clear; it didn't seem to have an *agenda,* unlike most of Bear's product (Orange Sunshine, Purple Haze, Blue Cheer, White Lightning). Through the afternoon and evening I blithely tripped on; as the shadows grew longer, tremendous thunderheads blew in and out, and music flowed from the stage: Santana, Mountain, Canned Heat — and suddenly, it was night, and our turn to play.

What can I say? It was a dark and stormy night. In spades. Let's take it from the ground up: The stage, a huge heavy structure, was sliding through the sea of mud *very slowly,* propelled by the very efficient sail-like properties of the monster light-show screen. At the current rate of travel, it might have arrived in the vicinity of the front row of the audience by the next morning; either the screen had to come down, or the wind had to stop. Even without the wind, the stage felt tremendously unstable and rickety. Onstage, our equipment had been loaded onto the rear half of one of the big turntables; it made about a quarter turn and collapsed, because of the great weight of our gear. Shouts of recrimination flew back and forth, but to no avail; the gear was unloaded from the table and reassembled in front of the momentarily quiescent screen.

Back down in the mud, the electrical ground had failed completely, producing in the sound system (and all the band gear and monitors) a sixty-cycle hum the size of New Hampshire. Compared to the background hum you'll hear in any electrified edifice, this was a saber-toothed crotch cricket of a hum: almost obliterating any signal passed into the system. A steel pole fifty feet long was sunk, seeking dry ground. Not a chance.

At the front of the stage there had been lights set to illuminate the audience; these had gone off and would not return. We went on in a howling wind, the screen flapping behind us and blue balls of lightning scurrying across the stage. The simple act of plugging in one's instrument became fraught with peril; we were all still playing high-impedance instruments, so the differential in electrical potential was large enough to make any shocks potentially lethal. Bob steps up to test his mike — and a big blue spark blows him back to the amp line flat on his ass. He bounces back up, his eyes bulging, yelling, "I didn't even touch it!" Yipes. I manage to plug in my bass without loosing any demons, and out of the hum comes a sharp burst of static: then, "Roger, Charlie Tango, [static] I'm landing now" — the command radio signals from the chopper fleet are homing on my pickups and playing through my speakers. Double yipes.

Bear is frantically trying to do something, anything, about the ground loops; then suddenly there's a mysterious voice raving over the PA — but nobody onstage can see anyone at the mikes, or hear exactly what's being said. I look over at Jerry; for the first time ever, I see fear in his eyes: This is truly out of control, unlike the Acid Test or any of the more benevolent scenes we'd experienced. It does seem as if Nature is working against us, but as I look at Mick and Bill I see a quiet determination; Bob, Pig, and T.C. too. Jerry shakes it off and counts into "St. Stephen."

Curses! We're playing into a light-sucking black hole; not only is it pitch black in front of the stage, but the PA is so loud that we can't get any sense of *auditory space* — just the sound of our amp line, the drums and vocal monitors, and a huge roar deeply penetrated by the all-conquering sixty-cycle hum. "St. Stephen" isn't going over, guys — and after only two verses we lurch into, of all things, "Mama Tried," a Merle Haggard outlaw ballad. We get through that without much trouble; right then all the stage power goes off. I stand there, looking helplessly around at the other guys, while over the PA the mysterious voice returns — "well are we are we — our timing is a bit off, because uh, because the only place, you know, where we, where we, you know, feel comfortable is in home, you know, and, but, heh heh, and when the family is a big one, we'll feel, uh, even when we're like this, and the rain comes down, and everyone's, um, in terrible shape." Simultaneously, voices can be heard backstage screaming, "The stage is collapsing!" The PA is buzzing like some demented ten-ton insect, and our amps still don't work. Plus, it's pitch-dark onstage and off, except for a few work-lights and the status lights on the PA amps; *and* the wind is slowly pushing the huge screen askew, diagonal to the amp line behind us. At least the stage seems to have stopped moving . . . and then the amps come back on. Yay, Bear! OK, let's play "Dark Star" — whadda we got ta lose?

The Phantom Rapper has disappeared, somehow, as mysteriously as he burst forth, and we get spacy with "Dark Star" — what the hell, if we can't see who we're playing to, we can at least play for one another. We don't even know if the PA is sending out music; hum is all we hear from that direction. So we get small and introverted, exploring meticulously microdetailed spaces, ever more tightly convoluted, through the first verse and out into a more solidified jam — and then, instead of the second verse, a diagonal sidestep into Jerry's new slow ballad "High Time." We'll try anything, especially now! "High Time" sails out into the blackness, accompanied by the crackling voices of the chopper crews; we still can't hear any audience response over the hum, so let's bring it home — Pig! "Lovelight"! We pull off a pretty respectable "Lovelight" under the circumstances, stopping and building up again on Pig's cue: "Now — wait a minute!" After two or three of those, we start winding down on Pig's rave, "That's all I neeeeed" — I look at Bob and Jerry. An unspoken agreement passes between us: Let's cut our losses and blow this joint. We very slowly fade the song waaay, waay down — into blackness and hum. Thus spake the Grateful Dead, at the biggest gig so far.

The event at Woodstock generated many different responses — from the outside world and from the artists themselves. As I watched TV news the next night, the main thrust of the reporting focused on the impact of the festival on the local area: a tremendous influx of people, clogged roads — and garbage. I've rarely seen Walter Cronkite so indignant as when he described the "tons and tons" left behind, while the screen showed the trash-filled mud slopes of the main amphitheater. Crosby, Stills, and Nash, on the other hand, were ecstatic, celebrating the festival as the most loving, peaceful, and significant gathering yet of a new generation; Joni Mitchell wrote a song, "Woodstock," that described the helicopter "bombers riding shotgun in the sky/And they were turning into butterflies/Above our nation." For us, also, the reactions were varied. It's clear in retrospect, at least for me, that Woodstock was a peak of empathetic coexistence among the attendees; that level of pristine, loving compassion would never be reached again.

Some artists gave career-defining performances at Woodstock: Santana; Sly Stone; Crosby, Stills, and Nash, for example. Once again, as at Monterey, we seemed to find ourselves unerringly in the crosshairs of chaos. At least, we thought optimistically, that particular combination of factors (weather, power failures, timing) that bedeviled us at Woodstock seemed unlikely to rear its head again.

The Charlie Manson Memorial Destruction Derby
and
Hippie Love–Death Cult Festival

The path that led us to the disaster at Altamont began, innocuously enough, with Rock Scully's trip to London in September '69, just two months after the Rolling Stones' free Hyde Park concert in memoriam Brian Jones. Rock's overt mission was to try to set up a similar event there for three San Francisco bands: the Grateful Dead, the Airplane, and Crosby, Stills, and Nash (who qualified as a San Francisco band when Nash and Crosby both moved into the area after Woodstock). His covert mission was to deliver gifts of the finest LSD to the various movers and shakers of Swinging London, so naturally he was busted going through customs. During the process of securing his release, Rock made a connection with Sam Cutler, the Stones' stage manager, and instead of a free show in London, the idea became a free concert in San Francisco, at the end of the Stones' upcoming U.S. tour, featuring the Stones and some local bands.

Having planted that seed, Rock returned home, only to find that things were getting a little strange with Lenny ("Nothing weird here, guys, I send *all* our business correspondence postage due, and no, you can't see the books — you wouldn't understand them, anyway. . . . Isn't this great? I love being a hippie"). At a local gig, Pig's organ had been confiscated from the stage before the show, in payment of an old debt; still, not a ripple of alarm disturbed the calm surface of our detachment.

We saw the free Stones concert as an extension of what we'd always done in the Panhandle — unannounced appearances, short and sweet, in with two trucks, set up and play for an hour and a half, maybe two, unplug, and split. We failed to take into account that the Stones were filming their tour, and they saw the free event as the logical climax of the film, the bigger the better. For reasons of their own, the Stones announced at a press conference in New York that they would close their tour by playing a free concert in Golden Gate Park on December 6, thereby guaranteeing both the magnitude of the event (three hundred thousand would eventually attend) and the impossibility of holding it anywhere in San Francisco, as the Board of Supes immediately issued a statement refusing the use of the park for the concert.

So instead of a modestly scaled free concert in congenial surroundings, we were suddenly committed to a monster event — essentially the setting for a film shoot, which would be a factor in the negotiations for the next site chosen — Sears Point Raceway, in Sonoma County.

The owners of Sears Point, a company called Filmways, had bid for the Stones' L.A. gigs through their affiliate Concert Associates, but at the last minute, the gigs went to Bill Graham. Now, Filmways, in return for allowing the concert to take place at Sears Point, wanted a piece of the film distribution and a huge insurance policy. Not a chance, replied the Stones. So, just a week before the scheduled gig, there was no venue.

On Thursday, December 4, two days before the concert date, a venue in Alameda County was volunteered — a half-mile oval racetrack and destruction derby site called Altamont Raceway. Rock and Michael Lang, from the Woodstock team, checked it out, reporting that it could be done. The setup team went into afterburner mode, siting a stage within twelve hours and cobbling together a PA from elements donated by the Dead, Quicksilver, and the Family Dog. Meanwhile, the Hells Angels motorcycle club had been asked, not to do security (they said, "Nobody hires the Angels to do anything"), but to see that no one messed with the generators supplying the power for the bands (and the film gear), just as they had after the power failure at the Be-In. They agreed, in return for one hundred cases of beer.

The stage was set, then, for the concert to go on as planned: Santana would open, followed by the Flying Burrito Brothers, Jefferson Airplane, Crosby, Stills, and Nash, the Dead, and the Stones. A great lineup, all would agree. But the featured performer that day would be Murphy's Law: Whatever can go wrong, will go wrong. All week, we had been getting calls from local astrologers, including Ambrose Hollingsworth (who had cast the horoscope for the Be-In). Unanimously, their verdict was, "What are you doing? The moon will be in Scorpio! That means really bad news! You have to stop this!" But the event had taken on an unstoppable momentum. From the moment of the Stones' announcement in New York, thousands of people had begun their trek to the Bay Area. As soon as the final venue was announced, concertgoers began to arrive at the site even as the stage was going up and the PA was being assembled. By sunrise on December 6, the day of the show, there were one hundred thousand people on site, with more arriving every minute, parking their cars by the side of the highway and walking over the dusty hills to the racetrack, just as at Woodstock. Even before any music had started, the tone of the day was set by early arrivals kicking down the temporary fences and simply flooding freely onto the site.

For us, the day starts relatively normally; we congregate at the studio and ride into town together to take a helicopter from the Ferry Building Heliport. As we stand around waiting for the bird, a long black limo pulls up and out climbs Jagger, wearing a cape and a shirt with the astrological sign of Leo embroidered on it. "Whoa, heavy," I whisper to Jerry. "You and Mick, both Leos!" We crack up, and Lenny boldly strides up to Jagger with "Hey, Mick! Have you met Jerry?" and then takes him by the arm and drags him over to our little gaggle, with a flourish presents an obviously embarrassed Garcia, and stands by smiling while an awkward silence ensues. Eventually, Jagger shrugs off the situation, and with a wave and "see you around," climbs into his chopper and lifts off for the gig.

After waiting another hour or so, our helicopter finally arrives; we cram in and take off. Flying over the site, I see a gigantic dust bowl filled with people, with the stage situated at the bottom of a hill. The air is full of *grit,* as if tires were burning; we later learn that farmers in the Central Valley have been burning chaff from their crops all month. While we're disembarking, Santana drummer Mike Shrieve runs up, grabs Jerry and me, and, screaming over the chopper noise, tells us that Marty Balin of the Airplane has just been beaten up by some Angels as he tried to prevent the beating of a spectator in front of the stage. My response: "Hells Angels beating on musicians? That doesn't seem right." After all, the San Francisco bands and management teams had been on good terms with many of the Oakland Angels. I couldn't quite grasp what was going on down by the stage.

As we leave the helipad, we're directed toward the downhill path to the backstage area. I decide to check out the crowd vibe, so I take another path and begin picking my way down through the audience, carrying my bass over my shoulder. I don't realize that Jerry is following me closely until I hear his voice responding to someone's greeting; I turn quickly, just in time to smack poor Jer in the chops with the end of my bass case. No harm done, except for the shock; but it starts to feel awfully weird to me right about then.

I think that was when I made the decision not to take any acid that day; and was I ever glad I hadn't. As Jerry and I stumble down through the crowd, people are calling out things like "They're going nuts down there!" and "The Angels are out of control!" Jerry looks at me and says, "Hey, man, are the Angels ever *under* control?"

We approach the stage and see that it's about three feet high, just low enough to make it easily accessible from the crowd; the Angels have parked their bikes in front and around the sides, as if they expect three hundred thousand people (surging toward the stage under the influence of too many drugs, too much alcohol, and too loud music) to respect, or even notice, that the bikes are meant to serve as a barrier. Since his bike is more important to an Angel than just about any-thing, the bikes serve more as provocation than as protection — the thousand or so freaks whose life mission it is to rush the stage keep making the mistake of trying to climb over the bikes to get there. These poor people are brutally beaten with pool cues, over and over again. It was to help one of these hapless fans that Marty had made his dive into the crowd, and been hammered to the ground for his trouble — thank God he didn't knock over a bike on the way down.

Jerry and I carefully make our way around to the back, giving the stage a wide berth, and climb into the back of our truck, where the roadies and equipment cases were hiding. Crosby, Stills, and Nash are playing their set, but the crowd hasn't mellowed out at all, and nei-ther have the Angels. We learn that most of the actual members and officers are attending a high-level meeting somewhere in the South Bay, and are expected to arrive later. The Angel presence at Altamont therefore consists mostly of "prospects" — wannabe Angels who are acting without supervision.

The prospects go wild, beating back wave after wave of deranged fans, as Crosby, Stills, and Nash finish their set with only minor in-juries to the band — Stephen Stills is bleeding from being poked by an Angel with a bike-wheel spoke — and now it's our turn to go on. Our gear has been stacked on the stage since early morning; I attempt to leave the truck and cross the stage to get to my equipment, but a patrolling Angel blocks my path: "Get back in the truck!" Outraged that *anyone* would try to keep me from my instrument, I draw breath for a reply, and then I see the *pool cue* coming out from behind his shoulder. Oh, shit. I mumble something like "OK, OK" and turn away, just as another Angel steps in front of me and deftly redirects my would-be assailant's weapon, simultaneously pushing me back into the truck.

The band cowered in the truck trying to rationalize what we all knew: We're not playing this gig. My excuse: The music pulls everyone toward the stage, forcing the frontline freaks into the waiting clutches of the Angels, thus perpetuating the cycle of violence. Better to cut it short, try not to prolong the agony. What we didn't know was that the Stones were waiting for sundown so the lighting for their film would be optimum; by the time that became apparent, the violence had increased to a point where we were just too scared to risk our asses on that stage. Not that we admitted that to Sam Cutler, the Stones' road manager, when he came to see what was up; we just flat refused to play. In unison.

There we stood, as the demonic red sun slid below the hills, watching ignorant armies clash by day like a battle out of *Lord of the Rings,* both sides so ugly you couldn't tell the Orcs from the Uruk-hai. The crazed victims would rush the stage, be beaten back, and rise out of the bloody dirt to do it again — and again, and again.

For a full two hours we wait and watch, while the light slowly fades. At last, the stage lights burst into life, instantly transforming the hellish scene into an almost normal rock 'n' roll stage; the horrific tableaux beyond the reach of the lights suddenly seem less important, because — here come the Stones! They take the stage; Mickey and I scramble up on a stack of amps behind them — let's see if these guys soothe the savage beast. Wrong. No music could have transformed that scene; as we would soon see, it was a ritual sacrifice in the making.

Under the circumstances, all the Stones could do was play, and play they did. A little tentatively, I thought, at the beginning, but with the undiminished head-breaking action beginning to creep in around the edges of the light bubble, understandable. I think they started with "Jumping Jack Flash," although I distinctly remember hearing "Brown Sugar" and "Midnight Rambler." The real action peaks after "Sympathy for the Devil": As they finish the song, there's a wave of bodies rushing the stage; they are savagely repulsed. Jagger and Keith try to cool the crowd down, but no good; there's nothing for it but to continue. They kick into "Under My Thumb," and now they're playing for their lives; Mickey and I look at each other in amazement — this is really rockin' (and what does *that* mean?). In the middle of the song, we're looking out over Jagger's head into the crowd and see a sudden whirlpool of activity — a flurry of fists, a flash of reflected light, a glimpse of green jacket — then the turbulence subsides and there are only dancing fans. Curiously, after this incident (in which we later learned a man had been stabbed to death), the violence seems to diminish somewhat. The Stones play on, stronger than I've ever heard them play before or since; clearly, they are playing for their survival, as if they know that if they don't deliver the shit, this crowd will rip them apart.

Before the Stones' set finishes, we're off the stage and running for the chopper. The flight back is very subdued, our thoughts and emotions numbed by the magnitude of what we'd seen; it's enlivened only by a zodiacal astronomy presentation by M.G. Somehow I forget to ask her the main question on my mind: Which one is Scorpio? (Right there, behind the moon.)

In all fairness, the Stones were just as naive about the true nature of the Hells Angels as were we. The British version of bikers was descended from the "rockers" of the fifties; they were mostly about wearing leather and riding two-wheelers, bar the occasional rumble with the "mods" (who were mostly about wearing pseudo-Edwardian clothing, ur-hippies, you might say). The London branch of the Hells Angels had, in fact, acted as security at the Stones' July '69 Hyde Park concert, and behaved peacefully there — it's easy to see how the Stones could have made their assumptions.

The Grateful Dead should have known better, but several factors clouded our minds and prevented us from seeing disaster approaching: the fact that the band wasn't directly involved in the planning of the event; the lack of communication between our team and the Stones *and* between our management and band. I didn't know about the movie, for instance, until we were told after Crosby, Stills, and Nash's set that the Stones wouldn't take the stage until sundown.

Today, I regret that we didn't play. *Pace* what I said just above, the music might have been able to at least modify the rhythm of events in some way, to slow, or even stop, the incessant flood of violence. We'll never know. In the final analysis, we were afraid to stand up for our belief in the power of music and the spirit of our community to turn back the tide of hate and transform it into love. Not our finest hour.

It's interesting at this remove to contrast Woodstock and Altamont — indeed, one can't seriously discuss one without the other. They seemed, even then, to be two sides of a coin, and the passage of time has only strengthened that impression. One could perhaps describe them as the "Utopian" (Woodstock) and the "atavistic" (Altamont) facets of the emerging rock culture.

Woodstock, held in high summer in the expansive, radiant sign of Leo, felt like a turning point, the cusp of a new stage of human evolution, the culmination and exaltation of the Haight-Ashbury spirit, achieving, in three days, what took three years in the Haight: a tolerant, loving community with a unified consciousness of the potential available to us as a culture. Some song titles reflect the nature of the event: "I Want to Take You Higher," "Somebody to Love," or "Turn on Your Lovelight."

Altamont manifested as practically the polar opposite; held as fall turned to winter, in the deeply conflicted sign of Scorpio, it raised its ugly head like a throwback or regression to an earlier stage of consciousness. Even some of the Stones' song titles agree: "Gimme Shelter," "Let It Bleed," "Sympathy for the Devil."

More than two thousand years ago, Plato warned us of the power of music to "unsettle the most fundamental political and social conventions."[1] The ability of music to touch our very souls is at once its delight and its danger; the nature of the message wrapped in its seductive glamour can be anything at all. Music doesn't care. Like any of humanity's prototypical tools — language, technology — it can be directed to vastly different ends.

---

[1] Plato, *The Republic* (360 BCE).

In January 1970, after a blissful week of music and sailing in Hawaii, I flew from the islands to New Orleans for our first gig in the storied Big Easy, the birthplace of jazz. After checking into our hotel on Bourbon Street, I joined my roommate, Bear, who was out on appeal bond and could travel freely, in his nightly search for steak. It's always an adventure to eat in public with Bear, as the quality of conversation is almost balanced by embarrassment when he inevitably finds fault with the preparation of the food. Returning to the hotel, I was still grumbling from the spectacle of Bear placing his steak in the ashtray because it wasn't cooked properly.

As we entered the hotel, two Deadheads approached us, warning us of police surveillance. The Airplane had been busted in New Orleans just a few weeks before, and we'd had warnings from the musicians and from Bill Thompson, their manager. A security person from the hotel had even warned Pigpen, but since Pig was so squirrelly about drugs anyway, we just shined it on, stumbling blithely into the trap.

Sure enough, as soon as we get back to the hotel room after the gig, there comes a knock on the door. Before we can open it, a key turns in the lock, and in come New Orleans' finest, flashing badges and chuckling at the success of their high-profile bust. They toss the room and our luggage thoroughly, confiscating everything that might be drugs, including my asthma medication. Everyone except Pig and T.C., whose room is clean, is piled into prowl cars and driven to the jailhouse.

About fifteen of us — the band (except Garcia, who was pulled in later), roadies, and management — are herded into what looks like the main office for processing. After the usual fingerprinting, mug shots, etc., we're individually taken to the jail area and put in cells — but not before the ever-irrepressible Bob Weir somehow manages to handcuff one of the attending officers to his own chair.

By this time daylight is just beginning to filter through the dirt on the chicken-wired windows; I roll over and try to get some shut-eye, but — no such luck. *Brraaappp!* The sound of a billy club tenderly stroking the cell bars brings us all back to grim reality: Guess what, guys? It's time for the Perp Walk! The cops have decided to parade their captives in front of the local crime photographers. Perhaps they felt that the shame of it all would cause us to see the error of our ways. Most likely, though, they just wanted publicity.

We're rehandcuffed, this time to each other in a daisy-chain formation, and led out the back door of the jail onto a loading dock, where the press corps awaits. The shot that made the next issue of *Rolling Stone* features me — in the center, arms stretched out, hair hanging lankily down, eyes unfocused (they had also confiscated my eyeglasses), mouth agape — the very image of the drugged-out rocker. Actually, I was running on fatigue fumes by that time.

As soon as our close-up is in the can, we're sent back to our cells, where some of us manage to gather a few winks before the promoter comes through with bail. On the way back to the hotel, we drive by a formidable mossy, windowless structure surrounded by chain-link fence, and the cabbie glances back at us: "You know, you boys lucky they didn't take you there" — nodding at the building — "that's the Parish Prison." The tone of his voice as he speaks the words *Parish Prison* sends a chill through my veins: This guy knows from experience.

That night, we play a strong first set and are poised to fly into the second when the equipment goes haywire. We finish off the show acoustically, and I'm more than happy to go home early and crash.

There's nothing scheduled for the next day at our venue, the Warehouse, so we announce a special "bailout" performance; Fleetwood Mac, our mates from the two previous gigs, are still in town and come over for the fun. It's only toward the end of the set, though, that Peter Green from the Mac joins us for "Lovelight." Fleetwood Mac at that time were primarily a blues band, not the pop powerhouse they became in the late seventies; Peter's powerful, cogent playing makes our band focus more on leaving room for one another, always a good thing. During the jam I look over and crack up at the sight of Mick Fleetwood, who dances onstage, shirtless, with drumsticks in hand, drumming (on every available surface) his way randomly through the band. A sign hangs around his neck reading: OUT OF ORDER. This, not unexpectedly, provides ample fodder for Pig's closing rave, and we wind up the show on a very high note.

During the New Orleans shows, T.C. had approached us with the news that he had just been offered a very stimulating project: a musical called *Tarot,* of which he would be composer and musical director. We all agreed that with the move away from balls-against-the-wall free-form weirdness toward simpler songs and musical storytelling, this might be a good time for him to move on. With our assurances that he would always be welcome to sit in, we parted ways.

Back in California, Bear was rousted at his home on Ascot Road in Oakland and jailed for possession of a roach. Since he was out on appeal bond from his federal acid trial, his bail was revoked, and he went immediately to jail. When the appeal was denied, Bear was transported to Terminal Island Federal Penitentiary in San Pedro Harbor to begin serving a three-year sentence.

Meanwhile, strange rumblings regarding Lenny's fiscal policies were beginning to bubble to the surface of our awareness. Lenny had temporarily taken over the management of the Family Dog, and when Chet Helms of the Dog asked to see the books and was stonewalled, a meeting was held with Chet and the Dead's management. Everyone agreed that suspicions (from as far back as the previous December, when Pig's organ had been repossessed from the stage) were on the verge of being confirmed, and when Jerry's check for his soundtrack work on Antonioni's *Zabriskie Point* was delivered to the office — and then disappeared — we knew it was finally time to take action.

The whole band, crew, and management team met and decided that it was time for Lenny to move on, but out of respect for a band member's father, he could have a week to come up with the books. What trusting souls we were — right after Mickey and I conveyed that message to him, Lenny (and all the money) fled to Mexico with his girlfriend, a local bank teller who had been helping him funnel our money into a personal account in a Lake Tahoe–area bank.

So there's Lenny, on the beach south of the border with his ill-gotten gains and his beehive-hair girlfriend, while up north his son Mickey is suffering the tortures of the damned — kicking himself every which way including inside out. He had been devastated when Lenny had refused to show him the books. He knew right then that his own father had been stealing from us, and from him. Mickey was thrown into a black depression by this realization. He had known that his dad was mixed up in some less-than-savory business practices before, but Lenny had convinced him that he'd reformed, seen the light, found Jesus — take your pick, it was all bullshit. While others raved about the Hells Angels' bounty-hunting skills (three months after Altamont!) or hiring private investigators, Garcia, philosophical as ever, stated simply, "Sooner or later, his Karma's gonna get him." And it was so. Two years later, Lenny stood trial for embezzlement and did some jail time, which he spent preaching the gospel to his fellow inmates. We managed to get back about one third of what he'd stolen, but nothing could compensate Mickey for the knowledge that he'd brought in someone who stole from us — and that person was his own flesh and blood. We all bent over backward to assure Mickey that he wasn't being held responsible for Lenny's misdeeds. I think he believed us, but it didn't seem to help much.

The real-world result of our brush with the charlatan Lenny (aside from the fact that M.G. and Jer couldn't buy the house they'd lived in and come to love, or our inability to pay salaries or operating expenses) was the radical restructuring of our management team. Old friend Jon McIntire, who had been working for us in various capacities, agreed to step up as "band manager," responsible for record-industry negotiations and communication central. We hired Sam Cutler away from the Stones to be road manager; old friends David Parker and his wife, Bonnie, came onboard as accountants, and Rock was in charge of tour and record promo (paid by Warner Brothers). As always, we expected to be briefed occasionally by Jon, but otherwise — just do it, man.

With the lineup change, the stage was set for a new version of our music: Acoustic sets were introduced, and a decidedly country flavor pervaded many of the new songs. Jerry was to call this period the "Bakersfield era" — after the town in California's San Joaquin Valley that spawned such speed-country artists as Merle Haggard and Buck Owens. The song lyrics reflected an "old, weird" America that perhaps never was ("Lot of poor man got the Cumberland blues — he can't win for losing"; "You told me good-bye/how was I to know/you didn't mean good-bye/you meant please/don't let me go/we were having a high time/living the good life/well I know").

The stripped-down sound that was emerging from the new songs would find its full flowering on a new album being recorded at Pacific High Studios beginning in February 1970; we'd call this one *Workingman's Dead,* and it would signal our commitment to a new simplicity and directness of expression. The almost miraculous appearance of these new songs would also generate a massive paradigm shift in our group mind: from the mind-munching frenzy of a seven-headed fire-breathing dragon to the warmth and serenity of a choir of chanting cherubim. Even the album cover reflects this new direction: The cover for *Aoxomoxoa* is colorful and psychedelic, and that of *Workingman's Dead* is monochromatic and sepia.

For me, already reeling from the bust and its aftermath, the management crisis, and the departure of my longtime girlfriend, it was a real relief to be able to go into the studio and focus on music: Every day I drove from Marin down to San Mateo, listening to the rough basic tracks we'd already made and happily singing along, learning my parts as I went.

Hunter is also in residence at the studio, tweaking his lyrics as necessary. Our entire creative team has now solidified — band, lyricist, tech crew — and we're working together in a harmonious atmosphere, undistracted by any psychedelic craziness. Gone are the designer hallucinogens; now there's only the music, the tape, and us.

Walking into the studio, I hear Bob and Jerry picking away on acoustic guitars, going over "Uncle John's Band," one of the songs scheduled for the day. I tune up my bass and join in. Like most recording studios, the room has no windows, so we've brought in candles and draped colorful cloth over some of the baffles. Mickey is perched on his stool in an isolation room, surrounded by percussion instruments, which he will be scraping, shaking, and bashing. These sessions have proved to be a lifesaver for Mick; instead of obsessing about his father's crimes, he can lose himself in the music and the warmth of our companionship. Billy and Pig show up, we lay down a couple of tracks, and then it's time to sing a little.

Bob, Jerry, and I line up in front of the mikes to sing "Uncle John's Band." We're recording these vocals in real time, singing together rather than one at a time. We'll then double our voices — singing the same parts, on three new tracks — in order to create what's called a "stack." This creates a choir effect, but with the clarity of solo voices, since each voice is on a separate track and can be mixed individually.

For me, this is the first time I've been able to make a real musical contribution by singing. The new songs seem to demand that they be expressed by massed voices, and we're happy to comply. Our three-part harmonies are consciously designed with the melody as the lowest part, but the high parts tend to be heard by a listener as melodic, so I'm working hard to make my parts as interesting as possible.

I've often said that there's nothing more exhilarating than improvising in full flight with like-minded musicians; the same can be said about singing three- or four-part harmony. Jerry's sweet, reedy tenor; Bob's rich, conversational baritone; and my stratospheric alto: The blend felt almost alchemical. From one who lived to push limits, I'd returned to the heart of all music and fallen under the ancient spell of humanity's oldest instrument: the human voice.

The shows, too, were changing radically: "Dark Star" and "The Other One" remained as vehicles for extended jamming, and "Not Fade Away" replaced "The Eleven" in the "St. Stephen" sequence. "Dancing in the Streets" and "Good Lovin'" were expanded to include exploratory jams (and raves from Pig, in the case of "Good Lovin'"). First (and occasionally second) sets were made up of discrete songs with beginnings and endings. Even more extraordinarily, some shows played out without any extended jamming at all. This period would also see Bobby come into his own as a unique and visionary rhythm guitarist. His playing had finally delivered on its latent promise; he would become the tonal glue, the gravitational force, that kept Jerry and me from spinning together into deep space.

One thing for sure: in our dire financial situation, we better play some gigs PDQ, and gig we did: in 1970, 142 shows, the second highest number in our thirty-year history as the Grateful Dead. We were playing well together, and the new direction was very exciting. We felt like a rock band again — lean (even with two drummers) and mean. We were back to having fun, that's a fact. I for one no longer felt the pressure to storm heaven; I found that I'd rather relax and let heaven find me.

Many of the shows we played that spring have entered history carrying the epithet "legendary" — not only because people had them burned into memory, but because they were recorded from the audience as part of a new phenomenon, the tapers. These fans arrived at the show loaded down with portable cassette equipment, microphones, and lots of batteries; they would set up in the most acoustically promising location (usually right in front of the soundboard) and proceed to record the entire show. Since we had from the beginning tried our darnedest to not play the same show every night, the Grateful Dead were a perfect resource for tapers. An entire tape-trading culture was to grow from these tentative beginnings. The technology became more and more sophisticated, and networks of fans sprang up who were dedicated to trading the tapes of their favorite bands. Those who would allow taping, that is; our philosophy was, as usual, expressed most pithily by Jerry: "As soon as we play it, we're done with it. Let 'em have it." Actually, we weren't done with it; we made our own tapes, starting early on, and would frequently audition them to mine ideas from the jams. Many of these tapes would somehow be disseminated into the trading stream, and later we would also authorize our sound mixer to feed his board signal to selected tapers, in the interest of clarity. It's interesting to speculate about the influence of these trader networks on the programmers who designed such file-sharing peer-to-peer software as Napster, LimeWire, or Kazaa — software that does the same thing digitally.

In February 1970 we returned to New York City for a run of shows at the Fillmore East that have passed into Deadhead legend. We were playing two shows a night, sharing the bill with a Southern California band called Love. Opening the show was a then relatively unknown band from Macon, Georgia — the Allman Brothers Band.

"Hey, Phil, make sure you check these guys out," Jerry said to me, referring to the Brothers, on the way to the first gig. "They're kinda like us: two drummers, two guitars, bass, and organ, and I hear they jam hard." Prophetic words, as we were to discover that very night.

The first show went pretty smoothly. We lit off a barn-burning "The Other One" in the middle, and closed with "Casey Jones." Backstage between shows, we met Gregg and Duane Allman and their drummers, Butch Trucks and Jaimoe. It also turned out that our new friends from New Orleans, Fleetwood Mac, were in town — playing somewhere else the next night — and they fell by the Fillmore to say hello.

The Brothers kicked off the midnight show with a blistering set, including their popular instrumental "Mountain Jam." The song is derived from "There Is a Mountain," the Zen Buddhist tune by Donovan: "First there is a mountain, then there is no mountain, then there is," and the theme is actually quoted by Jerry in a jam on "Alligator" recorded for *Anthem of the Sun.* The Grateful Dead had played around with it for a while in live performance, so it was a very pleasant surprise to hear that the Brothers had also discovered the tune and developed its potential.

During our set, we're tiptoeing through a quiet part of "Dark Star" when Duane Allman comes onstage and plugs in. I'm fixated on the fingers of my left hand, so I don't see him at first. Jerry plays a minimal version of the melody in place of a sung verse, and the first notes of Duane's slide guitar creep out of his speakers. I look over, startled: Jerry, that prankster, hadn't told me that he'd invited anybody to sit in. Duane, a lanky towhead with a walrus mustache, is a little tentative at first, but soon gains confidence and begins adding thoughts to the flow. The music grows — and then falls back into a very sparse, quiet space. Jerry takes the music into the minor tonic, and the thread becomes more and more tenuous as the dynamic remains quiet. Peter Green from the Mac plugs in just as I'm pulling the music into the dominant minor; both he and Duane seem to feel more comfortable in this space. Peter even starts to take the music into a "Smokestack Lightnin'" groove. Jerry, as deferential as ever to honored guests, steps back into a rhythm role and lets the newcomers wail. Duane steps up with some tonally ambiguous slide, while Peter and Bobby crunch away at the rhythm, aided by Jerry. The drummers and I pump up the groove a little higher, and Jerry and Duane trade a few rippin' licks. The dynamic is still fairly quiet.

Bob, meanwhile, has been hinting at a different direction — simply by playing one extra chord, he takes us into a full-blown "Spanish Jam," a four-bar pattern we'd borrowed from the Miles Davis/Gil Evans album *Sketches of Spain,* while Jerry and Duane continue to converse. Gregg Allman slides onto the organ bench and lays down some sustained notes, and then some rapid figurations. The dynamic builds, then quiets; Duane and Gregg trade some figures. Butch Trucks joins on drums, as Mickey attacks his gigantic gong, unleashing waves of colored noise. Duane leaps in with a slashing, brassy figure that evokes the blues. Gregg answers, and the dynamic grows louder. Bob is thrashing away for all he's worth. By this time we have a hybrid meta-band onstage, lacking only one element — Pigpen.

Peter plays a huge climactic passage, and underneath the ending of his phrase, Bob and I slyly insert the opening riff of "Lovelight." Mick Fleetwood and Danny Kirwan, the other Mac guitarist, find room to join the festivities. We sail into the vocal at a steaming tempo. From here on out it's a surprisingly coherent free-for-all, with five guitarists, four drummers, organ, and — Pigpen roaring over it all. We go through the two verses of the song itself at least three times. Gregg takes a verse, sounding like a fifty-year-old black man even then. The band breaks down, and it's Peter and the drums, with interjections from everyone. The chord pattern changes slightly; Pig and Gregg trade vocal licks, while the guitars lament behind them. Pig takes it out and back, calling for the band to "wait a minute!" and telling his story. His lover got "box back nitties and great big noble thighs" and "wriggles like pigs fightin' in a sack."

Berry Oakley, from the Brothers, takes over on bass about halfway through. I just want to listen to this for a while, I tell him, as he plugs into my amp. The "Smokestack Lightnin'" theme returns, and the band amalgamates it into the "Lovelight" pattern. My mind starts to stretch out of shape. Everyone on stage is flat-out wailing. Danny, Duane, and Gregg take it into the closing fanfare, but Pig isn't quite done yet, exhorting everyone to "take yo' hands outa yo' pockets." The music builds to a crashing finish, and Bobby jumps to the mike and rounds it off: "From all of us to all of you, thanks and good night."

The audience slowly files out as the musicians gather behind the amp line, congratulating one another and reveling in the glory of it all. Someone opens the loading dock door behind the stage. I walk outside — it's daylight, and snow is falling gently on the streets of New York. The other musicians straggle out. We stand there, our breath steaming, and look east down the crosstown side street. A distended orange sun is rising between the buildings, casting lurid shadows on the fresh snow. I grab Bob and Jerry in a group embrace: *This is what it's all about.*

Back home, we played a four-night stand at the Fillmore West, when we were faced with the unenviable task of following the great Miles Davis and his most recent band, a hot young aggregation that had just recorded the seminal classic *Bitches Brew.* As I listened, leaning over the amps with my jaw hanging agape, trying to comprehend the forces that Miles was unleashing onstage, I was thinking, *What's the use? How can we possibly play after this? We should just go home and try to digest this unbelievable shit.* This was our first encounter with Miles's new direction. *Bitches Brew* had only just been released, but I know I hadn't yet heard any of it. With this band, Miles literally invented fusion music.[2] In some ways it was similar to what we were trying to do in our free jamming, but ever so much more dense with ideas — and

---

[2]Jazz music using funk, R & B, and rock rhythms.

seemingly controlled with an iron fist, even at its most alarmingly intense moments. Of us all, only Jerry had the nerve to go back and
meet Miles, with whom he struck up a warm conversation. Miles was
surprised and delighted to know that we knew and loved his music;
apparently other rockers he'd shared a stage with didn't know or care.

In the nation at large, storm clouds were looming; there was widespread unrest in colleges and universities over the farcical trial of the
Chicago Seven (for alleged conspiracy to disrupt the '68 Democratic
Convention) and the ongoing imprisonment of Bobby Seale, a Black
Panther leader. When on May 4, President Nixon ordered troops into
Cambodia, a supposedly neutral nation bordering South Vietnam, the
campuses erupted with strikes and protests; that day, four students
were killed by the National Guard at Kent State University in Ohio,
and two more were killed on May 14 at Jackson State in Mississippi.
These events provided the background for our tour of colleges in May,
from Alfred College in Alfred, New York, through Wesleyan; MIT;
SUNY Delhi, in New York; Worcester Polytechnic, in Massachusetts;
Kirkwood, in Missouri; Temple; and Fairfield University in Connecti-
cut; students were on strike everywhere, enraged at the widening of
the war and the erosion of civil liberties at home. Some things never
change; as I write this in the spring of 2004, Americans are once again
protesting the widening of a war and the erosion of civil liberties at
home.

The student strikes were erupting as we pulled into Cambridge,
Massachusetts, for a scheduled gig the next day at MIT's gym. When
we were asked if we'd consider a free concert in support of the striking
students, we jumped at the chance. We set up on the steps of the main
library and played a single set. Hadn't we done this before, striking
students and all?

I spent that evening at the MIT computer science lab, late into the
night, playing the world's first computer game (Space War) together

with Ned Lagin, a musician and computer scientist studying there. Ned had sent us a three-page single-spaced letter the previous year, describing how the intersection of music and computer technology could change the way we listened and made music. Both Jerry and I had been impressed with the quality of Ned's thinking, and when Ned introduced himself to Jerry at the free gig, Jerry yelled over to me: "Phil! This is the guy! Remember the letter?" Indeed I did; it was a pleasure to meet him at last, and we discussed the potential of his letter far into the night, while playing Space War over a hot cathode-ray display.

Looming on the horizon was one of the great rock 'n' roll adventures of all time: the Trans-Canada Festival Express. The brainchild of Thor Eaton, the heir to the Eaton's Department Store fortune, and promoter Ken Walker, the idea was to bring the "Woodstock" experience of a major festival with an all-star lineup to the major cities of Canada — one at a time, rather than throwing one huge gig in a field somewhere. Good idea, but they missed the mark somewhat; Canada isn't the United States by a long shot, and as we found out at Altamont and elsewhere, "Woodstock" doesn't seem to travel well, in space or time. The kicker for us, and for the other artists invited, was that we would be traveling together across the vast expanses of our neighbor to the north, by train.

All of the artists involved — the Grateful Dead, Janis Joplin, the Band, Traffic, Ian & Sylvia, Buddy Guy, New Riders of the Purple Sage, Delaney & Bonnie, and Mountain, among others — were of that generation that still considered trains as magnets of adventure and romance, much of our music celebrating the "high lonesome sound" of train whistles in the night. Riding the rails, like running away with the circus, was a reasonable alternative to the nine-to-five gray-flannel treadmill that had consumed the majority of our contemporaries. The train spoke of freedom, of mythical journeys and heroic quests "across the immense and lonely visage of America. . . . [The train] making its great monotone that is the sound of suspended time."[3]

There we would be, all these musicians — crammed into a train with individual sleeping compartments, two bar cars, and a dining car — traveling together across Canada for ten days, with five big festivals scheduled along the way: Montreal, Toronto, Winnipeg, Calgary, and Vancouver. The Dead, and everybody else, jumped at the chance.

Problems arose right away. The Montreal festival had to be canceled because of conflicts with their big midsummer holiday, St. Jean-Baptiste (one down and four to go). We eventually flew to Toronto at the end of June 1970 to start the festivities off with the first big show.

During the events of May '70, general disenchantment with the behavior of those in authority (any authority) began to spread out from the college and university strikes in the United States, reaching Toronto's Rochdale College right after Kent State; the students there set up a protest organization called the May 4 Movement (M4M), named after the date of the Ohio massacre. When the festival hit town with ticket prices of either eight, fourteen, or sixteen dollars (I've heard all three quoted by people who were there), it seemed "totally reasonable and just" to M4M to issue an ultimatum with demands to the corporate pigs that were ripping off the people (never mind that a ticket bought you an all-day show with eighteen artists, including ten or twelve of the top acts on the planet).

The sheer outrageousness of the demands guaranteed that they'd be rejected out of hand; the show went on, then, with about two thousand five hundred protesters agitating for free entry. Throughout the day little flurries of action were continually breaking out as people climbed fences, broke through gates, and generally crashed the party

---

[3]Thomas Wolfe, *Of Time and the River* (New York: Charles Scribner's Sons, 1935).

any way they could. Jerry was prevailed upon to speak to the crowd, promising, to general disbelief, a free concert for the next day, naming the time and place.

That's what happened; we played in Toronto's Coronation Park the very next day for free, along with the New Riders of the Purple Sage, Ian & Sylvia, and James and the Good Brothers. Nice day — and not a bad show, either, for about two thousand people — probably all the same folks who wanted in for free the day before. And then — it was time to *get on the train, and RIDE!* (Two and a half days to our next gig in Winnipeg? Where's the bar car?)

I don't remember who it was that broke out the first guitar, but suddenly both bar cars seemed to extrude amps and instruments from the very walls, and before we'd cleared the Toronto city limits, the monumental, historic, never-ending transcontinental jam was under way. At first there was a "country" car and a "blues" car, but as we thundered on through the night, musicians started drifting from one to the other, initiating an almost molecular process of cross-fertilization. Jerry was in his element — playing acoustic, electric, pedal steel, and even banjo; Bobby was everywhere, singing all the goofy jug-band songs he could remember; Pigpen was ecstatic, hanging with some of his idols in the "blues" car. Drummers were reduced to hand-clapping and seat-pounding as the train hurtled on — over mountains, across valleys, past lakes and rivers, and on into the West.

We were expecting more break-ins at the Winnipeg show; thankfully only about one hundred protesters showed up, chanting "Make it free" while we played "New Speedway Boogie" loud and long: "One way or another, this darkness got to give." The show came off with no other incidents as such, except that the crowd was really small. It was clear after Toronto that the promoters were going to take a bath, and it's to their credit that they went ahead with the last two shows anyway; they could easily have canceled the whole thing (or just canceled the train and flown us) and lost less money. The magic of the open rails lured them in, I guess, and so out of Winnipeg we chugged, bound for Calgary, on the last and wildest leg of our journey.

The jam had grown to epic proportions by this time; if one sat in the dining car, between the two bar cars, one was immersed in different strains of music (country, blues, R & B, rock) swirling through the cars, fading and swelling as vestibule doors were opened and closed, all modulated by the "great monotone" of the wheels, drumming on the rails like swinging robot rudimental drummers from the asteroid belt.

Strangely enough, all this energy and fun was being fueled by alcohol, the usual recreational tools having been left behind for fear of border inspections. Stranger yet, no one became belligerent or mean behind their booze. Everybody onboard was a happy drunk, at least until the next morning when we all, hungover or no, had to get off the train for the last time and face the early morning sun with slowly peeling eyeballs and pounding headaches. You'll understand our consternation, therefore, when the announcement was made: We're running out of booze! Thank all that's holy there was no emergency cord on that train. I can just see the whole thing coming to a screeching halt — sparks flying from the rails as the huge train slides to a standstill in the middle of nowhere, without a liquor store in sight, or for a hundred miles.

We agreed upon a plan. "When is your next stop?" "We don't have another stop until Calgary." "You do now. What's the nearest big city?" "Uh — Saskatoon." "How far?" "Two hours." "OK — Saskatoon it is. Pass the hat!" And the hat was passed — garnering some eight hundred dollars in donations to the cause. That doesn't seem like enough to buy out an entire liquor store these days, but back then, if it was a *small* liquor store. . . .

The train slides to a stop at the Saskatoon Station, discharging an inordinate number of loopy musicians onto the platform; a small group (mostly "management") detaches itself from the gaggle and heads off up the street to the only lit-up building around, the government-run liquor store. (I wonder if somehow they radioed ahead, or was the store always the only one open after dark?) Most everybody drifts back onto the train; a few snatches of music can be heard through the open windows. The raiding party returns, staggering under the weight of their booty. They climb aboard; the train pulls away.

A three-gallon bottle of Canadian Club blended whiskey is installed on a makeshift altar in the "country" car. The bottle comes equipped with a pump dispenser; during the course of the night many on the train (including, in spite of my protestations, myself) will come to kneel in front of the sacred spout to solemnly receive at least one ritual libation (accompanied of course by much whooping and yodeling). After my turn, I hang out for a while until the music starts circling endlessly around the "Falling, yes I am falling" motif, randomly punctuated by fits of helpless laughter. I stumble back to my compartment and fall into the bunk (where I won't get much sleep). I've left my door open, and my peripheral vision keeps being triggered by strange shapes flowing along the corridor outside. At first they seem like curiously elongated tortoiseshells, then like a python that had just eaten a couple of small sheep. I ask myself, "What *was* that whiskey dosed with?" Sure, I saw capsule fragments at the bottom of the bottle — but this is more like some exotic South American vine extract than any acid I've ever tried. Finally, my vision snaps back into focus on the here and now, and I realize that what I thought were semimythical creatures are actually Garcia and the Band's Rick Danko, crawling along the floor of the corridor. Obviously, they're far beyond knee-walking drunk; I had never seen Jerry that plastered, before or since. They reach the end of the corridor, and since they can't get up high enough off the floor to reach up and open the door to the next car, they puddle up against the door and try to get around each other in order to go back from whence they came, all the while emitting sounds combining elements of singing, hiccupping, and howling at the moon.

I had to turn away from the implications of that vision, and mercifully passed out soon thereafter; I awoke to the awful burning brightness of the morning sun full in my face as the train shuddered to a halt. Last stop! Calgary! Everybody off the train! Oh, please God, not right now; can't we just shut the shades and stay here? Alas, no. Outside, the faces tinted in various shades of green provided mute witness to what must have been the most egregious collective hangover ever experienced by mankind (with the possible exception of the Israelites on the morning after the dance around the golden calf). Every footstep crunching in the gravel beside the tracks rang in my head like a bell being machine-gunned right over my head. The sun shot splintered shards of light directly into my brain, accompanied by garbled shrieking from my optic nerves.

Luckily, we were afforded some recovery time in hotels before the final show; nonetheless, everybody looked just a little burned out when we assembled for the ride over to the venue. Hangovers notwithstanding, all the bands played really well at that show, as if to give validity to the depth of meaning and feeling of comradeship we'd all felt wrapped around us while on the train. Janis in particular was in fine form, presenting the promoters with a case of tequila at the end of her set (and receiving a birthday cake and a quart of Southern Comfort in return). The final all-star jam brought a semblance of closure to one of the finest experiences any of us would ever have. But it was the end of the bus ride back to the hotel that capped the whole trip: as we pulled up to the hotel entrance and began to disembark, some cowboy (in town for the big rodeo, no doubt) made a comment about Sylvia Tyson's attire; her husband, Ian, ever quick on the trigger, instantly jumped the guy, and my last image of the Trans-Canada Festival was of these two, locked together, rolling over in the street, punching merrily away at each other as the remaining musicians cheered them on. I stepped carefully around them and walked into the hotel. Personally, I couldn't wait to get up to my room and sleep off the residue of that morning's monumental hangover.

Electric set, Warfield Theatre, September 1980 (© Jay Blakesberg)

Acoustic set, Warfield Theatre, October 1980 (© Jay Blakesberg)

Berkeley, 1981 (© Ed Perlstein)

Red Rocks, July 27, 1982 (© Bob Minkin)

Dead Heads, the Greek Theatre in Berkeley, June 1986 (© Jay Blakesberg)

All dressed up, no place to go. "Throwing Stones" video shoot, Oakland, California, November 5, 1987 (© Jay Blakesberg)

Jill with Grahame and Phil at Frost Amphitheatre, Stanford University,
May 1987 (© Jay Blakesberg)

Jerry and Phil in 1967 and 1987 (© Herb Greene)

Robert Hunter and John Barlow in 1987 (© Herb Greene)

Touch of Grey: Brent Mydland, Bob, Grahame Lesh, Phil, Bill,
John Cutler, Jerry, Mickey, 1987 (© Susana Millman)

Dylan and the Dead, July 1987 (© Jay Blakesberg)

Brent at Frost Amphitheatre in May 1988 (© Jay Blakesberg)

Tom Constanten in
1988 (© Jay Blakesberg)

Phil, Bob, and Jerry, the Greek Theatre in Berkeley, 1989 (© Jay Blakesberg)

Grahame Lesh playing backstage at Frost Amphitheatre, 1990 (© John Werner)

Vince Welnick and Bruce Hornsby in 1991 (© Jay Blakesberg)

December 1992 (© Jay Blakesberg)

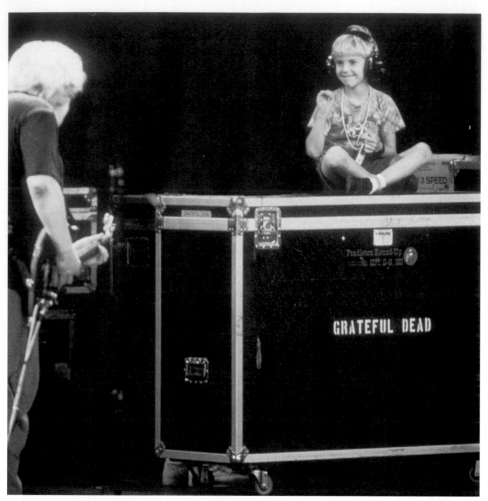

Jerry and Grahame Lesh, 1993 (© Susana Millman)

Las Vegas, May 15, 1993 (© Jay Blakesberg)

Garcia Memorial in Golden Gate Park: David Graham, Jill with Brian on her back, Grahame, Phil, August 1995 (© Jay Blakesberg)

Garcia Memorial, Haight Street, August 9, 1995 (© Jay Blakesberg)

Phil Lesh & Friends, Maritime Hall, San Francisco, February 15, 2001
(© Jay Blakesberg)

Phil Lesh Day in Berkeley, 2001 (© Stephen Dorian Miner)

The Sweetwater, Mill Valley, California, June 10, 2001
(© Jay Blakesberg)

Bill and Mickey in 2002 (© Bob Minkin)

The Dead onstage, Oakland Coliseum, December 31, 2002 (© Jay Blakesberg)

Phil, Bob, Mickey, Bill, May 2003 (© Jay Blakesberg)

Undying love, Bob and Phil in 2004 (© Herb Greene)

Phil Lesh & Friends, Warfield Theatre, December 18, 2004
(© Bob Minkin)

Lesh family: Brian, Phil, Jill, Grahame, 2004 (© Herb Greene)

While on the road earlier in the year, I had received word from home that my dad had been diagnosed with prostate cancer and had undergone surgery. As soon as I got back, I drove up to Napa (where my folks were living then) to visit him in the hospital. Since I'd finally left home at the age of twenty (after two failed attempts at independence), I hadn't spent much time visiting with Mom and Dad, certainly not as much as I should have; that no doubt contributed to my feelings of guilt and apprehension as I approached the hospital. Also, the relationship between Dad and me had been on a roller-coaster ride ever since my entry into adolescence. It was only within the last year or so that I'd felt he had come to accept me as a person in my own right, and not as merely his wayward child.

My earliest memory is of being cradled tenderly in his arms as he sat in the big chair by the huge console radio in our living room; I'm staring at a brilliantly colored faux Tiffany lampshade showing quaint Dutch landscapes with windmills. (That same lamp stands today on my son Grahame's bedside table.) I loved him unreservedly then, as a child will. When we went on our Sunday drives with my grandma Bobbie and Mom, I would stand on the seat next to him with my arm around his neck and watch him drive.

The last time I'd seen him had been the preceding Christmas; I'd gone over for dinner, and it struck me forcibly how he'd *shrunk* — he looked so much thinner and shorter than I remembered him. Of course, at age thirty thoughts of anyone's mortality rarely enter one's head; I assumed that Dad, at age sixty-five, was just getting old.

Dad was a guy who worked hard all his life, and the way I saw it, he didn't have much to show for it. I felt that he'd been beaten down by life and never had any kind of aesthetic or spiritual payoff from his work to make it all seem worthwhile. Mom and Dad had lost their business during World War II; when he then went into teaching, he ended up coming home pissed off: "My students don't want to learn anything — I don't know what they're doing in my class, or any class, for that matter." Even when he went back into business, events seemed to conspire against him. He bought some office machines from a former student, and they turned out to be hot. He was prosecuted for receiving stolen property, and the costs of his defense doomed his new business.

As I walked into the hospital elevator, the smell of a chance wisp of cigarette smoke spun me instantly back to my childhood. Every morning, my dad would get up, light a cigarette, and head for the shower; I had to get up right about then, too, to get ready for school. Since Dad had to leave first, he always took the first shower, and the combination of cigarette smoke and steam from the shower became fused in my memory. The smell has ever since evoked my dad, my home, the downstairs hall with the bathroom at the end, and the innocence of childhood.

I walked into Dad's room — he had a private room looking out over the Napa countryside — and saw with a rush of relief that he was in a good mood, full of wisecracks and black humor: "I told my doctor I didn't know whether to call him Dr. Swift or Dr. Armour"; not bad for a man who'd just had his prostate cut out and his testicles removed. My respect and love for him peaked right then. This was the Dad I remembered from the good days, full of sardonic humor and not at all sorry for himself.

We sat around for a while, jiving about this and that, and when it was time for his regular blood draw, in came a drop-dead gorgeous blond candy striper with the syringe and accessories. Dad saw my eyes bug out, and immediately greeted her by name, saying, "This is my son Phil; he's in the Grateful Dead." For some reason, I was embarrassed as hell; maybe I thought he was explaining why I looked so weird. "Aw, c-come on, Dad," I stammered, "she probably never heard of us." A statement that she wisely neither confirmed nor denied, thereby depriving me of the chance to chat her up with a backstage invitation; she finished her work and left. It was not until I'd said my good-byes and was driving out of the hospital parking lot that I realized: He really *is* proud of me, that I'm in a popular band and have made a name as a musician. How come I couldn't see that? It was a classic example of an all-too-human tendency to misread situations negatively, respond in kind, and then see the light after it's too late.

Between that time and the end of the summer, I'd been fooling around (on acoustic guitar) with a chord sequence that had sprung into my mind one day that spring. It's funny how songs occur, or develop: each in its own way, as if it were a living thing, an organism, with its own rules of growth. This particular sequence was a repeated phrase with deceptive cadences leading to three different endings: one leading back to the beginning, the others leading first to a chorus and then, in the second instance, to a coda. By the beginning of fall, it had cohered into an entire song structure complete with melody, lacking only words. I made a rough cassette with just guitar and my melismatic vocal, and presented it to Hunter, who I felt was the only man for this job. Hunter has said elsewhere that I had asked specifically for a song for my father;[4] actually, I merely mentioned casually that I'd be working out the vocal as I drove to visit him. One way or another, that must have been a catalyst for his imagination — a day later, he pre-

---

[4]Robert Hunter, *A Box of Rain (Lyrics 1965–1993)*: 26n.

sented me with some of the most moving and heartfelt lyrics I've ever had the good fortune to sing. The result was "Box of Rain," probably my most well-known and best-loved song, and also the first song on which I sang lead vocal. To this day, I'm asked to sing and dedicate this song to those who are recovering, sick, dying, or who have already passed on.

As summer of 1970 passed imperceptibly into fall, we went into the studio again to make our new album, *American Beauty*; the recording process, although much streamlined from earlier efforts, would be marked by the shadow of personal loss — for both Jerry and myself. Sometime in August, Jerry's mom, Ruth (also known as "Bobbie" to her family), was involved in a horrific automobile accident on Twin Peaks, and hospitalized in critical condition. In a kind of curious symmetry, while I was driving several times a week to Livermore (where my parents had moved after Dad's surgery), Jerry likewise was taking every spare moment away from the sessions, joining his brother Tiff to visit his mom at San Francisco General.

I got the inevitable phone call one September afternoon at the studio: "Phil, you have to come quickly — your father is dying!" The doctors had told my mom that he was terminal; I left the studio immediately for the nursing home where he was to spend his last days.

So our vigil began; Mom and I would take turns sitting with him — calling for the nurse when his pain became too great, wiping the sweat from his face, trying to converse when the medication allowed him to surface briefly from the twilight zone. One morning as I was sitting next to the bed, he suddenly opened his eyes, looked right at me, and proclaimed: "You know, I've finally figured it all out." Figured it all out? "Figured out what, Dad?" I blurted through my confusion. "It's the Russians — they've been stealing all our material and taking it back there," he intoned portentously, and sank back into the morphine haze. My mind staggered like a malfunctioning gyroscope: Russians? Material? *What* material? Of course, cosmic cowboy that I am, I was expecting some deep revelation from beyond the veil, and what does he give me? Perhaps his greatest put-on: He and I were political polar opposites, and he was always tweaking my head about it. I sat there with tears running down my cheeks, totally blown away by the intensity of my own feelings. I'd never realized before in my adult life how much I loved this man, and never have I loved him more than at that moment. What a shame it took so long for me to see, I thought. Right then my mom came in to take over; it was time for the shift change. As I got to the door, I turned back and called out, "I love you, Dad," but he didn't respond, and I'll never know for sure whether or not he heard.

After that, Dad seemed to stabilize a little bit, and Mom and I agreed I would go back to work at the studio, finish mixing our album, and remain on call. The very next night, I got the call; as soon as I picked up the phone I knew — he was gone. My mom managed to tell me, between bursts of tears, that he went peacefully in his sleep, and that his last words were "What are we waiting for — let's get this show on the road." *Let's get this show on the road!* If Dad had a tombstone, that's what I'd want to see engraved on it.

That thought didn't help much at the time; my heart was flooded with sorrow and regret, especially since, at the end, I'd not been able to tell him that I loved him. I don't know how I got through whatever it was I was supposed to be doing at the studio, or even if I did anything at all except stare dumbly into space. Somehow, I was able to get home and fall into bed, thrashing and flailing about as I tried to get some sleep. That night I had a very powerful dream; an ordinary straight-backed brown wooden chair stood in the center of a field of gray, and in the chair, facing me, sat Dad, looking as he had in his prime, before the disease had ravaged him. A rushing flood of relief and love filled my heart as my disembodied dream-self rushed to embrace him. Everything passed between us without words being spoken. He let me know without a shadow of a doubt that everything was all right: He loved me, he knew that I loved him, and he was on the right path. His last message was of Mom — "Take care of your mother" — as the vision faded and I found myself alone in bed, staring through the window into the brightening light of dawn.

My dad's wish had been that his body be cremated and his ashes strewn in the ocean; Mom and I agreed that I would take his ashes up in a plane and scatter them over the Pacific. After we landed, I bid him au revoir one more time, then fired up the car and drove out of the parking lot into a new chapter of my life.

The magnetism of the scene at Wally Heider's recording studio made it a lot easier for me to deal with Dad's loss and my new responsibilities. Some of the best musicians around were hanging there during that period; with Paul and Grace from the Airplane, the Dead, Santana, Crosby, Nash, and Neil Young working there, the studio (with its three main recording rooms) became jammer heaven. When you'd finished up your work on one track, you only needed to stick your head into the next room to find some outrageous collaboration wailing away. At the same time as I was arranging to take over my mom's support, I was playing on albums made by David Crosby (*If I Could Only Remember My Name*) and Graham Nash (*Songs for Beginners*); I was also making music with artists like Neil Young, Joni Mitchell, Paul Kantner, David Freiberg, and Mike Shrieve, and working on *American Beauty* with the Dead. Thank the Lord for music; it's a healing force beyond words to describe.

Even then, the death wave hadn't hit its peak. In mid-September, one of our gigs at the Fillmore East was darkened by the news of Jimi Hendrix's death in London; ten days later, Jerry's mom passed away peacefully in her hospital bed; and finally, on October 4 at Winterland, we got the news of Janis Joplin's death from a heroin overdose in a motel room in L.A. I was surprised, not knowing she used heroin. Janis had always seemed to be living her life on fast-forward; we were all devastated, but Pigpen took it especially hard. By this time we were all in a state of extreme apprehension, metaphorically looking over our shoulders and wondering: What next?

American Beauty is considered by many to be our finest album. Certainly it contains a great many of our best-loved songs: Of the ten songs on the record, eight would remain in our active repertoire for our entire performing career. "Box of Rain" was my first lead vocal, and the song itself served as a perfect lead-in to the emotional land-scape of the album. "Sugar Magnolia" was the vehicle that defined Bob's role as rocker, and "Sunshine Daydream," its companion jam in live performance, provided Bob with ample opportunity to shriek ec-statically and generally let it all hang out. "Operator," Pigpen's first solo songwriting effort on record, was a portrait of Pig himself, sitting with a guitar and musing on what might have been. The five Hunter-Garcia ballads are among the finest products of their collaboration: "Friend of the Devil," "Candyman," "Ripple," "Brokedown Palace," and the stunning "Attics of My Life," all featuring our new-found de-light in harmony vocals.

The song that caps the album, and arguably defines it, is "Truckin'," the closer. We took our experiences on the road and made poetry: all the cities fusing into one ("Chicago, New York, Detroit, they're all on the same street"), the loneliness of street life ("most of the time they're sittin' and cryin' at home"), the omnipresence of drugs ("livin' on reds, vitamin C, and cocaine"), being busted ("Set up — like a bowlin' pin"), and the line that passed into the collective lexi-con, "What a long, strange trip it's been." The last chorus defines the band itself: "Truckin' — I'm goin' home/Whoa-oh baby, back where I belong/Back home, sit down and patch my bones/and get back truckin' on." Get back truckin' on — that's all we knew.

After finishing up mixes on *American Beauty,* we were eager to hit the road on our next tour, which started about a week later, playing colleges and theaters all over the East. It was about this time that the Dead began to emerge as the engine of choice for aesthetic exploration among college students hungry for the unknown. In my view, it's always been one of the functions of art to provide experiences that evoke danger and uncertainty, and to resolve those uncertainties into a higher perspective that embraces the paradox of chaos and order.

To a young person at that time, a Grateful Dead show could offer this kind of adventure in a protected environment, gathered together with like-minded people in a community of kindred spirits. We played long shows, so those who were tripping could peak and return; the music wove a web between the poles of dragon's-breath wrathful-deity space jamming and simple tunes telling stories full of weird characters and situations out of American legend, and it generally resolved in the end to raucous, shake-your-bones-and-dance rock 'n' roll fireworks. It's not surprising that the band became more popular outside the big urban areas (Boston, Philly, New York); we were offering something rarely available in the button-down culture of the time (or anytime since, for that matter) — a chance to take a chance, to go on an adventure of sorts with a large group of one's peers, and to return to reflect and to tell the tale the next morning.

It didn't hurt that tapes of our shows were now being traded widely around the college circuit. In what remains the best decision we never made, allowing tapers to record and trade our shows essentially usurped the function of studio records with live performances. Since no two shows were alike, every show that went forth and multiplied itself on the trading tree was another advertisement for our live shows. Every friend or sibling of a Deadhead that weaseled a copy of a favorite tape and passed it on was contributing to the growth of the community (and to the size of our audience).

We closed out the year with more gigs at home, and began the new year of 1971 with more gigs in January — up and down the West Coast — and in February it was back to the East Coast for a series of gigs at the Capitol Theater in Port Chester, New York. These shows were interesting because they incorporated an ESP (extrasensory perception) experiment. Conducted by Mickey's acquaintance Dr. Stanley Krippner, the audience was asked to "send" images (projected on-screen in the theater) to a dreaming research subject at the Maimonides Medical Center in Brooklyn. The experiment was statistically successful enough to be written up and published in a formal peer-reviewed journal of psychology — but that was just a small part of the significance of these shows.

Even though we had done our best to buoy him up, Mickey had been sinking into a terrible depression ever since Lenny had ripped us off and split with the money. By the time we got to the Capitol he was in a state of acute paranoia, sleep deprivation, and suicidal agony. Stanley Krippner hypnotized him to help him get through the first show, but afterward he was still so desolate that Stanley drove him out to his mother's on Long Island, where he finally was able to get some sleep — for three days. When he woke up, he decided to leave the road — never a favorite part of it for him — and work out his destiny at home on his ranch, with the explicit understanding that he was more than welcome anytime he wanted to rejoin us, wherever we were.

This development left us effectively a quintet again, with only one drummer — but what a drummer. Billy's playing had evolved so much during the eight-limbed drum-octopus period that he was easily able to drop right back into his original role as the powerhouse of the band. Spiritually, Mickey's departure left a big hole in the band's aura; his boundless enthusiasm and demonic energy were a large part of our emotional gestalt, and for the first few months after that, we didn't play as well as we could have. We were in essence tiptoeing around the hole he'd left.

With the huge new catalog of Hunter/Garcia tunes, Jerry was emerging more strongly as a front man, and I began to notice a kind of withdrawal in Pig. His spirits seemed good, but he was playing less organ onstage, or for long stretches he would play congas, or tambourine, or not at all. In retrospect, it could also have been the on-set of health problems. He had been drinking every day since early adolescence, but it had never seemed to impair his performance. He would still sing a couple of songs every night, but he hadn't played much of a role in our last two albums, contributing only one song.

Bobby, on the other hand, seemed to be growing into his musical role. The increased transparency of the band's texture meant that I, for one, could hear what he was playing more clearly than ever. I found myself astonished, delighted, and excited beyond measure at what he was doing. Bob's guitar playing, like his sense of humor and attitude toward life in general, is quirky, whimsical, goofy — and rich in nu-ance and allusion. Harmonically, he grasps and extends the implica-tions of what he hears in a unique and provocative manner, enhanced by his prestidigitatorial ability to play on guitar (with only four fin-gers) chord voicings that one would normally hear from a keyboard (with up to ten fingers). This period would see the manifestation of the "turn on a dime" version of the Grateful Dead, a superbly respon-sive musical organism with lightning-fast reflexes. Bob's new promi-nence meant that we now had an equally balanced texture of mixed metaphors: the bass as the anchor, Bobby's rhythm guitar as the hawser, and Jerry's lead as the sail. Billy provided the rhythmic driv-ing force (or wind), and Pig soared over it all with his outrageous raves. Got that?

Around this time we also gained a new lyricist in Bobby's fellow high-school prankster John Barlow, born to a ranching family from Wyoming and a budding poet. Bobby's songwriting relationship with Hunter had long been fraught with tension and ambiguity. Bobby couldn't understand why he couldn't revise or modify Hunter's words himself; Hunter wanted his lyrics to be sung as written. He already had to put up with Garcia's input during the process itself, that was bad enough, and he was damned if he'd accept revisions from Bobby. Two more stubborn head-bangers you never saw. It finally came to a head backstage at the Capitol Theater when after an argument, probably about Bob's addition of a line to "Sugar Magnolia" — "[She] jumps like a Willys in four-wheel drive" — Hunter turned all responsibility for Bob's lyrics over to Barlow, with the words, "Take him, he's yours." Luckily, John had already written a lyric for Bobby, inspired by the mother of all tequila hangovers. This would become "Mexicali Blues," one of Bob's best cowboy songs. So began a collaboration that would last for decades and provide the Grateful Dead with some of our finest songs.

However, the "death wave" wasn't quite finished with us. That spring, both of Bob's adoptive parents died within a week of each other. She went first, on his birthday, and he followed her a week later on *her* birthday, a truly poignant example of life writing. Bob tends to keep his feelings to himself even when he's backed against the wall, but he did convey his sense that this beautiful symmetry was the final, and highest, earthly manifestation of their deep love for each other. In retrospect, it seems as if most of us had to grow up some that winter and spring: Jerry and Bob had lost both parents; I was now supporting my mom after Dad's passing; only Pig and Billy still had both parents.

Earlier that spring, we'd made a momentous financial decision. Since the sound systems we'd been using everywhere (usually provided by the house or by the promoter) were so problematic, we bought the Alembic PA that Bear and Ron Wickersham had been developing for use locally and took it on the road with us. This necessitated an increase in the size of the crew. With this system, bigger equaled better, louder, and cleaner. Bear's goal was, as always, sound that was transparent, clean, undistorted, and very loud. Eventually incorporating Bear's most extravagant concepts (for example, thirty-two-foot-tall bass columns and a center cluster for vocals), this system was to grow and evolve into the fabled "Wall of Sound."

Starting with the February shows at the Capitol Theater, we also began recording shows for an eventual second live album, featuring new tunes that we hadn't yet released on a studio record. After we'd pranked poor Joe Smith from Warner Brothers for the last time by insisting that the album be called "Skull-Fuck" (and getting the response "But — but — we won't be able to sell it at — Sam Goody! JCPenney!"), we eventually caved and let our attitude be adjusted. It would be released as — duh — *Grateful Dead.* The heads always referred to it as "Skull and Roses," after the artwork, drawn by renowned San Francisco poster artists Kelly and Mouse from the *Rubáiyát of Omar Khayyám.* It also featured our first appeal to our fans to communicate with us — "Dead Freaks Unite! Who are you? Where are you? How are you? Write P.O. Box xxxx, San Rafael, Calif." The response to this little blurb was overwhelming. Eventually we gathered a mailing list of about 150,000 names, which became the basis for our fan club (the Deadheads) as well as the core database for our future mail-order ticket plans.

One day in June '71 an offer came in out of the blue for us to play a big festival near Paris. It turned out that some fashion designer was angling for the post of minister of youth (can you imagine a Department of Youth in the U.S. Cabinet?) and, as part of his campaign, was producing a rock festival. Someone must have decided that it would be hip to have at least one American band; why they chose us I'll never know. Nonetheless, we jumped at the chance.

Upon arrival, we learned that the festival had been rained out (*oh, monsieur, je suis desolé*), but one of the promoters had offered to put us up until the time for our flight back. We accepted gladly, even though the place was some distance outside Paris. Leaving the airport, we passed through some rather interesting places: Versailles (our driver, a Parisian friend of McIntire's with strong leftist leanings: *"Voilà, Versailles. Roi Soleil — merde! Pfui!"*); Pontoise, a pleasant-looking suburb on the river Oise, a tributary of the Seine; Auvers, where we saw a church that still looked the same as it had when painted by Van Gogh almost a century earlier; and finally, Hérouville, a farming hamlet that was home to the Château d'Hérouville, an early sixteenth-century feudal manse now remodeled as a recording studio (Elton John, among others, recorded there later in the seventies) by Michel Magne, a film composer.

No doubt the ulterior motive was to introduce us to the studio, which was large, well-appointed, and state-of-the-art. But what remains with me is the outdoor setting: the landscape, the tranquillity, and, above all — the light! I did spend some happy hours jamming in the studio with musicians such as Jerry Granelli, the great jazz drummer (who was to have performed at the festival with the Light Sound Dimension, the multimedia group he formed with guitarist Fred Marshall and light-show pioneer Bill Ham), and members of a French band called Magma, who really stretched me out musically.

We couldn't sit around there very long without mounting an expedition into town. Here we were — if not exactly country bumpkins, for sure a bunch of smartass middle-class hippies who grew up on the legends of Paris in the first thirty years of the last century, when the very name reeked of freedom, romance, and creativity. Early one morning, we split off in several directions. Bob and Jerry headed for the Tour Eiffel, and I set my course for one of the pinnacles of Gothic architecture, the cathedral of Notre-Dame de Paris. For some time, I had been reading in an alternate history of consciousness, embedded in which was the concept that perhaps the so-called progress of civilization as we knew it wasn't quite as linear as we'd been taught in school — that earlier cultures might have been vastly more advanced in some areas of wisdom than we. The research I'd been doing in sacred geometry and ancient earth science had revealed the existence of a completely new perspective on spiritual history, especially the knowledge that many Christian holy places in Europe, including Notre-Dame, had been erected over "pagan" sites of worship, and those in turn were sited upon or near places of geomantic power, involving currents of telluric energy and underground springs. Inside the great cathedral, I stood in a space at once immense and intimate, illuminated by what seemed to be thousands upon thousands of candles. Floating down from somewhere miles above was the sound of the choir. The great rose windows seemed to vibrate as I turned from one to the other, and I found myself suddenly outside the church, blinking in the light, not remembering how I got there or how much time had passed. Two hours, I was told.

Back at the château, the band shared tales of their respective adventures, and the place started buzzing with plans for a solstice party. On June 21, 1971, we set up our gear in the courtyard of the château, along with the Light Sound Dimension guys, and played an outdoor show, in the twilight of evening, to what must have been most of the population of Hérouville — about two hundred souls. It was a return to the days of the knight in his castle providing a feast for the locals (from whom he derived his food and taxes). The tables groaned under the weight of the food, the wine flowed freely, and a fine old time was had by all — especially one governmental dignitary, who was dandling a sixteen-year-old girl on his lap with a distinctly nonavuncular look on his face, while locals and visitors alike took turns shoving each other into the pool. Vive la France! Vive l'amour! Vive la différence! While it lasted, a triumph of international solidarity.

Two days later, we're on a plane back to the States, where we and other bands preside over the end of an era: the closings of Fillmore West and East. Bill Graham, I think, wanted to expand out of the brick-and-mortar landlord role and promote on a larger stage. Much to no one's surprise, he soon began promoting shows at larger venues (including San Francisco's Winterland ice rink) all over the Bay Area and East Coast. We knew him, then, as he'd always thought of himself: "the Sol Hurok of rock."

On September 17 we got a nasty shock when Pigpen was hospitalized for a bleeding ulcer. Tests showed he was also suffering from liver and spleen problems. When I went to the hospital to visit and give blood, I was shocked to be told that his chances weren't good — but he rallied somehow and began to recuperate.

We had a mammoth tour booked for the rest of 1971, lasting right through to New Year's with only a couple of weeks' break; we were now facing the prospect of doing it without Pig. It would have been better for him if we'd just canceled the tour and let him recover all his strength at his own pace. But we just couldn't see our way clear to do that; touring was all we knew. It was agreed that Pig would rejoin the band when he felt up to it. Without realizing it, we put a lot of pressure on him to hurry up and get better.

Jerry soon found a possible substitute for Pig — a piano player named Keith Godchaux, who (sort of) approached him at one of Jerry's solo gigs. A curious story, for sure: Keith, almost painfully shy, was too embarrassed to even talk to Jerry, so his wife, Donna, got Jer's numbers and promised him "This is your piano player." They connected the next week, and Jerry invited Keith down to the studio — Keith showed up and played with Jerry. It must have been good. The next day when we all showed up, there's Keith at the keys, with Jerry sporting his Cheshire Cat–that-ate-the-canary grin. Introductions were made all around. All through the afternoon we played a whole raft of Grateful Dead tunes, old and new. That whole day, Keith never put a foot (or a finger) wrong. Even though he'd never played any Grateful Dead tunes before, his consummate musicianship and superb training allowed him to pick up the songs practically the first time through. That's something that we could have expected, but what amazed us most was that everything he played fit perfectly in the spaces between the parts played by the rest of the band. Since Mickey's departure, we'd been struggling to redefine our nature, to fill in the hole that he'd left — and Keith turned out to be the missing piece.

Keith's persona, too, was a perfect foil for the often abrasive, in-your-face front affected by most of us. A small, shaggy, delicate, melancholic young man, self-effacing almost to the point of exasperation, he evoked in us a kind of tenderness that had been lacking in our music (and our relationships with one another) — something we hadn't known was missing until it became part of our gestalt. At first, his playing was so smooth, so *harmonious,* that even in the wildest free-form improvisations or the most raucous rockers, his presence served as a gently beckoning gravitational force — reminding us to refrain from drifting off into our own personal ego-spaces.

Keith turned into a fire-breathing demon about halfway through the fall tour — not only following the band effortlessly through all our endlessly bifurcating highways and byways, but grabbing the ball and running with it, leading us into unknown regions and setting the stage for what many heads consider the peak years of the Grateful Dead. With Keith, we became the *turbocharged* turn-on-a-dime Grateful Dead that had only been hinted at before, but the music also became warmer and more organic, almost but not quite filling the hole Pig's absence had left.

We were all delighted to hear that Pigpen was flying out to rejoin the band onstage in Boston, but I was shocked when I saw him — he was shrunken and fragile-looking. However, he still managed to muster the energy to become his old jovial self again while he was doing his showstoppers like "Lovelight" or "Good Lovin'."

We ended 1971 with a New Year's Eve show at Winterland, featuring the New Riders of the Purple Sage and the fine local band Yogi Phlegm (essentially the Sons of Champlin without the horns). An old ice rink, Winterland had been host to many skaters, amateur and professional, over its history; but ever since '67, Bill Graham had been rockin' the rafters almost every weekend with some of the hottest and largest shows ever held in San Francisco (I myself heard Led Zeppelin and Cream for the first time there). A huge dirigible hangar of a building, it had the kind of acoustics that admitted of only one approach — play *really loud.*

During a break from touring, Bobby went into the studio to labor mightily on a solo album — with his deadline about two and a half weeks away. Long gone were the days of infinite studio time, mainly because we finally figured out that we always had to pay for it, somehow. One by one, we sidled into the studio, saying things like "Bob, I really like that tune — got a bass player for it yet?" or "Hey, Bob, need some keyboards on that ballad?" Drawn in by the new songs, we eventually assembled the whole band (minus Pig, who was still trying to regain his health) at Wally Heider's and finished the album (released as *Ace*) in a burst of enthusiasm. Bob's songwriting had taken a great leap forward with Barlow as his lyricist, and the material reflected his emergence in the band's live performances as a hair-on-fire rocker.

Jerry, on the other hand, had moved out to Stinson Beach on the Marin coast during the previous summer and, as was his wont, had almost immediately become the focal point of informal jamming with the local musicians. David Grisman, a mandolinist and friend from the early bluegrass days, had moved out there with the Rowans, a family of musicians he was comanaging (Peter, the eldest, was a fine guitarist/singer/songwriter; the younger brothers, Lorin and Chris, had an acoustic guitar/duo thing going, also writing their own stuff, and like singing brothers everywhere, they had a strikingly pure and unified vocal blend). After a lapse of about ten years, Jerry was again playing bluegrass banjo, so it was only natural that David and Peter would end up most days over at Jer's new place jamming. When the three of them needed a bass player to complete the ensemble, they called on John Kahn, another local who would become the backbone of almost all of Jerry's non-Dead musical efforts. When the decision was made to play a few bars and clubs just for the fun of it, "Old and In the Way" was the name they chose. Jerry also ended up coproducing an album for Lorin and Chris Rowan, as well as sponsoring them as an opening act for some of his local gigs.

As for me, I was living up in the hills in Fairfax, in a little cottage surrounded by redwoods. Room service was unavailable, so I was forced to eat most of my meals downtown. I had several girlfriends but no serious relationship, and I saw my mom periodically in between touring, rehearsing, and recording. Truth is, the Grateful Dead pretty much consumed my life at that point. The band was still, after seven years, the most exciting thing, musical or otherwise, that had happened to me, and I had little interest in the world outside of it.

Mickey wasn't in the band at the time, but he was a brother, and I made frequent trips up to his ranch in Novato to hang with him. He'd built a studio in his barn, and just about any day or evening musicians could be found there — John Cipollina from Quicksilver, Barry Melton from the Fish, the horn section from Tower of Power — jamming away, or actually recording tunes for Mickey's first album, entitled *Rolling Thunder.* His mantra — "Always record more than you erase" — was wood-burned into the top frame of the control-room window, along with the First Law of Rock 'n' Roll: "Lay it down dirty and play it back clean." Mickey had asked me to do some mixing on his record, most memorably on a smokin' horn-band instrumental called "Deep, Wide, and Frequent" (from the old joke "I'm gonna cut ya three ways . . ."). So there I am, the tracks are all laid down, I'm mixing away — running pass after pass through the tune getting the balance *just right* — with Mick hovering over my shoulder like Dracula sighting in on a pulsating neck vein (understandable, his first record and all). For my part, I was looking for a tasteful, elegant mix of this howling carnivore of a tune, just to have some kind of balance between its wall-toppling drama and the straitlaced retentive stranglehold demanded by the very process of recording. But no, it was not to be: At each and every tom-tom fill Mick would lunge over my shoulder and shove the faders as far north as they would go (it was then my job to bring the tracks back down), not only bringing them up into the distortion range, but virtually ensuring that the record stylus would jump out of the groove at those moments (for Mickey, a consummation devoutly to be wished). It was just like Charlie Brown, with Lucy holding the football: "I promise I won't do it this time." "Yes you will." "No I won't." "Oh, OK, here we go" "Augh! You did it again! *You did it again!*" "I lied." Endearing and frustrating at the same time, that's our Mick — hell, that's *all* of us, now that I think about it.

Singing high harmonies was starting to irritate my throat, so during a series of gigs in late March we invited Keith's wife, Donna, to sing with the band, and we had a new band member. At midnight on All Fools' Day, the entire Ship of Fools crew filed onto a British

Airways 747 bound for London and a much-anticipated European tour. This being the Grateful Dead, we of course had our entire tribe along for the ride. This included some members of the infamous Pleasure Crew, notably Marina, an oil heiress from New York. Marina was so used to instant service that when we got to our hotel in London, she mistook Garcia for a bellboy — and imperiously ordered him to bring her luggage in from the bus. Jerry, all-around good guy that he was, never even blinked, and we all cracked up at the sight of him staggering into the lobby loaded down with matching Louis Vuitton suitcases.

We opened the tour at the Wembley Pool, a chilly, cavernous sports facility, with two shows; the English musical press went wild. *THE DEAD STORM BRITAIN* was the headline in *Melody Maker* (they must have come to the second show, which was enhanced by the fact that our fingers had warmed up by that point). After those shows we had two days off — just enough time for Jerry, M.G., and me to take a trip out to Salisbury Plain, west of London, to visit Stonehenge, Glastonbury, Avebury, and Silbury Hill. The three of us had become fascinated by the lore and legend surrounding this area and while on the road had shared many books about its connection with Arthurian legend.

Towering over the town of Glastonbury and the abbey grounds is a hill so artfully shaped it might almost have been made by the hands of men: This is Glastonbury Tor. Surmounted by a tower dedicated to the archangel Michael, it still shows traces of a ritual path spiraling up and around the sides of the hill; it is this labyrinth that Jerry, M.G., and I found ourselves treading as we climbed laboriously toward the top. The path was very steep; at each doubling back of the maze, one of us would cut corners and climb up to the next level, laughing at the irony of yet again taking shortcuts to spiritual awareness. It's said that in olden times pilgrims would dance and sing their way up this path as a penitential meditation; it's pretty difficult, especially for out-of-shape hippies, to emulate that degree of commitment.

After Wembley, we played a gig at the other Newcastle (upon Tyne: that's right, the one with the coal), and then undertook a voyage across the North Sea to Copenhagen. We had acquired two buses, which quickly separated out into "Bozos" and "Bolos."[1] This came about when somewhere north of London the crew brought out Bozo masks (*where* did they find that stuff in England?) and wore them as we passed through the pitiful remains of Sherwood Forest and into the city of Nottingham. Needless to say, the reaction of the unsuspecting populace was hilarious at the very least ("Cor! Look, Mum, they're all plastic!").

At the port of Newcastle, the buses drove onto a monster ferry-boat, and I disembarked to straggle up to my stateroom. The voyage was to be overnight, and since the rooms were cramped and airless, I ended up standing at the stern rail with my roadie, Kidd, watching the sun sink into the mist, generating richer and richer bands of color beyond the flocks of seagulls following the ship.

After a quick gig at the university in Aarhus (a cafeteria with a *very* low ceiling), we returned to the Tivoli Gardens in Copenhagen for what came to be known as the "Band of Bozos" gig. The performance was to be broadcast on Danish TV, so once again the masks came out — and this time the whole band became Bozo, a bright and shining moment. It didn't last long, though; the plastic chrome-dome channels sweat right into one's eyes, and it's hard to sing with that bulbous nose bumping the microphone; Jerry was the first to cave, sending the mask sailing back over the amp line just before digging into a screaming lead. I think the rest of us held out for the rest of the first set, but after the break, Bozo was history.

In Hamburg, I'm confronted with some almighty weirdness: my doppelgänger. We're checking out the hall where we're to play: the Hamburg Musikhalle, home of the NDR Symphony Orchestra and

---

[1]Non-Bozos? Anti-Bozos?

the Hamburg Philharmonic; one of those bands is rehearsing excerpts from *Carmen* in the hall. I decide to cruise around outside the auditorium. I'm in the foyer, reading a plaque about favorite son Johannes Brahms returning in triumph to his hometown, and M.G. comes rushing down the balcony stairs — "Phil! Come here! You've got to see this!" What? What? I follow her up to the balcony, where Jerry, Bob, and a couple of roadies are standing open-mouthed and pointing toward the stage. At first all I see is the forest, not the trees — an orchestra playing — but then Jer says, "The cellist!" I look down at the solo cellist — and he is me. Same face, same hair (only shorter), same build; when they break and he stands up — the same gait, the same posture — I'm flabbergasted. I had read, of course, that everyone has a double somewhere, but I'd always thought of that as a folk legend — until I saw mine. I decide that I must come face to face with him somehow — so I run downstairs to the backstage area.

Having left my bell-bottoms and paisley period behind, I'm now dressed like an American cowboy — boots, jeans, checked shirt, Levi's jacket — everything but the hat. You can imagine the thoughts running through the minds of this man's colleagues, their heads snapping around in double takes as I pass through them. Backstage, another entire orchestra is rehearsing in a huge room; the other musicians are dispersing. I never found this guy, but oh, how I wanted to shake his hand and find out his name. Could it have been Lesch? Lösch?

On to Paris, where it seems that the revolutionary spirit of 1968 had not entirely disappeared from the streets; an individual complaining loudly and at length that we had no right to come there and not play free "for the people" confronted our crew during the load-out. Not only that, but he followed us back to our hotel (the Grand Hotel, not exactly the place that a "people's band" could afford to stay) and continued his harangue from the plaza in front of the main entrance. Now this person was clothed in a *very* nice lavender jacket, and happened at one point to tempt fortune by standing directly under the window of the room occupied by roadies Rex Jackson and Sonny Heard. Someone suggested that the color brown would make a fine old contrast with the jacket; and presto! Out the window and over the head of our fine French friend went the warm remnants of Rex's room-service chocolate ice cream. The howls of outrage could have been heard in Berlin, but we were soon to learn that there would be a price to pay for our little moment of euphoria.

Our next scheduled gig was at the university in Lille, just south of the Belgian border. Imagine our consternation when we discovered that someone had insinuated dirt into the fuel tank of our equipment truck as it sat trustingly on the streets of Paris; when it was time for the gig there we were, but our gear — amps, guitars, drums, PA — was still several hours behind us in a quickly rented backup vehicle.

We held a quick council of war to decide our course of action. Should we just not show up? Should we send Rock to take the heat? As usual it was Jerry who insisted that we do the right thing; some of us (but not him) must go there and try to explain. So, picture this if you will: a smallish venue filled with students; the promoters, students themselves, freaking up the wall, their investment totally blown; the band, crew, and management on the stage trying to explain in one and a half languages (English and Franglais); the mood of the students growing ever more restive and ugly; the only refuge a small dressing room at the back of the stage. As the protests grew more and more intense (the students, predictably, had briefly turned to arguing among themselves), we slipped one by one into the relative safety of the backstage shelter, and as the door began to cave in under the onslaught, we decided to opt for discretion over valor, and leave. Unfortunately, the only window was one story from the ground; luckily, there was a drainpipe next to it, and a truck conveniently parked at the end of the pipe, so down we went — shimmy down the pipe, jump to the truck, crawl to the ground, sprint for the bus — all the time laughing hysterically at the sheer absurdity of it all. Bobby was the last man out, having sent the ladies ahead; as the door blew open, his defiant shout rang through the air: "We'll be back, and we'll play for free!" For free! Lavender Velvet was going to get his wish, though he probably never knew. . . .

It was a brisk spring Saturday when we finally pulled into the center of Lille to keep our promise of a free concert: on a sparkling afternoon in the central park of the town, we played to workers carrying lunch pails, baguettes, and carafes of *vin ordinaire;* mothers with their babies in perambulators; and, of course, hundreds of students, many more than could have been crammed into the tiny hall where we'd originally been scheduled to play. Clouds came and went; at one point it rained, so we covered the gear, retreated into the trucks, and waited it out. Sure enough, the sky cleared rapidly, and the audience was still there, so on we played in the glorious spring light. The landscape, the flowers, and the people seemed to radiate a simple joy in just *being.* Afterward the student promoters embraced us tearfully — they hadn't believed up until the moment we pulled into town that we would actually make good our promise. It was one of our finest "music for the people" moments, if I do say so myself.

I hadn't hung out with Billy much outside the shows, as he was married with children, so it was an unexpected pleasure when he and his wife, Susila, asked to join me on a side trip to attend the legendary Monaco Grand Prix. All we had to do was get to Orly Airport in Paris, two and a half hours away, in time for the flight. With Billy driving, Susila riding shotgun, and me navigating from the rear seat, we made pretty good time to Paris — but as we hit the city, traffic began to accumulate. Never fear, the Gang of One is here — Billy took us up the Champs Élysées, around the Arc de Triomphe, and through downtown Paris like smoke up a chimney; we made the flight with plenty of time to spare. After that, the race itself would have been anticlimactic, except for one thing: it rained. Summer, in Monaco, the pearl of the Mediterranean, and it rained.

Back to Geneva, fly to London (with Keith Richards in the seat next to me; we talk mostly about what a drag commercial air travel is), play four shows at a theater called the Lyceum, and fly home to resume the endless tour.

Pigpen came home from the tour looking frail and thin. It turned out he'd picked up hepatitis A in Europe. Hepatitis was the last thing Pig needed right then — he clearly couldn't go out on the road until he was completely recovered.

Naively, we thought that three weeks was enough time for Pig to get better. We just couldn't bring ourselves to believe that his illness was as serious as it would turn out to be.

On a brighter note, we were very happy to hear that Bear was getting out of prison and coming back to join the sound team. Bob Matthews had been doing the front-of-house mixing, with Betty Cantor making tapes; Dan Healy had sworn to upgrade the sound system ASAP. With Bear's return, we had three really strong skill sets working together: Matthews/Betty mixing the real-time house sound; Healy the supremo hands-on troubleshooter and acoustical analyst; and Bear the wild-eyed radical visionary idea man. Trouble was, each of them wanted some of the other's turf: both Healy and Bear, for example, wanted to mix real-time.

As a preliminary step in the right direction, Bear and Ron Wickersham came up with the concept of "noising" the venue before the show: a process by which noise with a specific frequency content (so-called white noise) would be blasted from the PA into the room; special microphones and frequency analyzers would read the peaks and valleys and determine what frequencies were favored or hindered by the acoustics of the room. That known, it should be a simple matter to determine which frequencies should be boosted and which cut in order to render the room musically transparent. Healy is the guy who went out and found the hardware to make it happen (all of which existed but had never been used for music), put it together, and made it work.

These tools led to the use of sound-deadening material (stage curtains and the like) in many of the arenas we were now playing, while the concept itself spread out, to other bands and sound companies, and was continually being refined and upgraded by all. Today, every self-respecting sound company has a completely computerized multichannel audio analysis system as an everyday component of its PA.

If there ever was a Grateful Dead "business plan," it consisted solely of an attitude. Although we had to be a "business" in order to survive and continue to make music together, we were *not* buying into the traditional pop music culture of fame and fortune, hit tunes, touring behind albums, etc. Therefore, we were constantly besieged with business plans from employees and friends. To begin with, our road manager, Sam Cutler, started up a booking agency, and two of our office staff opened a travel agency, both devoted exclusively to, and dependent upon, the Grateful Dead.

In our naïveté, the band thought that we could control all this without falling prey to the infighting and dissension that comes with the territory. At the same time, no one in the band wanted to be bothered with the boring details of such control — preferring, in the time-honored way of artists, to delegate the hands-on nuts-and-bolts stuff to someone trustworthy, like Lenny, or Ron Rakow, formerly of the Pleasure Crew, the Carousel Ballroom, and a casualty of the Wall Street stock and bond wars. At Jerry's behest, Ron came up with a plan, formalized in his proposal, "So What Papers," in which he put forth his ideas for marketing and promotion. These ideas rested solidly on the need for him to take over our management for everything except touring, meaning he would produce and market our

records — at first Grateful Dead, then any solo or outside collaborative projects. We already owned our own sound system. Booking and
travel were in-house. It seemed as if being our own record company
would be worth a try. No one could see a downside.

The big question: How would we distribute the records? Rakow's
original scam was to sell the records from ice-cream trucks — Ding-
a-ling! Getcha Fudgsicles here, and don't forget to pick up a copy of
the new Grateful Dead album! Right. Good for some yuks, but seriously impractical. In the end, we settled on a more traditional model:
the Dead would finance and produce the recordings, and United
Artists Records would manufacture and distribute.

But first, we had to score enough money for the start-up, and
Rakow decided to approach a Boston bank for a line of credit. Suddenly, our gigs were infested with swarms of suits. Rakow led them
around raving about his latest idea, the obsolescence of vinyl records
in relation to the new "holographic" technology he was investigating.
The music would be encoded, somehow, onto a pyramid-shaped object, made of a material that hadn't been invented yet, and read by —
a laser! As a visual aid, Rakow would brandish a nonfunctional cardboard model of the player, complete with a cute little cardboard pyramid inside. Maybe it was the lure of the bright lights, or the roar of
the greasepaint — as Jimmy Durante used to say, "Everybody wants
ta get inta de act" — because I can't imagine that these sobersides
thought that we were a sound investment. Nonetheless, there they
were, dazzled by simultaneity and blinded by multiplicity, buying
right into the Acid Test business model: Throw money at everything,
but don't bother looking to see if it sticks. Rakow also hustled some
funds by leasing our foreign distribution rights to Atlantic Records,
so we were ready to roll with our new record company.

On March 8, 1973, one of the office girls called me in tears,
telling me that Pigpen had been found dead on the floor of his little
apartment in Corte Madera. I sat down hard at my kitchen table, re-

membering my last visit with him. When he greeted me with a hug, I had to be careful not to squeeze too hard; this once robust man was now skin and bones. The official cause of death was listed as internal bleeding from an esophageal hemorrhage. Pig's passing devastated me, but I didn't yet comprehend the magnitude of the hole that had just been blasted in the Grateful Dead.

Two days later, a large wake was held at Bobby's house in the hills above Mill Valley. The place was wall-to-wall people, but I stayed close by my old pal Bobby Petersen, who'd been a kindred spirit to Pig. To numb my pain, I tried to match Petersen drink for drink, but soon decided I'd rather just go home. On my way out the door, Jerry turned to me, saying in a dark tone, "That motherfucker — now *he knows.*" Knows, that is, what, if anything, is on the other side of death.

Pig hadn't performed with us since June, and one would think we'd had plenty of time to get used to his absence. Going on stage without Pigpen was clearly difficult for the whole band. Before our first performance after his death, I had the first and only attack of stage fright in my life. Even if Pig hadn't been physically present, we were still expecting him back at any time. Now that he was really gone, I felt an aching loneliness on stage — as if I couldn't put a foot right. Over the years, I realized that Pig would always be with us, and his spirit would live in our music.

After a sporadic spring of touring and some early summer shows, we rolled into upstate New York for what we expected to be a tidy little one-day festival with the Allman Brothers and The Band at the former U.S. Grand Prix racetrack near Watkins Glen.

Close to one hundred thousand tickets had been sold, and we were looking forward to a pleasant afternoon and evening with two of our favorite bands. By the time we got there on Friday the highways had been closed and reopened already, there were about two hundred thousand people camped out at the site, and many more were expected overnight. The general consensus among musicians and management:

It would be a good idea for each of the three bands to do an extended sound check, so as to keep the natives from becoming restless. The Band went first, and in keeping with their predilection for short songs, played for forty-five minutes to an hour. The Brothers were up next, and jammed out their stuff for a good hour and a half. Not to be outdone, we went up and had a blast doing two short sets, playing about two hours and sounding a lot better in the cool of the evening than we did the next day, when the overnight rains combined with the midsummer heat and humidity had rendered the speaker cones soft and soggy.

By the time we got there the next day, the crowd had tripled itself. The stage was set up in the infield at its lowest point of elevation, surrounded on all sides by trees and grassy slopes. The racetrack itself encircled the top of the bowl, occasionally dipping down into the "amphitheater" area. Compared to Woodstock, where we couldn't see anything beyond the front of the stage, at Watkins Glen I was staggered by seeing the open areas on all sides completely covered by human bodies, blankets, banners, etc., all the way up to and over the skyline, and the surrounding tree branches burdened with hundreds of concertgoers seeking a better vantage point. The steepness of the slopes and the exponentially increased population density, combined with the typical East Coast summer mugginess, made for an oppressive, claustrophobic setting. The high point of the day for me was the festival closer, a riotous superstar jam featuring members of all three bands playing the crowd-pleasers "Not Fade Away" and "Mountain Jam." There was a special feeling of camaraderie between the Brothers and us: We'd just lost Pig, and they were still reeling from the loss of Duane Allman and Berry Oakley. Despite the large crowd, it was very warm and intimate on stage playing with our old friends.

As soon as we got back from the East Coast and dried ourselves off, it was into studio B at the Record Plant in Sausalito to record our first album for the new regime. Hopes were high; we had what we thought was a bunch of great material, and the studio atmosphere was very congenial (several of us spent many happy hours frolicking in the studio's huge hot tub). We'd learned to break in the material at shows (under fire, as it were), rather than try to work it out at rehearsals, or in the studio at tremendous expense. Perhaps the studio vibe was *too* comfortable — the performances on the record fell far short of the intensity we could bring to the music in live performances. Still, the album, *Wake of the Flood,* did fairly well commercially (thus lending credibility to Rakow's business model) while being savaged by the critics ("hippy-dippy" was the kindest epithet employed by *Rolling Stone* magazine in its review).

Undaunted, we pressed onward with our various explorations. Jerry worked with Old and In the Way, his bluegrass band, and with Merl Saunders and John Kahn in an electric unit. I worked with Mickey and our old friend from MIT, Ned Lagin, at Mickey's ranch, trying to evolve an improvisational electronic music with synthesizers, modified bass, and percussion. And raving together we fantasized about our next outrage: the Wall of Sound.

For some time, we'd been running up against limits in reference to our sound equipment. The amount of gear needed to amplify the sound clearly and distinctly was outgrowing the size of the stages available to us. Luckily, we were starting to play larger venues, where the stage was built of scaffolding brought in for that purpose. But this development created further problems (besides increased expenses): We now needed more speakers and amplifiers to project the sound farther still. The delay towers first seen at Watkins Glen provided a partial solution, but the sound coming directly from the main-stage towers was still unsatisfactory. The "recording" model — mixing the different instruments and voices together into a mono or stereo mix — created too much distortion at the volumes necessary for large venues. Bear's solution was to isolate each instrument and voice into its own channel, amps, and speakers, projecting them separately from a common location: behind the band. In this model, each instrument — two guitars, bass, keyboards, drums — would have its own individual speaker stacks, basically one on each side of the stage. In each stack the lower half would serve as a monitor for the players, and the upper half would project the instrumental sound out past the sound-and-light booth to a point where delay towers would be unnecessary.

The sticking point in this concept was the vocals — how to project them from behind and above the band without being obliterated by leakage and feedback. Someone in our crack sound crew — Bear? Healy? Matthews? Wickersham? — came up with the idea of differential microphones (basically the same paradigm that later created noise-canceling headphones): two microphones placed close together, one out of phase with its mate. The singer would sing into the mike that was in phase with the system, while any sound (leakage, feedback) that went into *both* mikes would be eliminated by phase cancellation. Simple, elegant — and practical, especially if you had nothing better to do with your money. The vocals were then fed into a full frequency center cluster that dispersed the sound in a 120-degree arc from the centerline — easily heard on stage, and clear as a bell at one hundred yards.

So. The Wall of Sound. Forty feet high, seventy feet wide — six hundred speakers and twenty-five thousand watts of solid-state McIntosh power, all stacked in a single line behind the band. Six independent channels: five for the instruments and one for all vocals. Each instrument had two stacks, one on each side; for the bass, I had two thirty-six-foot-tall columns divided into four channels. At that time I was playing a quadraphonic bass, equipped with a special pickup and output preamp that allowed me to place the sound of each string in any of the four possible locations. Not that I used it all that much.

From a musician's standpoint, the most endearing aspect of the system was the control the band now had over the actual sound heard by the audience; the sound crew had eliminated the necessity for a front-of-house mixer, returning that responsibility to the musicians, where it belongs. Basically, the soundman's job was now to monitor the sound in the hall and to report back if any adjustments were necessary (e.g., more vocals, more drums, less piano, etc.).

We had finally achieved the alchemical ideal envisioned by Bear in the sixties:[1] The instrumental and vocal balance onstage (the microcosm) is unique and complete, sui generis, needing only to be transmitted verbatim to the larger audience space (the macrocosm) exactly as played by the musicians. It's probably no coincidence that the music we created playing through the Wall is regarded by most Deadheads as the pinnacle of our live performances; this period (about forty gigs) remains to this day the most generally satisfying performance experience of my life with the band. Playing Grateful Dead music through that system was both exhilarating and terrifying; the combination of the collective risk-taking inherent in our music and the knowledge that one's slightest move was being scaled up to almost godlike omnipotence was humbling (but rarely daunting, thank goodness).

The main drawbacks to this system were few but critical — the differential mikes that were optimum for phase-canceling weren't the best-*sounding* vocal mikes available, and the drums weren't projected quite as clearly as the electric instruments, probably as a result of distortion stemming from the many mikes necessary to capture the various components of the drum kit. The biggest boondoggle: the size of the system and the setup-time factor. We had to use two stages with two sets of trucks leap-frogging from show to show: While we were playing a show in, say, Philadelphia, our second stage crew would be erecting the stage scaffolding for our next gig in Boston. At the end of the Philly show, the system would be loaded into its trucks and sent off to Boston, while the Philly stage crew would dismantle and load

---

[1] "As above, so below," or in our terms: "As on the stage, so in the hall."

the stage scaffolding into its trucks and head for New York (the next gig after Boston). We now employed twice as many stage crew and truckers as before, meaning we had to play larger venues, sell more tickets, and play more often to be able to support the sound system. Luckily, our audience was continuing to expand; even so, the financial strain would eventually prove untenable, especially after we took the whole system on tour to Europe, where we (predictably) failed to break even. Ah, impetuous youth — where is thy sting? Right in the wallet, mate.

By this time the stresses and strains associated with large-scale touring — together with the devastating loss of Pigpen — were starting to create cracks and crevices in our unanimity of purpose. The expenses associated with the Wall of Sound meant that we were constrained to play only the largest venues — basketball and hockey arenas and the occasional football stadium — where the intimacy we'd prized in the ballroom era was a fading memory. The stages were ten to twelve feet high, further removing us from contact with the audience, who receded into a blur of shapes lacking any individuality. Our crew was twice as large as it needed to be, and could be quite surly. Simultaneously, the psychic atmosphere was beginning to cloud up with the emergence of cocaine as the drug of choice among the crew, generating an "us against the world" mindset.

The amount of security and backstage space needed in an arena had tripled from that of a theater or ballroom, and the band became more and more detached, withdrawing into the famous "bubble" of isolation out of the sheer desire for preservation of our energy and sanity. At that point I wasn't drinking or using drugs; to avoid the onslaught of backstage acquaintances, I would find a quiet room and read before the show.

Too many gigs, too much money spent, and too many people trying to get backstage all added up to a potentially explosive broth. Something had to give — so before it did, we made a decision to take some time off, pare down the sound system and the crew, and come back refreshed after a period of renewal, individually and collectively. Intellectually, it all made sense, but I was worried — I had put all my eggs in the Grateful Dead basket, and I had an unspoken fear that once it stopped, it would never start up again. As our last run, we booked five shows in October '74 at Winterland in San Francisco, after which — who knew?

But first, we decided to take the band to Europe for a whirlwind dash through the Old World — seven gigs in twelve days: three in London, one in Munich, one in Dijon, two in Paris. After the tour, I stayed over in Paris for a week, luxuriating in art exhibitions and fine food. Soon enough, I would be very glad I had taken that time to recharge.

In a scene that must have been reminiscent of the Mickey Rooney/Judy Garland musicals of the thirties and forties (I've got an idea! Let's put on a show!), Rakow, playing shamelessly on Jerry's well-known desire to direct films, had offered him the opportunity to learn on the job, as it were (an all-too-typical Grateful Dead paradigm). The idea was to make a live concert and documentary film, shot at our upcoming Winterland gigs. In a contentious meeting held at Bobby's place, which also included plans for a second record company (Round Records, for side projects), Hal Kant, our trusted long-time general counsel, raised some questions regarding the funding and possible conflicts of interest inherent in these proposals. Jerry jumped to his feet and flamed Hal: "Are you trying to say there's a burn going down, man?" Words that would return to haunt him soon enough. Hal, in his understated way, could only reiterate his concerns about conflicts, and when I added some questions of my own to the discussion, Rakow rounded on me with the words "It's a jungle out there, man — how about some support?"

With all dissent crushed, preparations for the film shoot/farewell concerts proceeded apace. Bill Graham was unhappy at the thought of Winterland being used as a film set, especially by the Grateful Dead, who he'd always thought were above such matters. Not that Bill's objections made the slightest difference — the juggernaut was rolling, and woe betide anyone who stepped into its path. The concerts themselves went off without a hitch, the high point being the return of Mickey, who showed up at the set break of the last show, complete with a drum set in the back of his car. He joined us for "Playin' in the Band" in the second set, playing his little heart out just like he'd never left. It was a bittersweet reunion, as the "hiatus" — which would last (with several interruptions) for almost two years — was about to begin.

Most of the band — Bobby, Jerry, Mickey, Keith, and Donna — had side projects of their own to keep them busy. With the exception of my experiments with Ned, I myself had no such outlet — I had never wanted to be in a band other than the Grateful Dead — so it was with a great deal of relief that I learned of the general desire (the record company needs product) to make a record of new material, starting from scratch, at Bobby's home studio.

With the exception of parts of *Anthem of the Sun,* most of our previous studio albums had been recorded after the material had been developed somewhat, either in rehearsal or in performance. This time, we wanted to start off just playing together, to see what would surface that could then be elaborated into more extended structures. In that spirit, Jerry brought in a strange, almost atonal melodic entity that would evolve into the title song and sequence for the album, and I had sketched out a little Latin-flavored seven-beat instrumental number, inspired by Shelley's poem "Ozymandias," called "King Solomon's Marbles." Besides "Crazy Fingers," his marvelous essay in smoky ambiguity, Jerry also contributed a triptych of already written tunes ("Help on the Way," "Slipknot," and "Franklin's Tower") that would become, in live performance, one of our finest exploratory vehicles. Bob had a beautiful guitar instrumental, "Sage and Spirit," and one of his stompin-est self-congratulatory rockers, "Music Never Stopped," to round out the album.

Bob's home studio was just large enough to hold all of us and the drums — minus our big stage amps, of course. This forced intimacy (no isolation booths or baffles, there wasn't room) really enhanced the process of developing the tunes. We had to play them like a band would onstage, milking them for all the expressive content we could find.

These sessions also marked the return of Mickey to our permanent lineup. I had asked him to come in and play timbales on "Marbles," and he then collaborated (playing and contributing sound design) on some of the more exploratory pieces on the album — for example, the ambient track of chirping crickets on "Unusual Occurrences in the Desert."

The insatiable appetite of Rakow's record company for product led us to release six albums in 1975/76 — Hunter's *Tiger Rose,* produced by Jerry; *Keith and Donna*; *Seastones,* my collaboration with Ned Lagin; *Old & In the Way,* Jerry's bluegrass band with David Grisman and Peter Rowan; *Blues for Allah,* the Grateful Dead studio album recorded at Bobby's; and the abysmal *Steal Your Face,* the "soundtrack album" from The Movie. The last is worth some commentary, since it has been justly reviled as perhaps the worst album we ever made.

The same recordings were being used for both the album and the film soundtrack — the quality of the actual tracks was wildly variable, the worst being almost unusable because of noise resulting from improper recording technique. It didn't help that the chief recording engineer for the filmed concerts disappeared during the actual filming, or that the backup vocal tracks had been recorded on a second machine and had since disappeared into the fabric of the universe. It didn't help that Bear and I, who were mixing, decided to master the whole thing in "quad" (an early four-channel surround format) and then fold the four channels into two for the stereo version; the result was a glutinous mud bath of sound, through which any music was scarcely discernible. Bear and I went to Rakow, telling him that the recordings were unusable. He brushed our objections aside, saying,

"They'll buy it anyway; we need this record." It's a wonder the record was ever finished; the fact that it was released — against my better judgment — shows how desperate we were for product to take up the slack from lack of touring income.

Meanwhile, postproduction on The Movie proceeded apace — a snail's pace, that is. Leon Gast, the original director (who had brought the concept to Rakow and Jerry as a simple video document of the last concerts only to see it blown far out of proportion into a megafeature), clashed with Jerry early in the process and withdrew. I don't think Jer had any idea at the beginning how much mind-numbing repetitive detail he would have to wade through just to storyboard the film's structure; the editing ended up taking more than two years, in the process scarfing down hundreds of thousands of dollars we didn't have.

Somewhere in the middle of the whole process, Jerry decided that what the film needed was a blockbuster animated opening. So he commissioned Gary Gutierrez, a San Francisco filmmaker, to create a cartoon sequence featuring a Harley-riding Uncle Sam skeleton and a bunch of dancing bears. Almost too cute, one might think, but it turned out to be one of the best parts of the film.

Meanwhile, the work on what would become *Blues for Allah* continued at Bob's studio, with various guests, notably Mickey, David Crosby, and John Cipollina, coming and going. As spring turned into summer, we managed to finish the recording of *Allah* to our satisfaction, and took the tapes into San Francisco for the final mix. We finished the mixing in July and went into rehearsal for a prerelease party — complete with a live performance of the whole record. The rehearsals for the release party were more fun that we'd had any right to expect. So far, the time off wasn't too bad for me — I was still playing the occasional benefit with the band, still recording, and now playing a gig.

During this time, Jerry had started seeing a young woman named Deborah, while M.G. took care of their two kids, Annabelle and

Teresa (and Sunshine, her daughter by Kesey), at home in Stinson. Women seemed to come and go around the Grateful Dead, but I was saddened to see a split between Jerry and M.G., whom I'd always thought of as a perfect match for Jerry. Deborah, with her black hair, black clothing, and black sunglasses, seemed to be the exact antithesis of M.G.'s hearty, outgoing manner.

When I arrived for rehearsal one day in August, I saw that the main soundproof door to Bob's studio was hanging herky-jerky by one hinge, the bottom one. Now, this door was at least eight inches thick, and solid, like that of a bank vault, only made out of wood. What could have happened? It was Jerry's birthday, and M.G. had brought the kids to see him, since he'd been staying with Deborah in her apartment off and on for a while. Jerry, M.G., and the kids were in the studio talking, and Deborah walked in and sat down next to Jerry, giving M.G. a possessive little smile. M.G., who is not a passive person, "just lost it," grabbing Deborah, picking her up, and throwing her against the door with such force that the top hinge was ripped out of its mooring in the doorjamb. It was all over by the time I got there, but it's a wonder that Deborah wasn't hospitalized from the impact. After that, she stayed away from our scene for a while, hanging with Jerry at his gigs and at her place.

For our party, we'd rented the Great American Music Hall in San Francisco — a nice intimate little place with room for about five hundred of our closest friends. We tried to integrate Mickey's crickets into the performance of "Unusual Occurrences," but during the course of the show, they escaped, one or two at a time, from their sand-filled box through the microphone hole. Healy, at Mick's insistence, kept running the cricket track louder and louder ("More crickets!"), as the crickets became fewer and fewer. To the best of my knowledge, they can still be heard chirping nightly from the highest rafters of the Great American Music Hall.

We played our last gig for nine months, a free concert with the Jefferson Starship, at Lindley Meadows in Golden Gate Park on September 28, and the hiatus finally began for real. For ten years, the Grateful Dead had consumed my every waking moment (and much of my dream-life as well). Now I was truly at loose ends. No musical projects except the occasional Seastones gig, living alone, and somewhat estranged from the whole Grateful Dead/Round Records/movie scene (although I did pay a couple of visits to the editing house where Jerry was struggling with the film, plodding frame by frame through endless reels). For a while I was occupied mixing the *Steal Your Face* album, but that too came to an end — and I was alone with myself.

As I was to discover, an idle mind is the devil's workshop. It's very difficult at this distance in time to analyze the motivation for my conduct in the next few years. It may be that I was feeling some degree of isolation after ten years of complete immersion in the band and its music. One thing's for sure — there are always plenty of people ready and willing to commiserate over a brew or two (or twelve) with a rock star who's feeling sorry for himself, or underappreciated, or frustrated with the way his life is going. So it was that I found myself spending more and more time propping up the bar at our local downtown Fairfax watering hole, a place called Nave's. I would drive down the hill to Nave's every night for dinner and a couple of beers. I had never been much of a drinker, scorning it as unworthy of my attention, but I rapidly settled into a routine of drinking all day, eating dinner, and drinking until the bar closed, whereupon I would then go home with any complaisant female I'd been able to pick up. You get the picture. I guess I wanted to live like a wild, irresponsible rock star: If I had the name, I might as well have the game.

Thus began my descent into alcoholism. Inevitably, I began to wake up in the morning with absolutely no memory of the previous night, but feeling a dreadful foreboding: What did I do that I don't remember? Whom do I have to apologize to today? Mickey remembers being called more than once to come get me, pour me into the car, and take me home when I was passed out at the back table. The recurring comment was "That's Phil Lesh from the Grateful Dead — what a shame!" True, but I was shameless — unthinking, unfeeling — and maybe oblivion was the point. But even though I knew deep down that I wasn't exactly having fun living this way, I just couldn't seem to break the cycle.

If there's one lesson I learned during the worst of this period, it's "never marry someone you meet in a bar." I was introduced to Lila one afternoon at my usual hangout; I was instantly smitten, and we eventually married. I now had a drinking partner, and it wasn't long before we added cocaine to the mix.

At the end of '75, Jerry was making a solo album with his new band. Four tracks had already been laid down when problems surfaced within the group. Rather than fire anyone, Jerry dissolved the band, and called on the good old tried-and-true Grateful Dead to finish the album. No problem — we had already played three of the four songs onstage with the Dead, and it wasn't much of a stretch to learn the last one ("Might As Well") and put the tracks down on tape.

We soon agreed that it was time to get back on the road and play Grateful Dead music again, partly because the individual side projects had lost their attractiveness for various reasons, and partly because we all knew that the Grateful Dead delivered the highest degree of aesthetic payoff. Rediscovering how much fun it was to play music together was a real lifesaver for me, and I found myself looking forward eagerly to the rehearsals for our upcoming tour.

Meanwhile, the situation with Rakow, the film, and the record companies continued to go downhill. Rakow had borrowed a large sum of money from unknown sources to finance the editing of the film, and never told us. We found out later Rakow also put some of our money into a Hells Angels film that was never completed. Jerry insisted that Rakow had to be trusted, and since his vote loomed larger than everyone else's put together, it put a lot of strain on the rest of us. It came to a head when Rakow sold the distribution rights for our new album (*Mars Hotel*) to United Artists and split with most of the advance — $225,000. He called Jerry and me into a meeting and attempted to justify his theft, saying that he was somehow "owed" this money. When I heard Rakow say, "You can't fire me, I cut myself a check, I'm splitting, and fuck you," I got up and walked out. We went back on the road in June '76, and in typical Grateful Dead fashion, we never spoke about the rip-off again. Just as it had been for Mickey, it was very hard for Jerry knowing he'd brought someone in who ripped the band off.

Sometime that fall, we shut down Grateful Dead Records (and its fellow traveler Round Records) for good. Rakow's defection had left everyone tasting ashes and bequeathed us a pile of debt; we simply couldn't afford to keep the doors open any longer. That left us without a record company, an essential income source in those troubled times. Fortunately for us, Clive Davis had just left Columbia to take over a small company (Bell Records, which he promptly renamed Arista) and was looking for "name" acts.

We met with Clive around the gigantic conference table we had recently installed at our Front Street rehearsal studio, and what a circus it was. On one side of the table: Clive and a couple of execs from Arista; ranged along the other side: the band, management, crew, and office staff — stacked ten to one in our favor. To their credit, the Arista guys were not intimidated by the massive forces marshaled across from them; they laid out their case clearly and carefully, leaving no detail open to misinterpretation. That day we actually struck up a verbal agreement, beginning a partnership that encompassed five albums, including two of our best, and almost nineteen years. Although Clive was hoping for a "hands-on" advisory relationship in which he would help choose material for our records (and perhaps even work with us in the studio), he was true to his word and never tried to push anything of the sort on us, eventually realizing that we would go our own way, no matter how much he cajoled our management to persuade us to do otherwise. He did request that we work with outside producers, and we agreed to do so, at least for the first few records, since we felt that we had temporarily reached the limits of our ability to produce ourselves. Over the next two or three years, with vastly differing results, we would make records with producers as disparate as Keith Olsen, Gary Lyons, and Lowell George.

Early in spring 1977 we had taken up residence in L.A. to make our first record for Clive and Arista, working with Keith Olsen at his favorite studio. The album, *Terrapin Station,* like most of our records, varied wildly in terms of material, but there were enough strong songs ("Estimated Prophet," parts of "Terrapin Station," "Samson and Delilah") to make it a fairly successful effort. However, the orchestral and choral sweeteners added to the title sequence by Olsen and Paul Buckmaster were a classic example of gilding the lily. The highlight of the sessions was the percussion overdub in which Mickey used a roadie's head as a drum, tapping it gently with a huge, soft gong mallet. The result was a most curious, unidentifiable, hollow-but-meaty, almost gourdlike sound.

In May, after two and a half years, *The Grateful Dead Movie* was at last ready to go. At tremendous cost, both monetary and spiritual, the editing was finished and the soundtrack was synced up. We were ready to release the movie — and to do it the Grateful Dead Way. Wishing to present the movie as a concert experience, Jerry enlisted one of our concert promoters to rent theaters (a process called "four-walling") and bring in special sound systems to enhance the sound quality. (This was before the era of universal multitrack movie sound.)

For the band, a dispiriting development during this period was the introduction into the scene of a form of heroin known as "Persian." Instead of injecting it, one would simply smoke it in a pipe, like opium, which it was purported to be at first. Jerry was still under a black cloud from the stress of Rakow and making the movie, and he was also having a hard time saying no to all of the demands made on him for his time and energy. He had started using cocaine, which allowed him to keep burning the candle at both ends, but found Persian to be a tool that allowed him to check out whenever he wanted to. As these things have a habit of doing, the drug gradually took over his life, first his domestic affairs, and then his music and his relationships with the other band members, to the exclusion of all else.

Ironically, even though the rest of the band was concerned about Jerry's heroin use, we were all self-medicating — some with pills and some, like me, with alcohol and cocaine. No doubt that affected my performance and my personality adversely, but I just couldn't see it from the inside. I was in an unhappy marriage and had come to depend on the slightly numb, detached feeling that alcohol provided to get me through the night — and the day. Any day. Every day.

At home or on the road, my routine was pretty much the same. I would drag myself out of bed as late as possible, depending on whether or not we had a sound check, and go out for breakfast, which usually included a beer or two. Arriving at the show, I would be greeted by many friends and acquaintances, all of whom wanted to party with me. Luckily, we had a dressing room that was well stocked with alcohol, so it was a simple matter to fortify myself, not for the performance, but for the extremely demanding social gauntlet that the backstage scene had become.

Even though he never said one word to me about it, I can't help wondering if Jerry, seeing me drowning in alcohol, uncaring and insensate, didn't seize upon that as a go-ahead of sorts. I sometimes wish that he hadn't had such mortal fear of being thought of as a "cop" —

if he hadn't, maybe he would have said something, and maybe I would have listened. It was not to be, but that didn't stop Mickey from commenting in his own inimitable way. One night we were playing along during the second set, and I started feeling tired — tired of being onstage, tired of playing — but I couldn't just stop and walk off, so I sat down on the edge of the drum riser and continued to play, albeit half-heartedly. Immediately, Mickey jumped up from his drum stool, leaned over his cymbals, and started drumming on the top of my head — hard. That woke me right up, and I stood up smartly as he sat back down with a satisfied smirk on his face.

That summer, however, we couldn't tour because Mickey had rolled his beloved Porsche over a cliff, at the exact point where a single tree could catch the car and save him from the rocks three hundred feet below. Luckily, he survived, but with a broken collarbone and considerable structural damage. He wouldn't be able to play again for at least three months. To fill in the time, Bob and Jerry went into the studio to cut new solo albums — Bob with Keith Olsen in L.A.; Jerry with his band at our Front Street rehearsal hall. Me? I went back to the bar and spent my summer cheering on the local softball teams from a carefully staked-out position right next to the cooler.

By early September, Mick had recovered to the point where he could play — just barely. This was all it took. If Mickey had been born a Native American, his name would have been "Pushing-the-envelope." So we returned to the road in September '77 with a huge outdoor gig in front of a hundred thousand people in Englishtown, New Jersey. The stage was set up in a big open field — so far, business as usual — but the security fencing was something new. Our promoter had brought in almost one hundred cargo containers, fourteen feet high and thirty feet long or so, and placed them end to end around the perimeter of the audience area. Slippery, impenetrable, and impossible to climb, even with crampons and an ice axe, they formed the most formidable and effective security barrier yet seen at any big outdoor rock show. When we drove in to the venue, I had to laugh out loud at the sight: clumps of would-be gate-crashers standing in front of these insurmountable objects, literally scratching their heads in confusion. Uhhh . . . looks like we'll have to buy tickets.

The sight of one hundred thousand people crammed into a finite area surrounded by walls of containers was quite bizarre; it reminded me of some kind of holding pen created by aliens out of a science-fiction story — Robert Sheckley's "To Serve Man" comes to mind. En-glishtown served as a promotional event — after a hiatus of more than a year and a half, to pull off a show on that scale augured well for our potential touring draw — and the record company jumped on it, run-ning full-page ads with pictures of the crowd featured prominently. The album (*Terrapin Station*) was selling moderately, and we were able to breathe a sigh of relief at the thought of maybe being able to pay off some of our debts.

Nevertheless, only three months after we'd returned to touring, the endless grind was starting to cast a pall over our spirits. Lila had divorced me for a Hells Angel, and though I was happy to be single again, for the first time in my life I was seriously out of shape, having put on thirty pounds from drinking.

I needed a mission, an adventure, something so far out of the or-dinary that it could shake up my entrenched habits, and maybe break up whatever it was that seemed to be holding my spirit hostage. The gods then delivered our longest, strangest trip: it began when Richard Loren, our current manager, and his wife, Elaine, together with a friend, Goldie Rush, traveled to Egypt for a vacation during the band's break from touring. Their little party ended up in the town of Luxor, and while floating on the Nile in a felucca, Richard saw a con-nection between the loose, laid-back lifestyle of the Egyptians and the spirit of the Haight (something we seemed to have left behind). His fantasy: What if we came over to play and brought a bunch of our friends along? It could be a "hands across the water" event, and we might even be able to reconnect to some of the spiritual roots that we'd let languish in darkness.

Ever since my visit to Stonehenge in '72, and my exploration into what survived of the ancient geomantic sciences, I had envisioned playing at one of the ancient world's places of power. Stonehenge itself, Machu Picchu, Avebury, the great gothic cathedrals (Chartres, Notre-Dame de Paris), all were impossible for various logistical and political reasons. But the greatest of all places of geomantic power and numinous mystery suddenly seemed attainable — the Great Pyramid of Giza, in Egypt. We enlisted the assistance of Jonathan Wallace, an old friend and editor of the influential investment journal *Middle East Economic Digest,* who put us in touch with Joseph Malone, a former State Department Middle East hand and an unapologetic Arabist. Joe and his wife, Lois, came onboard eagerly, and we set up an agenda of meetings in Washington DC to get the ball rolling. But first we wanted to try to get Bill Graham on the bus, so to speak; to that end Mickey and I visited him late one night at his Marin hilltop compound "Masada," bearing signs reading EGYPT OR BUST! and PA A MUST! Bill greeted us somewhat warily, and his only reaction after we explained our plans was a slow shake of the head and the words "You guys are totally insane." Undaunted, we asked Richard to follow up, but Bill merely repeated himself — and then asked if Santana (whom Bill was managing) could come along. Richard politely declined, and Bill took himself out of the picture. When Mickey heard that, he went totally orbital, calling Bill at 5:30 a.m. and screaming into the phone, "Fuck you, Bill! Just fuck you!" until he was gasping for breath — then in a complete about-face, crooned, "Bill! You still there?" "Yeah, I'm here." "Let's go out for breakfast." "OK" — and off they went, old buddies, like Bogie and Claude Rains at the end of *Casablanca.*

The Malones scheduled a series of meetings with various interested parties in Washington DC. For these meetings, held in March

'78, we nominated a team of Richard, Alan Trist, and myself; I dusted off my *very* conservative dark-blue Dunhill of New York suit and declared our team to be: the Men In Dark Suits (MIDS). (Code for pyra-MIDS, get it?) Joe and Lois first took us to the U.S. State Department (where the runes were consulted and it was mystically determined that we could adequately represent the United States abroad without embarrassing them or ourselves), and then to the Egyptian Embassy, where we met with Mr. Ghorbal, the ambassador (who, unknown to us, was then involved with the negotiations that would lead to the Camp David peace treaty between Egypt and Israel). In those days, international diplomacy was fueled by countless draughts of the finest Scotch whiskey; there we were, the rockers from the Haight, choking down expensive distilled spirits and talking around our real purpose like old Foggy Bottom regulars, as the ambassadorial staff worked overtime trying to determine just how subversive a presence we might be in their volatile political climate. The turning point came when Joe suggested that we turn over any profits to charity; half to the Faith and Hope charity, founded by Madame Sadat (the first lady of Egypt) to provide for poor children, and half to the Department of Antiquities, keepers of the pyramids. We agreed readily, and the bargain was sealed — from the U.S. side, at least. Our next step, with Lois as our escort and nanny, fly to Cairo and submit our proposal to the Ministry of Culture and Antiquities *in person.*

Egypt puts the zap on me the minute we walk off the plane — the light! The heat! The chaos! Inside the terminal, the tumult is virtually indescribable — persons of all ages, dressed in all manner of outlandish garb, rushing frantically to and fro, bearing suitcases, bags, loose items, and live animals; all screaming hysterically in several languages, none of which I've ever heard. The only evidence of potential order is the presence of many heavily armed soldiers, standing in clumps here and there, watching the passing parade with more than a hint of boredom. And then we hit the street. Pandemonium! We're assaulted by waves of "guides" offering their services; it seems that the experiences of a lifetime await, if only you, Sahib, will employ me as your exclusive escort (not to mention bargains: "Egyptian gold, Sahib, very cheap"). Lois quickly hustles us to a waiting car hired for the occasion, and we pull out of the airport into Cairo traffic.

Cairo may or may not be the most congested city in the world, but the bewildering variety of vehicles and conveyances encountered on her streets beggars the imagination. Trucks, foul-smelling diesel buses, handcarts, bicycles, mopeds, motor scooters, pedestrians (some carrying produce, textiles, or mercantile goods balanced on their heads), taxis, the occasional Big Black Government Car — all sharing or fighting for the two or three lanes available for traffic. It's as if the city is a gigantic souk; bargains are struck (between merchants, or with customers) in the middle of the street, and *everyone* seems to have something for sale. Did I mention that lane markers are universally ignored, as are stoplights, so that the center of the city is frozen in perpetual gridlock? Traffic inches its way through intersections like oozing mud.

When driving in Cairo traffic, the horn is as important as the steering wheel — and much more important than the brakes or turn signals. Much as in New York City, the horn is used to signal proximity ("I'm coming up in your blind spot!"), intent ("I'm cutting in front of you now"), dissatisfaction ("You !*^%^#$@$*#! You cut me off!"), and many other more obscure messages. The difference: In Cairo there are no noise laws, and the horn is one's main tool for plowing through traffic.

The exhilarating cacophony of a Cairo intersection still awaits its Gershwin, but suffice it to say that every conceivable pitch and timbre of car, truck, and bus (or wheeled vehicle of any description) horn is not merely well represented, but ubiquitous. It's a revelation to be hopelessly ensnared in the middle of a gridlocked intersection and to realize that one is in the midst of a huge music; the thousands of tones merge into a slow, deeply moving lament, the cri de coeur of a suffering planet.

Our first stop after freshening up at our hotel (Shepheard's, on the Nile) and breaking out the dark suits: the U.S. embassy, where we once again sat with the ambassador and his wife, sipping Scotch and confirming our appointments at the Ministry of Culture the next day. Somehow the State Department, in its infinite wisdom, had decided that what we wanted to do was mostly harmless, and that the great game of U.S. interests and policies would most likely not be derailed by our presence in Egypt.

Our business done for the day, Lois took us out to dinner at a popular riverside nightspot. Egyptians, like the Spanish, tend to eat supper late, in the cool of the evening; the place was jammed and noisy, with Arabic pop music blaring over tinny speakers and the hubbub of conversation flowing musically over the tables. Alcohol was served (uncommon for a Muslim country), and I had my first experience with Egypt's national brew: Stella Beer (this name was to provide much hilarity among our party, especially when sung or howled to the last phrase of Jerry's tender ballad: "Stella Brew"). Now, Stella Beer is no Heineken, even compared to Jamaica's Red Stripe. In fact, it tastes a bit like liquid iron, harsh and metallic. But it was ambrosia in comparison to the local red wine, which came in obviously reused bottles with no cork or cap. Perhaps because of this, none of us got too wild that night, knowing that our most crucial meeting awaited us in the morning. Besides, no one wanted to behave like an ugly American on our first night in town.

On the way back, we stopped at Giza to see the Sphinx Theater, our proposed venue, and the site of a son et lumière presentation given nightly in three languages. The stage is located at the front of the Sphinx temple, just to the left of the Sphinx itself if you're facing the statue from the front. The stage wasn't being used for the Sphinx show, so there were several rows of metal folding chairs set up in a small area at the front edge. We arrived just in time for the English-language presentation, and we slipped into our seats (we were the only spectators) just as a blast of cheesy martial music shredded the silence and a battery of colored lights swept over the ancient statue. "I AM THE SPHINX!" screamed a stentorian voice. "I HAVE ENDURED FIVE THOUSAND YEARS! WHO WILL ANSWER MY QUES-TIONS?" A rhetorical device, no doubt, as the voice went on to an-swer itself, describing the origin and nature of the being depicted in the statue (according to currently fashionable received opinion). The voice then went on to become Rameses, who liberated the Sphinx from the sand; Cheops, who (supposedly) built the Great Pyramid; his son Khephren, "builder" of the second pyramid; and, finally, Mykcri-nos, "constructor" of the third and smallest major pyramid. These rulers got most of the credit for these great works, never mind that in scholarly circles some doubt exists as to the actual age and provenance involved in their construction. As the voice ran through its historical self-congratulatory routine, the same good old colored lights would illuminate the various structures in rotation — a drearily predictable sequence, producing an effect of artistic anesthesia. Even so, we left the theater babbling excitedly and throwing out ideas about lighting and sound for our performance, some of which would actually happen.

The next morning, we arrived early at the Ministry of Culture, where we spent some time shuttling around and cooling our heels in various suboffices before we were escorted with great ceremony into the office of the minister himself. We knew this was the big time be-cause an assistant offered us small glasses of hot sweet tea (the bever-age of choice in the Arab world) as Lois gave us a quick background on our host: Moishe Saad-ed-Din, a friend and adviser to Egyptian president Anwar el-Sadat; a published poet and writer, a constant voice for liberalization, and a former head of the secret police.

The man himself greeted us warmly; we sipped tea in a small alcove and exchanged pleasantries while Lois sketched a quick presentation of our plans. "You wish to donate fifty percent of your profits to Faith and Hope? That speaks well. You must OK it with Ahmad Fawzi, Madame Sadat's personal secretary. I'll arrange for a meeting tomorrow. And," — turning to me with a searching look — "have you found that your music changes when you play in different parts of the world?" "Indeed we have," I replied, "and that's precisely why we want to play at the Great Pyramid." He sat back with an "I thought so" expression on his face, smiled, and gave us his blessing: "I wish you good fortune. May I suggest you take some time to visit the Pyramids now? You may wish to acquaint yourselves more closely with them to confirm your suspicions." When we invited him to the performances, he smiled again, saying, "Oh, I'll be there — you'll see."

Our meeting had ended early, so we had the rest of the day and that night to spend at Giza, the plateau outside the city where the mighty pyramids stand. No amount of reading and perusal of diagrams and charts (and I'd done plenty of both) could have prepared me for the sheer *presence* of the Great Pyramid. It's so *there* that it wraps space around itself — even its shadow has weight and volume. It's an immense, brooding presence, yet curiously uplifting, as if, unseen, deep in the Stygian intergalactic blackness of the hulking structure there glows a torch burning with a white-hot flame, the color of the Pyramid clad in its original raiment — polished white limestone.

As we walk into the gigantic shadow, I pray that this colossal structure is more than just a priest-king's ego trip. All the reading I've done leads me to hope that I'll receive a sign, some signal from the higher intelligence that seems to have guided the builders. We move closer to the entrance, where a clump of djellaba-clad locals, presumably guides, await us. At the sight of us, they seem to confer briefly, and one of their number detaches himself from the group and approaches. "Good day, gentlemen, welcome to Giza. You would like to see the Pyramids? Explore the interior, perhaps? It is no longer permitted, alas, to climb to the top." Alas. We strike a bargain — his services for the day for five Egyptian pounds. We begin with a walk around the perimeter, looking for any trace of the famed casing stones, but only gaping sockets remain where gleaming limestone once stood. We complete our circumambulation and climb laboriously up several courses of masonry (each course just high enough so that one is required to scramble up on one's belly) to the forced entrance blasted by Caliph Al Mamoun in the seventh century CE.

The only concessions to modernity and the volume of tourists offered by the Ministry of Culture and Antiquities are a rickety wooden stairway running the length of the Grand Gallery and strings of naked white lightbulbs strung everywhere; the light throws the angles and planes of the interior into garish relief, like some demented op-art installation. We climb the Gallery, detour into the so-called Queen's Chamber, and ascend to the structural and mystic heart of the Pyramid — the King's Chamber.

The King's Chamber is empty, except for a stone coffer just large enough to hold a human form (the presence of this "sarcophagus" is the main evidence for the "tomb" theory of the Pyramid espoused by most academic Egyptologists).[1] This is the room where, in 1797, Napoleon spent the night; when asked what befell him in the Great Pyramid, he replied, "I would tell you, but you would think me mad." This is the room where, according to one theory, initiates into the Osirian mysteries were brought to the point of death in order to be reborn into a new and higher life. We've read of the remarkable acoustic properties of the Chamber, so we begin to hum and chant, and sure enough, the sound resonates so fully in this small space that a much vaster space slowly opens in our minds. We close our eyes; we might well be in an underground cavern, or a great cathedral. Our voices find the resonant tone of the Chamber: The sound expands into infinity,

---

[1]There are, of course, many other theories regarding the actual purpose of the Pyramid — ranging from "stargate," or "initiatory temple," or "cosmic energy-transformer" to "Tesla device" or "astronomical observatory."

and we begin to hear strange, occult harmonies resounding above our fundamental chant-drone. The energy is so strong that the sound grows louder and more complex without any of us doing anything — the feedback system works perfectly. The sound orders itself into celestial music, with so many layers one can't possibly comprehend it all. I'm straining to hear more deeply when our guide abruptly enters — and the magic is gone, the thread snapped. We shake ourselves like dogs and stumble outside into the white heat of the Egyptian afternoon, having had at the very least our suspicions confirmed: This place *is* magic, and hey, how about the King's for an echo chamber?

Our last meeting in Cairo was with Ahmad Fawzi, Madame Sadat's personal secretary and a popular radio host. Still full of cosmic feeling from the previous day, I optimistically offered a jocular greeting, something along the lines of "Yo, I hear you've got the hottest show in town." A cold look. "Are you with the embassy?" "No, sir, I'm with the Grateful Dead." (You know, the crazy American rock band that wants to play here and donate to your boss's charity?) A sigh of resignation. To business, then — we were told that the first lady looks favorably on our plan, the Ministry of Culture and Antiquities has confirmed, and we're ready to go. Discreet high fives all around. Our telegram to the folks back at Grateful Dead World Headquarters read:

> Two count them Two open air concerts at the great pyramid sphinx theater in lower Egypt confirmed repeat confirmed for September 14 and 15. Steering committee landing Thursday SFO with signed repeat signed agreement.

Business successfully concluded, it was time to take a break and spend some time in what Richard called "the real Egypt." When in Luxor on his previous vacation visit, Richard had befriended Atti, the owner of a fleet of Nile pleasure craft, and we were to spend a day on the Nile with him. So we hired a car to take us south, up the Nile to that ancient seat of the Pharaonic priesthood, just across the river from the Valley of the Kings. The ride up was uneventful, in spite of our driver's penchant for speeding at what seemed like ninety miles per hour through small villages, dust spewing from the tires, chickens and children and old men scrambling out of the way (and occasionally a clenched fist waving in the mirror). We did try to stop for lunch in a town called Assyut but quickly decided not to try the local diet. When I looked up the town randomly in my Baedeker, I discovered that it was the birthplace of Plotinus, the third-century Alexandrian Neoplatonic philosopher. History loomed large everywhere here.

In Luxor, we connected with Atti and met his family, all of whom (the men, that is) were part of his boating company. It's relevant to note that the Egyptian people I met on these visits — from the Minister of Culture to guides at the Pyramids to Nile boatmen in Luxor — were to a man and woman welcoming and open. The most often heard phrase upon meeting was "Americans? Welcome!" Immediately we were ferried across the river to see the legendary Valley of the Kings, Queen Hatshepsut's temple, and the Colossi of Memnon, erected during the Old Kingdom. It is said that every day, these huge statues would greet the rising sun with song. Song from stone, a poem in itself.

That night, we explored the temple of Karnak at Luxor. The setting was almost as impressive as the Pyramids: the gigantic stone columns of the temple, the colorful reflections from the water, and, above all, the brilliance of the night sky (seen from as far south as I'd ever been). Immediately above my head as I stared, transfixed, shone a cluster of blue-white stars, seemingly so close as to be reaching down to us. "What's that?" I asked, awestruck; "The Pleiades, the Seven Sisters," answered Alan. "Normally, one can only see six, but from here . . ." We looked again, counted, and lo, there were seven. It's easy to see why the stars played such an important role in the Pharaonic religion; the extraordinary clarity of the sky makes it seem as if they are in residence here on earth.

On our last night in Luxor, Atti held a dinner party for us on his biggest, most luxurious boat. One of his brothers cooked a stunningly delicious lamb kebab over an open fire pit built into the deck, and we cast off into the westering light of the sun, over the most romantic of all rivers, sailing past riverbank scenes unchanged for five thousand years: a farmer plowing his field with oxen, women doing laundry by the riverside. This, then, was the real Egypt; pharaohs, kings, prophets, and presidents may come and go, but the Nile, in an ageless rhythm, continues to provide sustenance for its people. At sunset, as if in affirmation, the people on the neighboring boat broke out some instruments and began jamming! A flute or oboelike wind instrument, two small hand drums, and voices punctuated with clapping hands — human beings making music for the sheer *joy* of it: No doubt revisiting old favorite songs (and adding bawdy lyrics), they played far into the night with an exuberance and élan that took our breath away. It's a happy thought: Even if there were a culture in which there were no professional musicians, everyone would make music as well as they could anyway, without thinking of personal recompense, because music is ambrosia for the soul.

When we returned to Egypt in September, the whole world had changed. Egypt's leader was in Washington DC negotiating with the Israeli prime minister the first peace agreement between an Arab nation and the state of Israel. The atmosphere in Cairo crackled with anticipation and excitement, and as Americans, we were welcomed with occasional effusions of thanks, as if each of us as an individual was responsible for bringing the promise of peace. We descended upon the people of Egypt like a plague of Pranksters: band, crew, family — *and* the largest Pleasure Crew in history, some two hundred fifty strong (including Bill Graham, Kesey, and many other old friends), to serve as our built-in audience in case we didn't sell any tickets. We bunked up at the Mena House Hotel, literally in the shadow of the Great Pyramid. After crashing for twelve hours from jet lag and the after-effects of a wild predeparture party, I threw back my curtains to admit the glorious Egyptian sunlight, and there it was, filling the frame of the window with its incomparable gravitas, gathering the light into itself, the shape that had haunted my dreams since our visit in March.

We're now set to play three shows, the last of which, on September 16, coincides with a total lunar eclipse. The Pleasure Crew disperses into the souks and fleshpots of Cairo, in search of swag and hashish. The band mostly stays close to the Giza plateau, exploring the Pyramids and the nearby temple complex. The crew begins the setup, the logistics of which are complicated by a sixty-foot stretch of sand separating the trucks from the stage. Healy and some of his crew explore the idea of using the King's Chamber as an echo chamber; telephone cables are requested, and permission is sought.

We open the first two shows with a group from Hamza El Din's Abu Simbel school; they sing and play hand drums to set the mood rhythmically. On the third night, eclipse night, we postpone their appearance until just before the eclipse, at the beginning of the second set. Over the past two shows, I've been noticing an increasing number of shadowy figures gathering just at the edge of the illuminated area surrounding the stage and audience — not locals, as they all seem to be wearing the same garment, a dark, hooded robe. These, it turns out, are the Bedouin, the nomadic horsemen of the desert: drawn in by the music and lights (this is definitely not your usual sound-and-light show), each night they have remained to dance and sway rhythmically for the duration of the show.

Tonight, while the moon slowly disappears, the stars become even brighter and more colorful, their light burning through the sullen red glow of the occluded moon. As the last tiny corner of the moon's disc winks out of existence, a sighing wave of sound rises from the neighboring streets: The villagers have joined us, with homemade percussion instruments, pots and pans, shakers, and voices, to sing the moon back again. How many times have they done this over the millennia?

At the deepest point of the eclipse, the members of the Grateful Dead begin to trade places, one at a time, with the Abu Simbel choir. The chanting and banging reaches a peak and then subsides when the moon begins to recover some of her luster. The Grateful Dead play on, the Bedouins dance, the bats feed, while the moon returns to us — and still we play, and dance, and sing.

For a band that always blows the big ones (and this was arguably the biggest show ever for us, in an intangible sense) there wasn't a particular feeling of performance anxiety. The value of the moment didn't seem to depend on how well or badly we played according to our own lights; rather, it was more important somehow that we just be there and participate in the ageless ritual of the eclipse. The sad fact is, we didn't play well; the piano was out of tune, and Billy played with a broken wrist. The recordings we'd counted on for an album to partially defray the costs of the expedition turned out to be useless. But none of that mattered, then or now. We went there, we played, we donated, not just to Faith and Hope and Culture and Antiquities, but also the cost of a new soccer field for the kids of Mena Village, and came home in the hole to the tune of five hundred large. So what? We did it. Did what, exactly? I wasn't sure for a long time, but a few years ago I stumbled upon a Web site analysis of the astronomical and spiritual meaning behind the myth of Osiris and discovered that we had played a role in the return of the gods.

I learned that our name derived ultimately from a folktale about the resurrection of Osiris, and that our performance in Egypt in front of the Sphinx during a total lunar eclipse was the first, and totally spontaneous, raising of the Djed, the spine of Osiris, as the axes of the galaxy and of Earth's sky were turning into alignment. Our performance lit a fuse, and myth descended into reality. Let our chant fill the void, that others may know: In the land of the night, the Ship of the Sun is driven across the sky by the Grateful Dead.

We came right back from Egypt and trundled our cosmic asses into the studio to work on our album *Shakedown Street* — which we'd started earlier in the year with producer Lowell George. The album, with its cartoonlike cover, evokes the feeling of the scene at our studio-warehouse on Front Street in San Rafael. In marked contrast to our management office on the other side of town, which was in a beautiful Victorian house on a tree-lined street with restaurants and shops nearby, the studio was more of a clubhouse for the band and crew, surrounded by a gritty urban landscape of neon signs, shabby motels, and dilapidated storefronts. At the management office, friends and acquaintances could feel free to drop by, hang in the kitchen, and maybe even encounter a band member or two passing through. At the studio, only invited guests were permitted: mostly dope dealers, bikers, and other colorful characters who were constantly coming and going, giving the place an atmosphere of chaotic transition. When the band wasn't rehearsing or recording, we'd hang out in the front room where the big-screen TV was always on, although the view out the door was frequently more interesting than any TV show, what with all the action involving the cops and the local prostitutes and winos.

After five nights at Winterland, we embarked on a six-week cross-country tour, which would take us up and down the East Coast, through Mississippi and Texas to San Diego, and home to Winterland for the final performance at that hallowed hall.

But first, NBC TV's Studio 8H, at Rockefeller Plaza, once the home of the NBC Symphony Orchestra under Arturo Toscanini, was now host to a new breed of resident aliens: *Saturday Night Live.* We were asked to be *SNL*'s "musical guest" only because one of their best writers (Tom Davis, a friend of Jerry's and a major Deadhead) called in a marker on his boss — "For me, Lorne, for me."

The difficulties with live music on broadcast TV are legion, mostly having to do with sound. We have enough trouble making our records sound good — TV is orders of magnitude more difficult than recording studios. In the studio, there is at least some control over the mix, the instrumental sounds, etc., if one knows how to use that control. On live TV, the technology simply didn't exist then for subtle gradations of sound, and what control there was usually rested in the hands of the network sound crew — union lifers to a man — whose background was generally in film, radio, and TV news, and whose experience with music was limited. So we knew going in the sound would be shit. "Why are we doing this?" Jerry wanted to know. "Because it's *S! N! L!,* man!" This from a drummer. "And that makes it so cool we just have to do it?" "How about Tom Davis, who went to the mat for this?" Another drummer heard from. "Ahhh — rumbling grumblyguest . . ."

As jaded as we pretended to be, it was pretty exciting even so — Whoa, looky, ma! Big-time National TeeVee! The Dead will never be prime time material, but it was kinda neat to sneak into the late-show realm, even if what we played was hardly our most subversive stuff: "Casey Jones," "I Need a Miracle," and "Good Lovin'." I sent out for a T-shirt with "Hi Mom" silk-screened on the upper chest, even having the presence of mind to specify the *right* upper chest so the logo wouldn't be obscured by my guitar strap.

There's a run-through of one song for camera angles and lighting (oh, right, and a *sound check*), and we repair to a dressing room to await our appearance. The door swings open, and in cartwheels John Belushi, dressed in a garish purple evening gown, a feather boa, and pumps. (He's Elizabeth Taylor in a particularly gross sketch involving chicken parts.) He casts a raised eyebrow around the room and, raising a drumstick, gestures peremptorily at us all. "Just remember, when the little red light on the camera goes on — *TWENTY MILLION PEOPLE!*" He cuts and runs, pursued by a barrage of half-eaten fruit. Well, all right, then. Let's play.

The performance itself was mostly harmless, in that it was supposed to be a "promo" appearance, and we didn't screw up much. The fact is that live music on TV remains to this day a curiously unsatisfying experience, like cotton candy or Chinese food (except for performances that have been transferred to DVD and remixed). Maybe it's the awful sound coming through three-inch TV speakers; maybe it's the primacy of the visual element, so that as you stare in helpless fascination at a rock star's nose hair, brightly lit and in extreme close-up, the music tends to become less vivid.

But the best was yet to come — the Blues Bar. Belushi and Dan Aykroyd, in their personae as the Blues Brothers, had leased a hole in the wall downtown with the idea of turning it into a blues joint and having all the greats come to play when they were in town. It wasn't open for business yet, so all they had down there was some booze, a jukebox full of blues records, and a whole bunch of cocaine, in which, by that time, we were all indulging. Good enough for a party, we thought, so away we go into the downtown traffic, to find ourselves crammed into a tiny room with barely enough space for a stage and a bar, with the floors partly torn up — watch your step, here — and a trapdoor leading below, where the blow was done. "Can't do it up there — cops stop in all the time." My last vision of that evening is of Aykroyd bent over the open guts of the jukebox, tinkering with some mechanism, while his pants slid down his waist until he looked just like his butt-crack-flaunting repairman in so many *SNL* sketches.

* * *

By the first week of the winter '79 tour, it was apparent that Keith and Donna were melting down. This should have been clear to us for some time, especially after the night they turned the parking lot at our Front Street studio/clubhouse into their very own demolition derby. After a heated argument, they repeatedly smashed their cars into each other, then sped off just before the cops arrived. But the rest of us were, as usual, oblivious to anything outside of our own narrow solipsistic orbits. It came to a head one night in a hotel when Keith dropped a bottle of pills on the floor of his room; it rolled under the bed, and Keith crawled under after it, searching with a cigarette lighter. The bed, naturally enough, caught on fire, and Keith and Donna barely escaped the sudden inferno with their skins intact. The room was a total loss.

Keith's playing, once so perfectly fitted to our sound, had degenerated to the point that most of us were simply trying to "lose him on stage," in Bob's eloquent phrase. When we put their increasingly overt self-destructive behavior together with that, we knew it was finally time for a change. Never a paragon of self-esteem, Keith's increasing drug and alcohol use had put him in an almost vegetative state. His musical timing was suffering, and he had developed some annoying habits onstage, notably slavish imitation of Jerry's lead lines, a tic that began to irritate Jerry no end.

The Godchauxs' marriage looked to be on its last legs, and their infant son, Zion, was losing his parents. They couldn't bring him on the road, and they were gone far too often and too long to give him a home life. When Donna finally gave up and flew home early from the spring tour, the rest of us decided to act as soon as possible. Hey, we had a big summer tour coming up, and we needed to have a solid keyboard player. We met at Keith and Donna's place after the tour, and discovered that they too had come to the conclusion that the human cost of staying with the band was too high.

For some time, Jerry had been concerned by Keith's musical de-volution, and when playing a Jerry Garcia Band double bill with Bob's band, The Midnites, he had been impressed by the playing of Bob's keyboardist, Brent Mydland. Jerry asked Bob to contact Brent, ask him if he was interested, and send him some tapes so he could learn some of our stuff. The answer came in the affirmative; so when Keith and Donna left the band, Brent was ready to step right in and start working with us on a very high level. His superb playing and singing brought a new energy to the band, as if we were firing on all cylinders again, and his vulnerability and sweetness added a welcome ingredient to the gumbo of curmudgeonly abrasiveness that the band had become.

At the same time, we were trying to regain the edge in terms of our live sound, the absence of the Wall being keenly felt during this period of financial decline. Dan Healy and some colleagues from other San Francisco sound crews had formed a sound company, UltraSound, which would provide us with our finest PA since the Wall. The key to the system emerged in the person of John Meyer, a physicist and speaker designer whom Bear had discovered. John's new speaker/amp design — based on a method of time alignment that bordered on the inexplicable — provided us first with the massive "earthquake" sub-woofers so beloved of those Deadheads who found their spiritual home in the "Phil Zone" (that space in front of my position on the stage where the bass was most prominently heard), and then with a full-range system delivering sound that approached the transparency of the Wall. Over the next five years, that system was able to be pack-aged in a way that made it practical to use for touring, even in this era of lowered expectations.

In the first week of September '79, we played our first gigs at what would become my personal favorite among all indoor venues in the United States, Madison Square Garden in New York City. Playing in that building as it bounces up and down from the sheer stomping exuberance of the audience is a sensation that must be experienced to be believed. I say, "bounce up and down," and I mean that — literally. The Garden venue itself is suspended on huge cables from the roof of a surrounding but independent structure, basically hanging in midair above Penn Station. When the band is really rockin', it feels as if the bass and drums are driving the entire structure to dip and bounce in time with the music — somewhat disconcerting at first, but nevertheless tremendously exciting. Over the years, we would play more shows at the Garden than any other band (including one run of nine in a row while repeating only three songs).

Between tours (and sometimes during tours) we were trying to make our third Arista album, *Go to Heaven,* also our first with Brent in the band. For the first time since 1969, there were only two Garcia/Hunter songs ready for recording; Bob (three songs) and Brent (two songs) took up the slack, along with one song Billy and Mickey contributed and one rearranged traditional jug-band tune ("Don't Ease Me In"). The result was the usual mixed bag of stuff, made as commercial as possible by our producer, Gary Lyons, best known for his work with Foreigner. Clive Davis didn't help much by making a radio edit of one of the tunes — a process that always destroys any carefully thought-out musical structure, since the guiding parameters for radio edits are best exemplified by the concepts "the more choruses the better," or the panic-stricken "We can't go more than forty-five seconds without a chorus!" The cover, featuring us in Saturday Night Fever disco suits against a white background, reinforced the impression that we were "going commercial." Regardless of the reaction from hardcore Deadheads, *Go to Heaven* sold fairly well after its release in April 1980, making number twenty-three on the charts and recouping its studio costs. The critics savaged it, however; the least offensive description I saw was "cotton candy." Personally, I thought that the music was a lot better than the album cover — the Garcia/Hunter and Weir/Barlow songs were major additions to our repertoire, and Brent's two songs, in spite of having been written before joining the band, gave notice that a new voice had arrived.

Go to Heaven would also be our last studio album for seven years, as our disenchantment with studios, producers, and record company executives was complete; and besides, we had fulfilled the current Arista contract requirements with three studio albums in three years. All right! Now we can make some live albums!

Touring and more touring. We were playing in Portland on June 12 when Mount St. Helens erupted for the third time since May 18. The volcano had literally blown its top just at the time we were flaming our way through "Fire on the Mountain." The syncronicity of some of the lyrics still gets me: "There's a dragon with matches loose on the town/take a whole lake of water just to cool him down." We didn't find out until after the show, when we stepped outside the Memorial Coliseum to find strange gray flakes blanketing the ground and floating down from the sky — pieces of the mountain, fused into lava by the force of the blast, one hundred miles to the north.

During our July break, we got the word that Keith Godchaux had been in a serious auto accident. Early in the morning, after an all-night party session, a car driven by a friend (with Keith as a passenger) had come over White's Hill Road from West Marin at high speed. There was some roadwork going on there, and apparently the driver didn't see the warning signs, crashing into the back of the workers' flatbed equipment truck. Both were critically injured, and Keith died two days later from massive head injuries, never having recovered consciousness. I was terribly saddened; here was a man who'd had his dream come true, and it turned on him and destroyed him. The irony was undeniable: Drugs had helped us to create our group mind and fuse our music together, and now drugs were isolating us from one another and our own feelings, and starting to kill us off.

In September, we once again took ourselves and our recording gear into the Warfield Theatre in San Francisco for a fifteen-show run, aimed at presenting a new format — one acoustic and two electric sets — and making two live albums, one acoustic, one electric, from the recorded results. After a visit to New Orleans, our first since 1970, we went into Radio City Music Hall in New York for eight shows, ending on Halloween.

We had commissioned two posters featuring our now-familiar Grateful Dead skeletons (rendered Godzilla-size) for this series of gigs — one showing the Warfield and various San Francisco landmarks, and one showing Radio City and New York landmarks. When the rough design for the New York poster reached the upper echelons of the Radio City management, a great hue and cry went up. The executives of that financially beleaguered entity interpreted the skeletons looming over their site as a prediction of the death of Radio City, and in a scathing letter stopped just short of accusations of treason for being so un-American as to fail to have faith in the longevity of their institution. My reaction when shown the letter: "Un-American? Why, there's *nothing* more American than the Grateful Dead."

In order to save the dates, we agreed not to use the poster for the shows — but did use it later for two live albums, *Dead Reckoning* and *Dead Set,* one acoustic, one double electric. The rest of the year was taken up with more touring, working to integrate Brent into the band, and returning to Oakland Auditorium Arena for our second multinight New Year's run.

After a six-week break, the year 1981 started off with more touring. We tour, therefore we are. We considered ourselves a live band, i.e., playing for live audiences and dancers is what we did best and loved most, and most of our income ultimately came from touring.

We made a quick and dirty trip to England and Germany in March. After some shows in London for a warm-up, the grand finale was an international *Fernsehen und Rundfunk* (TV/FM) "Rockpalast" broadcast from the Grugahalle, in Essen, home to the Krupp arms dynasty. The broadcast was a double bill with the Who, with whom we'd enjoyed a more or less cordial relationship since our "Days on the Green" concerts for Bill Graham back in '76. They put on their usual explosive performance, while we strolled through a lackluster set — we've only once been able to perform at their level on a bill with them, and that was at one of the '76 shows. We had brought the extraordinary juggling/tumbling team the Flying Karamazov Brothers with us for the video; their antics considerably enlivened (and extended) the drum solo segment, during which they tossed bowling pins back and forth over the heads of the drummers. The Karamazov Brothers had performed a free show the day before in the central square; Billy and Mickey reciprocated in advance by joining them with hand drums. If you think the German public had a little difficulty understanding the Grateful Dead, imagine the sight of three outlandishly costumed freaks, dancing and cartwheeling around the central fountain in the square, slinging all manner of objects to and fro between them, to the feverish accompaniment of hurtling hand drums. *Donnerwetter! Eigenartig, nicht wahr?*

After a blowout all-nighter in the hotel bar featuring the crews of both bands at their drunkest, we flew back home to more touring: East Coast! West Coast! Midwest! West Coast! East Coast! And then it was back to Europe, a trip that yielded one of the last of our truly spontaneous moments. Jerry and Bob had played at the Melkweg nightclub and hashish den in Amsterdam on a night off earlier in the tour. When our shows in France were canceled, Rock decided, as sort of a stealth gig, to bring us back to the Melkweg for two nights, playing on borrowed instruments and amps. It was a total gas; I can't remember how long it had been since we played somewhere that small. We crammed onto the tiny, low-ceilinged stage and wailed our hearts out, to the screaming delight of the local audience, who were in shock from the startling spontaneity of it all.

Hoping for another adventure to recharge myself, as well as the band, I made an overnight stop at Glastonbury, in England, to discuss the possibility of playing the famed festival held at midsummer, our contemporary version of Druidical solstice rites. Alas, it never happened, but at least the festival is still happening, and bigger than ever, too.

I wasn't particularly looking forward to going home. I had asked my current girlfriend to move out by the first of the year, but we weren't there yet, and I could expect either a chilly reception or an empty house and *then* a chilly reception. Thank goodness, another tour in six weeks — and away I flew, back to the East Coast, then the Midwest, then home just in time for Christmas with Mom.

Over the New Year's holiday, a monster storm rolled down from the Alaskan gulf — or roared up from Hawaiian tropical waters, I don't know — and flattened the Bay Area for five days, leaving movement at a standstill and power outages, drowned streets, and downed trees everywhere. We were playing our annual five-night New Year's run, and I was barricaded in a room at the Berkeley Marriott for the whole time we weren't playing. The bridges spanning the bay and the Golden Gate were closed by the state of California sometime on New Year's morning — and I couldn't get home for two more days, having gotten so wound up on New Year's Eve that I'd missed the bridge deadline.

The band members weren't hanging together, as drugs and alcohol continued to isolate us from one another. I spent most of my time in the hotel bar. But in the mornings, little tendrils of thought began to surface as I lay there, my bones aching and my heart sick with remorse: You know, maybe this isn't the best life I could make for myself. In hindsight, I must have felt as though I'd finally hit bottom and there was no place to go but up. Something changed in me then, something that made me begin to strive toward the surface, after swimming so long in darkness and solitude. From such small beginnings can come major life changes, although I still had many years of soul-searching before I could consider myself on an upward path.

Hell is other people, says Sartre the existentialist. Not so, says Phil the psychonaut. Hell is yourself and only yourself: emotions, desires, hates, fears, ego, id, the whole churning astral soup, unrelieved by anything of the Other, of community, of sharing, of compassion, all of which I'd pushed away in my rush to embrace my own shadow.

But even before I'd begun to ask these questions of myself, I'd unconsciously taken a first step toward reaching out empathetically to other humans. For some time, I'd been eating my breakfast at a little place in San Rafael (where I'd moved after leaving Fairfax): the Station Café, owned by old friends, Mark and his wife, Karen. One morning just before Halloween (during the six-week break between Europe 2 and our East Coast tour), I was sitting at the counter there, gloomily muttering mindrot into a handheld voice recorder I'd bought in Edinburgh. My breakfast arrived, brought by my regular waitress, Jill, a slim young woman with warm brown eyes whom I'd gotten to know slightly over recent months. Without thinking (or even saying thank you) I pushed the record button, said, "And here's Jill's phone number," and held up the little machine for her to respond. After a startled glance, as if she'd never really seen me before, she clearly enunciated a number into the recorder — one that I knew (and she knew that I knew) was the number of the café where we were sitting — and finished with a little smile, as if to say, "Your move." I muttered something like "nice save" or "better luck next time" as I forced a smile and turned to my breakfast. But after that I kept thinking that she was looking at me a little differently than before. Not that I looked like much of a prize, thank you very much, with my booze-for-breakfast habits, puffy face, and thirty pounds of beer belly.

By the end of 1981, I was starting to feel trapped in an endless cycle of touring and recording. It seemed as if we were spending more time in meetings discussing recording and touring plans than we were on stage playing music. The band was touring ten months out of the year, a grueling schedule. We employed almost thirty people full-time and year-round, divided into three main areas of support: road crew, audio engineering, and management. Also, cocaine had become the drug of choice among us. Backstage, almost everyone had some. On many occasions, casual acquaintances would just walk up, wordlessly hand me a little bindle, and walk away with a wave.

The music was also showing signs of this pernicious influence — standing onstage during any number of performances I could see our chemistry cracking and crumbling. Even though everyone was playing individually as well as ever, none of us was really listening to one another much, only to our own frying brain cells. I was as much a part of the problem as anyone, falling into a stupefying cycle of booze and coke abuse: wake up with a hangover — have a line. Getting a little edgy — have a drink to smooth it out. Things start getting blurry — have a line or two to sharpen up the focus. Et cetera, ad infinitum. Kiss the once mighty group mind good-bye.

Lots of things had come to a head during our March '81 tour of Europe. Notably, one morning in Essen, Germany, Billy fired our manager, Richard Loren. The way I figure it, Richard had just left Billy's room on that fateful day when I arrived to say good morning. After some desultory conversation, Billy let me know that he'd just (wrongfully) accused Richard of stealing from us, and that he would be leaving our employ. "Well, *that* was a stupid move!" I remarked casually. *Grhgk!* With the speed of a striking rattlesnake, Billy grabbed me by the throat. My shock was so great I forgot to breathe for a second, and by then it wasn't easy. "A stupid move?" he inquired sweetly, leaning close. "*Grgghhkr* — yes! A stupid mo—uurgghknrm!" — he tightened his grip. His wife, Shelley, looked on aghast. Shock had turned to indignation, accompanied by light-headedness and a tendency for everything to turn pink, then red, as my oxygen-starved brain began to shut down. Suddenly the red light faded from his eyes and I was released. I left without another word. Stupid of me to use the word *stupid;* I really must practice Control of Tongue. I was still pissed when I got to the avenue, and when I saw Billy and he acted like nothing had happened, I gave him the cold shoulder. We played the show — but not well.

I was not very happy about the departure of one of the best managers we'd had. On the other hand, I was looking forward to the band making major management decisions. Not that we were particularly good at it; I just wanted us to take responsibility for ourselves. That way we wouldn't have anybody to blame when anything went wrong. The fun part was always making decisions for "trips," or just for sheer cussedness, regardless of how it would play in the music "industry." (Begin rant) Music industry. The image that comes to mind is an assembly line, which wouldn't be so serious if it affected only the mechanical process of distribution. The problem is that the content ("songs") is assembled in the same way as the medium of distribution: market-driven, prepackaged, modular, subliminally dumbed-down units of commerce. (End rant. Sorry.)

Unfortunately, the fun decisions weren't very practical anymore.

Several dozen employees (mostly old friends and new acquaintances that had signed on for the duration) depended on us for their livelihood, not to mention health insurance. This meant that we had to continue touring at the same rate, or figure out ways to earn more while touring less.

By this time, some members of our team had become concerned about an apparent replay of the tensions and pressures that had led to the original hiatus. No one wanted to see it all come crashing down again, and we knew we had to define the problem in order to solve it. Immediately after the spring tour of Europe, we held several consecutive general meetings, all well attended and intensely focused. In these meetings we organized a management committee (as opposed to having a single manager), which would refer its recommendations to the band. We commissioned a detailed report analyzing the responsibility relationships among the members of our team, and began to seriously discuss the possibility of less touring, so we could find some time to rebond with each other on a creative level.

Jerry neatly summarized the problem as he saw it in a preface written for the analysis of our business operation:

> Grateful Dead Productions, Inc. is a legal fiction, not a working reality. It doesn't represent our real work. Just because we have an office doesn't mean we have to feel we have to be office workers, nor [need we] identify ourselves as a Corporation because we *have* a corporation.
>
> We need to liberate ourselves from misunderstanding ourselves. We need to protect ourselves from believing that we are essentially a corporate entity.
>
> The reason for this attempt to describe ourselves is to free all the people in our organization from having to feel defined by what is actually an externally dictated fiction of convenience.

Bobby Petersen also weighed in with some words of wisdom, in his poem "For the Grateful Dead":

it gets lonely
in the high pines
& lonelier when
you finally get
to town
all that
goodness you
done stored up
be gone
in about 15 minutes
so you gotta go
through all that
sickness
& all that joy just
like pig did
wonderin'
what the fuck
am I doin' here & why?
when you damn well know
it's because we all love
each other

It was a classic double-bind situation: stay locked into our vicious touring and recording schedule or ease up on touring, which we couldn't do when we didn't have any funds set aside to keep our people employed and our team together, even on reduced salaries. So on we went, booking more tours and making live recordings at multinight stands in major cities. Incidentally, we were earning more as our popularity grew and we played larger and larger venues. Not that those earnings meant anything to the individual band members; it was mostly numbers on paper, since the band drew what was basically a maintenance salary, and all the rest went into the pot — for crew and management salaries, equipment expenses, etc. — to keep the trip going.

It would have been intolerable if occasionally the music hadn't, surprisingly, given me joy. After seventeen years, the music we made playing together could still surprise and astonish me intensely, if not as often or as consistently as it had in the beginning. In spite of the drug-induced isolation that was pushing us apart, every time I walked out on that stage I knew in my heart that the infinite potential present in that moment was available to us all, if we could only reach out and grasp it. That remained my goal — to walk out every night and play as if life itself depended on my every note, to wrest meaning from the jaws of entropy and decay, and to transform every place we played into a shrine of expanded consciousness.

Luckily, I had allies in this quest. Deep down, everyone in the band felt the same way, behind all the jiving and the superficial personas we brandished to mask our true natures. The music was still the reason we were standing onstage together every night. The proof was in the shows themselves. We now had enough material to really wring out the two-set format we'd been perfecting since the break, and for a while we really mixed things up, taking what might have been considered first-set tunes and plopping them down in the middle of the second set (but rarely doing the opposite). Somehow, in spite of our fragmenting personal relationships, we were able to hold on to the one precious thread of love and caring that would allow us to justify our trip to ourselves.

The real heart of the music seemed to manifest itself in the transitions between songs — the emotional and spiritual character of the whole show could be read from those intros and jam-out passages. These were the times — the only time, really — that we could speak to one another directly from our hearts, and put our differences aside to converse freely and honestly. In our best moments, all our individual quirks disappeared as if they'd never been. We were one in the music, and the music was playing us. To lose oneself completely in a spontaneous flood of music is one of the great human joys: one isn't creating, but being created — in fact, one no longer exists. At the same time, there's a give-and-take, a handing off of ideas that mimics the process of thought itself, as if we were synapses in a greater mind. Billy and I could lock in as if we shared a common heartbeat; Bobby and I left holes for each other's notes, creating an interlocking, constantly changing rhythm; I could entwine with Jerry and entrain with Mickey, and still have room to respond to Brent's interjections. It's not a question of dividing one's self: There is no self. There is only music.

Considering all our emotional ups and downs and roller-coaster drug use, it's amazing how powerful our underlying bond really was. If we could still play like this — communicate on this level — and do so more often than I had any right to expect, why heck, I could love doing this, and even grow in the process.

On another level, meanwhile, I had finally started to get lucky, which for me at that time was tantamount to a state of grace. My old girlfriend had finally moved out, and I was enjoying the "peace of solitude," while I continued to wrestle with my neuroses and my cast of characters (Dr. Lesh and Mr. Asshole — I was not a happy drunk). Every day I went down to breakfast at the Station Café, and it seemed as if Jill, with whom I'd struck out last fall, was sending me signals: a look here, a smile there — until one morning in February '82 I finally got up the nerve to invite her as my guest to our Warfield show that night. Now, bringing a date to a Grateful Dead show wasn't quite the bed of roses it might seem; notably, we had a crew full of predatory animals to whom any female was fair game, so I tried hard to keep Jill close to me that first night, going so far as to tell her not to go out front by herself. After the gig, I didn't want the night to end, so we drove to our studio at Front Street. Since there was no load-out, the crew was already there, cracking open beers and settling in front of the TV for an old Bogart movie.

Jill and I arrived and sat together in a big leather chair; on the small screen, Bogie and Bacall fell into an embrace. I looked at Jill — and we kissed for the first time. I felt as if I'd stepped into an open elevator shaft, and then been lifted up and transformed into a burst of pure fireworks. Somehow, we both knew: This one is the keeper. I'll never know what she saw in me then — an aging rocker, overweight and overmedicated — but is that not part of the glory of love? Sometimes love can penetrate the countless masks we use and shine its light directly on our souls, for those with eyes to see. Suddenly, gravity and gloom no longer had an exclusive claim staked in my heart, and that simple knowledge impelled me to start my long climb back up out of the bottle.

Jill and I fell madly in love and began spending virtually all of our free time together. In the spring of '83 she began traveling with me everywhere. In August '83 she was starting to burn out on airports and hotels, and was talking about going home. I dreaded the thought of going back to touring alone, so I stayed up late one night in Eugene, Oregon, concocting a plan: I would rent a car and we would drive, just the two of us, through Portland and Pendleton on the way to our next gig, Boise — and maybe even on from there.

Jill loved my plan, and we laughed and talked our way across the countryside, picking up local radio stations when we could, discovering incredible syncronicities between the places we were and the music we heard — the moment, for example, when at the climax of a track from McCoy Tyner's album *Dimensions* we topped a hill and saw the land dropping away ahead, opening vast western vistas, and to the east, a double rainbow. I do love these moments, even if they don't mean anything at all. We continued on, and while traveling from Boise to Park City, Utah, we saw a flying saucer streak across the sky in front of us.

Then, onward to three shows at the fabled Red Rocks Amphitheater in Colorado, the nation's most profoundly challenging outdoor venue. It's challenging because the music has to live up to the place itself, a former Native American sacred site. I had been talking up Red Rocks and the music we made there to Jill all the way from Portland, and I was going to make sure she got some great shows. With a crescent moon in the sky, I showed off for Jill by dropping bass bombs (loud, profoundly percussive low notes or chords) left and right. By the third show I was bopping around the stage with a fiendish grin on my face — it was that much fun.

Traveling out of Denver, en route to New Mexico, we pulled off the highway in the dead of night, finding a county road to take us far from the lights of the interstate. We stopped and got out, walking away from the car under the high plains stars. Not quite as intimate an experience as in Egypt, these stars, but more brilliant, more colorful, sharper and clearer. We at first stood transfixed, then climbed on top of the car to lie on our backs, drinking in the glory.

From the sublime to the twisted: next stop, Las Vegas, New Mexico, a single street lined with truck stops and fast-food outlets. We pull into the first gas station; I start pumping gas. There's a 7-11 equivalent across the street, humming with the comings and goings of the locals. Funny thing, every time I look over there, they're all looking at me. Is my hair really long right now? Nooo. Do I look like I'm not from around here? Yesss. Ok! Let's hit the road! I jump into the car and drive nervously out of town; Jill says, "Did you get the feeling we were being watched?" After some relieved, nervous laughter — I'm not paranoid after all! — I agreed that there must be so little action locally that *anybody* new stopping in town was BIG NEWS.

Onward to Santa Fe, where we'll play a gig, turn in the car, and get on a plane for Austin. After this show, our driving trip will be over. We cruise over the last rise before the turnoff in Santa Fe and — what's this? State police standing on the side of the road, waving everyone over? They pull seven or eight cars, including us, over to the side and give us all speeding tickets. Apparently they've been tracking us, along with the hundreds of Heads on their way to the show, for thirty miles by plane. So after traveling a thousand miles, the journey ends with a speeding ticket, literally within sight of our destination.

Over the next few years, Jill and I would continue our tradition by driving on tour as often as possible, usually on the East Coast, where the cities were closer together. We would leave after a show, drive halfway to the next show, stay in a small-town bed and breakfast or in a hotel by a lake somewhere, and then drive on, sometimes through a fall landscape glowing with color. Often we found ourselves in caravan with the many Deadheads cruising on tour. We would be rolling along and come up beside a car full of Heads; Jill matched speeds (she did a lot of the driving), and we cruised side by side for a while until someone in the other car looked over. I would put on my goofiest grin and wave; they would nudge each other and wave back or, in some instances, hurriedly scribble out a song request for the next show.

Frequently, after the show we would pull in to a truck stop and put away one of those classic trucker meals, complete with milk biscuits and country gravy. On one such occasion, as we walked in at 2:30 a.m., the dozen or so Deadheads gathered there stared in disbelief, then stood and gave us an ovation, startling the odd trucker or two into looking up from his food. Must have been a good show.

I began to notice around this time that the faces in the front row were the same at every show. It soon became apparent that there was a community of Deadheads essentially traveling with us, driving from city to city, attending every show, staying at the same hotels that we were, with tie-dye banners flying from the windows and taped music blasting from room after room. Heads camped out in the halls in front of their rooms or moved from party to party after the show. Returning from the show, I would emerge, more often than not, from the elevator to find our soundman Dan Healy sitting on the floor with his guitar, serenading the Heads in the hall.

As the number of tourheads grew, so did a support system of vendors and merchandisers, some of whom were earning their way from show to show by selling food, drink, posters, homemade stickers, or T-shirts in the parking lot before the show. Eventually, there was a vending area, with the population of a small town, at every venue. Affectionately dubbed "Shakedown Street" by the Heads, it became as much of an attraction to locals as the show itself. On many occasions there would still be several thousand people hanging outside while we played the show.

It's hard to overemphasize the importance of the Deadheads, not just to the band's "career," but also to the core values that made the music so unique. If the band onstage was a microcosm, the audience, and by extension the larger Deadhead community, could be considered a macrocosm.

The enthusiasm, openness, and, more important, the burning desire of our audience to be astonished, to be swept away, to be transported and transformed, if only for a few short hours, was truly what closed the circuit to create the music. Not the songs, of course, but the music of the moment: the way the songs were played; what was played between the songs; what expressive musical commentary was articulated during the songs.

The music wasn't, however, the only reason these folks came to our shows. The magnetism and drawing power of a large group of like-minded people can't be ignored. People came to our shows as if they were attending a family reunion. Their commitment was as much to each other as it was to the music.

As our audiences grew, the taper phenomenon exploded; by summer '84 there were so many microphone stands sprouting everywhere in the audience that Healy decided that we should create a taper section. Some tapers had been pretty aggressive about their right to set up anywhere, as a result sometimes interfering with the sight lines and enjoyment of others; so we gave them special tickets to their own little area, situated where the sound would be good and it would inconvenience the least number of other attendees. On any given day, one could see production manager Robbie Taylor moving among the tapers, checking the height of mike stands. On balance, allowing taping was maybe the smartest business move we ever made. We didn't anticipate, however, the expanding scale on which trading and distribution would take place. Today we don't feel right if we don't put up at least one song from every show for free download off our Internet Web site.

On a more personal note, being with Jill had unleashed the lovestruck fool in me. What could be more romantic, I thought, than to marry her in some beautiful old church in England, or in some fabulous French garden? I broached the thought gingerly, and was gratified to find that she loved my idea. We booked a five-week tour of Europe, complete with a few music festivals along the way.

We flew to Paris, where we were so jet-lagged coming straight from California that at first we found ourselves staring hollow-eyed out our windows at the rooftops as the magical Parisian dawn broke, then crashing during the best part of the day and evening. Eventually we synced up, and I delighted in showing Jill some of my favorite places: the Eiffel Tower, Notre-Dame, l'Orangerie, Monet's gardens at Giverny on the Seine outside Paris, and last and most gloriously, the town of Chartres, outside Paris, where we lit candles at the cathedral and shopped for lunch at the big open-air market, later stopping along the side of the road to picnic in a field in a classic "loaf of bread, chunka cheese, jug of wine, and thou" scenario.

We flew out to Salzburg the next day. I had obtained tickets for the second performance of a new opera, *Un Re in Ascolto,* based loosely on Shakespeare's *The Tempest,* the music composed by my former teacher Luciano Berio. Salzburg shimmered dreamlike in the misty dusk as we walked from our hotel along the river to the theater, where, as Jill went to freshen up, I encountered the man himself, Berio, sneaking out for one last Havana cigar before the performance.

I greeted him with "Mr. Berio," — bowing — "your former student." He looked closely at me through a wreath of smoke. Recognition dawned: "Phil! Hello!" and he shook my hand, asking, "How is Tom?" (T.C., my classmate at Mills with Berio, and one of his favorites). I assured him that Tom was doing well. With a preoccupied air, he stubbed out his cigar, casually reached over and straightened my formal bow tie (I'd bought a tuxedo just for this tour, but have never yet learned how to tie the damn tie), and, waving a jaunty farewell, returned to the auditorium.

From Salzburg we flew to Edinburgh, where on a romantic impulse, I decided I wanted to formalize our engagement. I got down on my knee, took Jill's hand, and confidently proposed. She gave me a loving look and said, "Yes, I will marry you."

I had another dream come true when we spent a week at the Bayreuth Festival in Germany, immersing ourselves in *The Ring of the Nibelung,* Wagner's vast operatic tetralogy. It was in every particular the tremendous artistic experience I'd hoped for; the composer's vision of a "total artwork" compellingly realized by the most dedicated artists of the day. We then drove on through Switzerland into France, to a little town on Lake Geneva called Thonon les Baines, where Bill Graham had offered us the use of his getaway house.

We reached Lake Geneva from the north just after sunset — the sky paling toward purple, the last glow reflected by the smooth waters, the lights of the picturesque lakeside villages beginning to dot the darkness of the shore. It was such a stunning sight that we pulled over, got out, and, arms entwined, walked to the edge of the slope. As the warm twilight poured over us, I turned to Jill: "We really owe Bill one, babe; now we'll have to name our firstborn son after him." We both laughed, imagining "little Wolfgang (Bill's birth name) Lesh." As it turned out, we did end up naming our firstborn Grahame, after family members on both Jill's and my side.

We drove into town to meet Bill's brother-in-law Jean-Pierre, who gave us the key to the chalet. We connected in a pizza/espresso joint downtown, where we cracked up as Jean-Pierre told the story of the only time Bill ever visited his hideout. "I'm always telling him, come over, come over! So he finally comes over. I pick him up, take him to the house, he stays up all night talking business on the phone, and takes the morning flight back to New York. Without sleeping!" For sure, that was the Bill we knew and loved.

We spent five glorious days in Thonon, shopping in Evian, boating on the lake, driving out to quaint little auberges on the back roads, plundering small-town markets for food. On our last morning we looked out the window to see two gorgeous swans circling by the little dock. As they passed back and forth on parallel tracks, their necks and heads periodically formed the stylized image of a heart. This became a symbol of our love.

It was getting to be time to go home for the fall tour. We got on the phone and began making inquiries about residence requirements for foreign nationals wanting to marry in Europe; alas, everywhere on the continent it was six weeks' residence. Where could we go in the United States? We had tickets on the Concorde, which flew from London through New York to DC, so we called New York: two days wait and a blood test; Washington DC: the same, but a kindly clerk told us to call Arlington, Virginia. They had no wait and no tests. We called Arlington and made an appointment for September 12 at 2:00 p.m.

Strolling through London, we found two gold bands nestled side by side in a shop window by the river. We tried them on, and they fit both of us perfectly. Jill found a wedding dress at Harrods, but we had lost our wallets in Switzerland and were lamenting the fact over tea at the Montcalm Hotel when we were approached by a distinguished-looking gentleman: "Excuse me, I couldn't help overhearing — are you folks in trouble? My name is Steven, and I'd like to help." Steven, an industrial executive, and his wife were also vacationing at the time; the four of us struck up a conversation, and when they heard the part about the wedding dress, their eyes lit up and they both insisted, "You *must* let us help you. It's what Americans do for each other." What could we do? We needed not only the dress, but taxi fare to the airport. Steven and his wife very kindly loaned us enough cash to cover everything we needed. We would never forget their kindness and generosity to total strangers.

After a speedy trip home on the Concorde, we met our friends Brian and Tita at the Watergate in DC. My old friend Alan Trist had flown over from England that same day, and would join us on the morrow. These three would be our witnesses.

The next morning, we made it to the courthouse in Arlington right about on time, but we still had to purchase the marriage license — and we were out of cash again. Brian came up with the twelve bucks, and we were back in business. We were now running late for our plane, but in a sure sign that our luck was holding, a very pregnant bride-to-be allowed us to slip in front of her in the line at the ceremony room. The justice of the peace was a narrow-faced man sitting behind a desk. We stood in front of the desk; he shuffled a few papers, found our license, and began. "Do you, Philip Chapman Lesh, take this woman, Jillspeck Wilfred" ("*Jillspeth Winifred!*" I stage-whispered) . . . etc. As he droned the final words, his phone began to ring. "I now pronounce you man and wife" — he picked up the phone — "Hello?" I turned to my bride, we kissed, and he hung up the phone with a crash. "That'll be twenty bucks!" Brian forked over the loot, and we rushed out to the airport.

We arrived at our home to find it blazing with light; close friends greeted us with champagne and flowers, and we wound down slowly, surrounded by the warmth of true companionship.

The fall '84 tour was our first as a married couple, and for me, the highlight was the night in Augusta, Maine, when Jerry, during the old folk ballad "Jackaro," turned to me as he sang the line "this couple they got married, so well they did agree" and, with a big grin on his face, actually *winked* at me.

On our fall '84 tour, Jerry's demeanor onstage had been alarming, to say the least. He would stand back from his mike, staring down at the floor, while listlessly going through the show without making eye contact with anyone, either in the band or the audience. At one show back east, our performance in the first set was so dispiriting that I went back to my dressing room in despair. I had learned to play the bass by tailoring my approach to complement and balance Jerry's playing, and my musical and spiritual bond was with him. I started to feel guilty about ignoring the elephant that was stepping on my foot; I could no longer pretend that Jerry was just fine. His time, once banjo-precise, was now wavering all over the place — faster, slower, often in the same phrase. He'd start tunes too fast and try to slow them down, then shrug and keep speeding up. The second set started poorly, but three tunes into it, Jerry seemed to come alive, and we locked into a familiar collective space, yet again finding new avenues to explore. Jerry was my drug, and I was hooked solid.

Even though he showed occasional flashes of his old self, Jerry's increasing heroin use was debilitating him to the point that his health was of major concern to us. His performances were perfunctory and lifeless, and he was increasingly uncommunicative and solitary offstage as well. He always insisted that he was just on a "maintenance" habit, but since there is no such thing (the dosage required to stay "straight" keeps increasing), every aspect of his life — health, music, personal relationships, hygiene — was beginning to suffer from neglect.

It's February 1985, at Henry J. Kaiser Convention Center in Oakland, and the Grateful Dead are about to go on for our second set. Jerry is locked in his private dressing room; everyone else is either onstage or on the way. I walk toward the stage and encounter my old and dear friend David Crosby, who had sadly fallen on hard times behind freebase cocaine. David doesn't look good tonight; he's very jittery, with occasional beads of sweat popping out on his forehead and then disappearing, like water on a hot griddle. The many small sores on his face and neck don't help either.

I have a sudden flash that he and Jerry should *see* each other. If they can feel mutual respect as they have in the past, maybe they can see themselves in each other, as in a mirror. I knock on Jerry's dressing room door, David in tow. Jerry yells something incomprehensible through the door, then opens it and slumps back in his seat. David may look bad, but he's a paragon of grooming and health next to the Hulk on the couch. They look appraisingly at each other — OK, what (drugs) *you* got? Break 'em out! The vibes start to get real thick; I leave, closing the door on them before they start patting each other down.

Eventually, our concern for Jerry's health led us to the dreaded Intervention. As bad as he had looked on the winter tour, his appearance was now truly frightening. His complexion had turned gray, he was bloated, always short of breath, and he rarely left his downstairs apartment. M.G. and the band, together with Hunter and some of the crew, converged upon his place. I joined in with some trepidation, as bearding the lion in his den is no small task. I wasn't surprised when at first he blocked the door with his considerable bulk and refused us admittance. We bombarded him with heartfelt and loving entreaties, which included the usual ultimatum: It's either us or the drugs. That seemed to make an impression, and he agreed to go with us right then to check out a treatment facility in Oakland, near Lake Merritt. On the way out the door, however, his true feelings reasserted themselves for a moment; when he and Kreutzmann arrived at the door at the same time, he roughly shouldered Billy aside with the words, "Out of the way, drummist dog!"

I volunteered to ride over with him, ostensibly as company. My covert reason was to make sure that he actually got there. The others all followed in their various vehicles. To this day, I don't think I've ever been so frightened in a car: not when a friend and I flipped his '53 Plymouth at seventy miles per hour on a backwoods gravel road; not when I spun my BMW into a pitch-black creek bank on Sir Francis Drake Boulevard after a late-night session; not when riding with Neal down the hills of San Francisco, cutting corners at sixty miles per hour — I knew *he* could see around corners. Perhaps Jerry was giving me a little payback for the embarrassment of the intervention. He would hurtle past some slower vehicle, cut over sharply into the next lane, and then apply the brakes real hard, just in time to avoid smashing into the rear of a truck. I had to wonder if Jerry was feeling suicidal — or murderous. I was shaky, and sweating bullets, when we finally pulled off at the Broadway exit in Oakland, and never in my life was I so glad to see a stoplight. At the clinic itself, Jerry signed up to go in at a later date, and I hitched a ride back with someone else. We all felt that at the very least we had voiced our concerns, and that even if he wasn't in a program now, he would be soon. No one wanted to burst that little bubble of hope.

Shortly before Jerry was due to go into rehab in Oakland, we got a call saying that he'd been arrested for drugs in Golden Gate Park. After we bailed him out, his roadie Steve Parish and I insisted upon driving him to his car, still parked where he'd left it. My motivation was, I guess, to make sure that Jer went into rehab as scheduled, but when we got in our car and I asked him about it, he gave me the most soulful, vulnerable look and said, "Please — don't make me go to jail twice in one day." My heart just about came unraveled; he *knew* that I couldn't bring myself to be a cop that day, especially for him.

Jerry eventually went into a drug diversion program and began trying to clean up. As his condition slowly improved, he began to enjoy his homelife a little more, with the help of Nora Sage, his nurturing housekeeper, who brought him art supplies to distract him from his habits. In time, she also encouraged him to market his whimsical artworks to great acclaim. He began to construct radio-controlled race cars, one of which he passed on to me. He also was building extremely elaborate model railroad setups based on products from Germany. The activity that really defined this period for him, though, was training his cat. He actually trained his cat to fetch. If I hadn't seen it myself, I wouldn't have believed it — he sat in his living room with a satisfied smirk, watching my jaw drop in disbelief as the cat picked up one thing after another and laid it at his feet.

At that time Jerry was still the voracious reader and cultural explorer I'd always known. When I heard that in June '85 the San Francisco Opera would mount a production of Wagner's *Ring,* my first thought was to invite him to attend with us. To my delight, he accepted readily; I reserved a box, invited the other band members and their families, and then begged management to cancel some shows that were scheduled during the cycle.

Jerry made it for the first three operas, the only one of the band besides me to see that many. Jill and I picked him up at his San Rafael house on opening night, and he came down dressed in a black T-shirt and sweat pants, an old leather jacket, and slippers. His first words to me as he looked at my suit: "You didn't tell me you were gonna dress up." "Don't worry — we have our own box." "A box at the opera?" (In a pompous-bullshit tone:) "This time you've gone too far!" "It'll be cool. Wait'll you see the spread we got for noshing between acts. They have a little anteroom in the box where they stash it, and you can just sneak back anytime." "Oh. Cool." We walk into the opera house without the slightest twinge of embarrassment (hey, it's a performance — as sure as it is at any show we play: the Grateful Dead Go to the Opera! In Living Technicolor!), and sure enough, when Jer sees the Swedish meatballs set out so temptingly in their little hot pan, he relaxes visibly and settles into an overstuffed chair to eat.

We created quite a stir among the other opera patrons. Mickey and Bob came for a couple of nights each, as did our old friend Bear, who spent the entire time lurching between trying to read his pocket libretto (with his special Eagle Scout Flashlight and Magnifying Glass) and trying to pick up Betsy Cohen, a friend of Bob's and a Stanford physics professor. Billy and Brent seemingly had no interest, but I was especially glad that Mickey showed up on the third night for "Siegfried."

In the final scene of act 2, our hero, after killing the dragon Fafner and winning the Ring, discovers that having tasted the dragon's blood he can understand the language of birds. He holds a brief conversation with a wood bird, and just at the most tender part, as Siegfried is singing about his lost mother, from behind me there comes a sound — part chainsaw, part the rooting of a wild boar searching for truffles. Oops — Jerry has fallen asleep and begun to snore. Mickey leaps to the rescue, jabbing him repeatedly with a salad fork while shaking his shoulders and urging him, half-asleep, back to the foyer. The occupants of the boxes on either side of us return their attention to the stage. I wonder fitfully if the snore was heard in the pit.

In the end Jerry didn't make it back for the final opera of the cycle, having made previous plans to take his daughter Annabelle to see Phil Collins at Oakland Coliseum. "What?" I asked when he told me. "You're going to pass up 'Twilight of the Gods' for Phil Collins?" "If it was just me — but I promised Annabelle." And he meant it, God bless him; Phil was her favorite singer, and here was something he could do for his child.

*   *   *

We celebrated our twentieth anniversary at the UC Berkeley Greek Theatre, one of my favorite places to play. The whole band was in good spirits, Jerry was slowly cleaning up, and while still not robust, was looking healthier than he had in the winter. Management began booking larger and larger places, and we were playing to more and more people. Jerry gradually returned to the level of musical creativity that was his natural habitat, and the gigs began to be fun again.

As Bobby settled more and more comfortably into his role as the flaming rocker in the band, he became considerably more overt in his showmanship. One of his favorite tricks, during the "Sunshine Daydream" jam part of "Sugar Magnolia," was to climb the scaffolding supporting the PA on the side of the stage while we were jamming out. He would scamper up two or three levels, hang by one arm with his guitar dangling from his neck, and descend just in time to make it back to the mike for the grand vocal finale.

One night at a local show, Brent and I pranked him good. He was two levels up when I looked at Brent and got the go-ahead. I cut off the jam and screamed out the count off for the vocal. Although caught by surprise, the band immediately knew what we were up to and jumped in on the first chord as Brent and I started the vocals.

I've never seen Bob move so fast: It was as if he hadn't transited through the intervening space between his place on the tower and the stage floor. Brent and I only had time for two vocal interjections before he was back at the mike, and I gave him a shit-eating grin as I relinquished his vocal line. The crowd went nuts. Jerry beamed merrily. Brent and I gave each other symbolic high fives, and we cruised through to the end of the song grinning insanely at one another.

Our old friend Danny Rifkin had recently brought us one of his finer concepts: a Grateful Dead nonprofit foundation. Our experience with benefits over the years had left us with mixed feelings — many of the benefits we were asked to do were simply impractical, or incompatible with our schedule. Our new plan was to set aside three to six shows a year and use the proceeds (the band's portion; the crew and promoters were paid) to fund selected nonprofits. The new entity would be called the Rex Foundation, in memory of Rex Jackson, our late lamented roadie and tour manager, who had been killed in a car accident in 1976.

The Rex board, which consisted of several band members, management, staff, and friends, scrutinized all suggestions closely; from the beginning we discouraged applications, preferring that a board member or someone from the immediate Grateful Dead family recommend any nonprofits for funding. Of course, the final decisions were made at sometimes contentious board meetings, but on the whole it worked very well. In the twelve years from 1984 through 1995 we gave more than seven million dollars to various causes, mostly in small chunks of five to ten thousand dollars. This resulted in a lot of surprised nonprofits; much as on the old TV show *The Millionaire,* a check would appear, and the Rex office would invariably get a call asking in bewilderment, "Are you sure there isn't some mistake? We didn't ask for a grant."

That same year we implemented another of Rifkin's ideas: Grateful Dead Ticket Service (GDTS). Danny figured that we could do the fans a favor by supplying tickets by mail order at a much lower service fee. We scheduled our tours far enough in advance so that orders could be mailed in and tickets could be mailed out in time. Despite many barriers thrown up by national ticket brokers, we managed to get it up and running.

Of course, the Grateful Dead Way is the more money you have, the more you spend. Whenever a member of the band, the crew, or the management team needed any money for a house payment, or a car, or a new stereo, it was no problem — our CFO Bonnie just put it "on account." A curious concept, that: borrowing against future earnings?

I had been sending monthly support to my mother for years, which always went "on account." One day I happened to ask Bonnie if I was paying taxes on what I was taking. She looked startled, as if it had never occurred to her before. She thought for a minute and said, "Let me get back to you on that." Not a good sign. Five days later, I got the word: No taxes had ever been paid on "on account" draws — and we hadn't declared those funds as income. This meant that not only did we owe taxes on the draws we had taken, but to be fair, we had to compensate those band members who didn't take large draws.

We began the process of bringing in professional accountants to fix the mess. Everyone agreed to a plan whereby we would institute a program of "tour bonuses" for the band and crew; taxes and reparations would be taken out of the bonuses given to the top spendthrifts (Jerry and me, in that order) and divided among the other band members, until parity was reached and taxes paid. After twenty years, we found it necessary to distribute our income in a more traditional way.

At the end of 1985, Jill had become pregnant but miscarried. After that, we began actively trying to start a family. When nothing happened right away, my mom gave us a jade fertility egg (I believe she ordered it from the Lillian Vernon catalog), and presto! Jill immediately became pregnant. Years later, we passed the egg along to Bruce Hornsby and his wife, Kathy, who had more serious fertility issues, and Kathy became pregnant with twins. The egg then went to our dear friends Jan and David Crosby, who had also had problems conceiving, and Jan promptly became pregnant. After their son, Django, was born, David sent the egg back to us, but by that time, our second son, Brian, had already been born, and we were not planning on having any more kids. We dared not even open the box, so we stored it away, knowing that its power would soon be needed by someone. Some time later, David called, asking if we would send it to another rock 'n' roll couple, who also successfully conceived. When asked if we wanted it back, we replied no thanks, it should be passed on wherever its mojo can do the most good. Each year, when I receive Christmas cards from these good friends with their family pictures, I take great pride in seeing these beautiful families — knowing that without my mom's fertility egg, things might have gone differently.

In anticipation of becoming a father, I quit using drugs completely, which wasn't hard, since my usage had dwindled dramatically, and I also began to restrict my wine intake to a couple of glasses at dinner — to quit drinking altogether was a much more difficult challenge.

On the '86 summer tour we were playing stadiums, headlining a bill with Bob Dylan and Tom Petty. It was tremendously hot that summer in the Midwest and East; Jill, who was pregnant, was having a hard time with the heat. But it was Jerry who really seemed to be struggling; onstage, he was red-faced and sweating, and I feared that he would blow a fuse.

Sure enough, a week or so after the end of the tour, I got a call from Nora; Jerry had collapsed at his home and been taken to the hospital in a diabetic coma. It was a harrowing week. At times, we weren't sure if he was going to pull through. It was a joyous day when I visited and found him sitting up in bed, with M.G. and Hunter in attendance. "Hi, gang," he said to me, waggling some fingers weakly, and I briefly wondered if he was seeing double — or had he mistaken me for Kreutzmann (to whom we frequently referred as "the Gang of One")? It was heartbreaking to see him so helpless and vulnerable, but at least it seemed to me that he was going to live.

Jerry had been so sick that his synapses got a little scrambled. As he recovered, he had to relearn some basic skills — like playing the guitar. His old friend Merl Saunders visited regularly to give him reminders, and he progressed rapidly — but it still was several months before he could play again. Grateful Dead Productions was in perilous financial straits, having canceled the fall tour. Management was so desperate that even before Jerry had completely recovered, they booked some shows for December 15, 16, and 17, in spite of the fact that Jill's due date was December 6. I had notified management that nothing would keep me from witnessing the birth of my first child: If Jill went into labor during a gig, I was out of there.

Not to worry — Grahame Hamilton Lesh arrived punctually on December 6. When I held my son in my arms for the first time, looking down at his infinitely precious little face, I felt my heart open; an outpouring of love unlike any I'd ever felt rushed through me. Now I know, I thought, what unconditional love really is.

When my son was born, I made a momentous decision. For twenty years the Grateful Dead had consumed my life. Over the years, I had witnessed the toll taken on the families and children of the other band members. I was determined that I was going to be a hands-on, available, full-time dad, and that nothing was going to stand in the way of my participation in all the large and small moments of my child's life.

It was a happy occasion when Jill and Grahame joined me at the Oakland Arena for Jerry's first show back with the Grateful Dead. The roar of joy that greeted him after he sang the line "I will survive" from "Touch of Grey" startled even him.

After eight years away from the studio, we decided to make a new album in January '87. We had the material, finely honed after months on the road; we had our crack sound crew itching at the chance to show off in the studio; and we had the place to do it live, thanks to Jerry and Bob, who came up with the concept. We would record all the songs playing together, just as in a performance; any clams could be overdubbed, or overlooked. I think all will agree that pristine perfection was not our strong suit.

We decided to record on the stage at the Marin Veterans Memorial Auditorium. The theater was part of Frank Lloyd Wright's plan for the Marin Civic Center area, and served for every kind of production, from the annual *Nutcracker* ballet to the Gyuto Monks, or Ali Akbar Khan. We rented the main auditorium for three weeks, brought in a recording truck, a mix board, and tape machines, set the band up in a semicircle onstage, and plowed ahead.

The best part of it for me was that I could walk to work. I'd been living since '81 on a hill overlooking the civic center, and it was a simple matter to walk down the hill at the end of my road, cut across a field, under the highway on an old railroad spur, and be there in ten minutes. The sessions were the most relaxed ever for the Grateful Dead, and everyone was in good spirits. We built in some time for just fooling around, in case lightning should strike and some great jam could be immortalized. Mickey proposed that we try to play in a totally light-free environment; we started off jamming with the lights on, and at Mick's signal the lights were shut completely off: pressure drop!

I don't know whether it was the darkness or the laughter that did us in, but as soon as the lights went out, what we'd been playing simply disintegrated in the most hysterical manner, rhythms stumbling, phrases twisted askew, so that within seconds we were gasping for breath, having descended further into low comedy than ever before. 'Twas the finest and most inventive train wreck I've ever experienced. We did, however, get the album title (*In the Dark*) out of it.

That pretty much set the tone for the sessions, and as work proceeded we could hear that lighthearted goofiness pouring out of the songs. We started to feel very good about this record. Arista Records was pretty pleased, too. We heard a story about one of their execs going bananas when he heard "Touch of Grey": "A fucking hit! The Grateful Dead wrote a fucking hit!" (Confound Your Expectations, that's our middle name.) When I brought the finished album home, Jill, Grahame, and I all danced around our living room to the strains of "Touch of Grey" — the first time in a while that I was able to relax and enjoy a finished record without any second thoughts.

Since the advent of MTV in 1981, the music video had become

the de rigueur form of promotion for the major labels, so naturally we had to do a video, right? No self-respecting single should leave home without one. The video featured us playing a gig and transforming into skeletons at the big final chorus "We will get by, we will survive." *In the Dark* hit number six on the album charts, and "Touch of Grey" was number nine on the singles chart — for one week. Having a hit was secondary, though, to having Jerry back, with his health, humor, and inventiveness fully restored.

The success of *In the Dark* was the beginning of what I call the "MegaDead" era. Suddenly we were drawing so many people to our shows that we now had to play mostly stadiums and huge indoor arenas in multinight stands. What's to complain about? one might legitimately ask; aren't you the live band par excellence? Don't you live to play for live audiences, and isn't your music at its best then? Yes, yes, and yes — to a point. But it's a very rare stadium show that can sustain the shared intensity of focus that's needed for ignition, let alone lift-off; the audience needs to *know* that they're making the music, too. The largest space we've been able to successfully and consistently levitate is Madison Square Garden, and that was mostly because of the "rockability" of the building itself.

The psychic connection and sense of community shared by the band and the audience is the key to our music and to the Grateful Dead "experience." This connection can be diluted by the presence of too many people; especially if people were coming to our shows because they heard that it was a great party, or because they heard that they could score drugs there (as opposed to those who came because they wanted to experience a transformation of consciousness as part of a larger community of like-minded souls). Many people found their place outside the shows, at the vending booths in the parking lot, or just hanging out and tailgating and never coming anywhere near the music.

As promoters and management continued to book us into stadiums, we sought out world-class co-headliners. Bob Dylan seemed to be a logical choice, and listening to him perform with Tom Petty's band the previous year had whetted our appetites. We had always wanted to play behind him like The Band did in the sixties. We were very pleased to find out that Bob was agreeable, and so we set up a short stadium tour — nothing too strenuous, about six shows with Bob, and a few smaller Grateful Dead gigs thrown in. In May '87 Bob came out to our studio, Club Front, to rehearse with us for the tour.

We were feeling especially frisky after the success of *In the Dark,* so each band member brought in long lists of their favorite Dylan songs. We went through about fifty songs in five days. By the end, I had a notebook filled with chord sequences, form diagrams, and lyric cues. It was impossible to memorize that many songs in such a short time. Rehearsals were big fun; we got to play behind Bob in some of his choicest ("Ballad of a Thin Man," "Memphis Blues," "Chimes of Freedom," "The Wicked Messenger," "Shelter from the Storm") and some of his most obscure ("Joey," "Man of Peace," "Heart of Mine") tunes, and also confirmed that, hey, this guy's at least as weird as any of *us.*

It only remained to make sure that Bob gave us a set list each show before we went on stage. Lotsa luck. At least twice Bob, that prankster, threw in a song we hadn't rehearsed. Playing with Bob really kept us on our toes, too; he was fully capable of deviating radically from the set list, and more than once left us slack-jawed in confusion as he switched songs in midstream. That seemed like poetic justice for a band that took pride in its flexibility and in not using a set list.

The tour as a whole went off pretty well, and we were even able to satisfy ourselves that some of what we did together was worthy of commercial release. For me, the big thrill was standing onstage backing Bob Dylan, like I'd always wanted to do, while Jerry sat beaming behind his pedal steel, healthy once again.

There are very few more accurate signposts for the state of a band's relationships than record albums; each set of recordings is a metaphor for the current status of the collective unconscious. Nowhere in the Grateful Dead catalog is this better represented than in our last two studio albums — *In the Dark* and *Built to Last*.

In the Dark represented the peak of our collective optimism following Jerry's cleanup and recovery in the previous year. It was recorded while we played as an ensemble, and the joy of communal music-making shines through every track on the album (even those songs that couldn't possibly be described as upbeat). Everyone felt connected — to each other and to the music — and as with all our best music, this album nullifies all heaviness of spirit; at least that's what it did for us when we made it.

In marked contrast to Jerry's exuberant resurgence, Brent was inwardly suffering from crippling insecurity and extreme sensitivity, especially to anything he saw as criticism. In true rock 'n' roll spirit, Brent took eagerly to self-medication as a method of dealing with his stress. His preferred anesthesia was alcohol, with a sprinkling of pills. He once showed Jill his pill stash: dozens of individual prescriptions, each with a slightly different effect. "I told the doctor I couldn't sleep, so he gave me this," holding up one vial. "I told the next doctor that

I was depressed, so he gave me this one," holding up another. By inventing symptoms, telling other doctors he felt fat, or skinny, he had accumulated an Alice-in-Wonderland stash of pills.

Brent's domestic situation was another source of stress. He'd married and had two lovely daughters, but his adoration, bordering on obsession, for his wife, Lisa, seemed only to drive a wedge between them. I don't know what it was that caused them to separate and come together again and again, but each time it was a little more intense — until Brent began responding by breaking things.

He never hurt anyone, but upon inanimate objects he would unleash violent rages. After a gig one night in Toronto in '87, we heard a loud crash from Brent and Lisa's room next door. Jill and I went over and knocked on the door; Brent answered, laughing sheepishly, Lisa behind him. Fragments of a mirrored door littered the floor. I took Lisa next door while Jill stayed with Brent. While I was gone, he picked up a machete-shaped shard of glass with his bare hands from the floor where it had fallen, put it on his shoulder, and marched back and forth, playing "soldier" with it until Jill persuaded him to put it down.

Brent seemed to bounce back from this low point with the help of John Barlow, who brought him lyrics and encouraged him as he entered into a prolific creative period. Their new songs brought him a welcome boost in his self-esteem.

By the time we began work on *Built to Last,* Jerry, to the distress of us all, had started using again. Given that emotional climate, it's perhaps not surprising that the recording process, originally envisioned as starting from where we left off with *In the Dark,* i.e., recording the songs as a band, all playing together, dissolved rather rapidly into Total-Overdub Land, a nightmarish brier patch of egotistical contention. It was agreed that we would proceed by accretion of layers; it was similar to the normal recording process (rhythm section; basic guitars and keys; lead vocals; instrumental leads; percussion;

backups and sweetening), but instead of doing one song at a time straight through, we recorded "sub-basic" tracks for everything — drums and guitar or keys — and attempted to overdub everything on top of those tracks, one at a time. Billy would come in and do all the drum tracks, then it would be my turn for bass parts, etc. None of the songs were performed as an ensemble; rather, the pieces were slapped on an assembly line and the song was manufactured — sloppily at that — without any development in live performance.

The material, which I felt was surely as strong as that of *In the Dark,* was never given full value by the band — not even later, in front of a crowd. The grooves never came to life, and the playing reflected that lack of unanimity. The total isolation of the recording process locked everyone into his own part in an unusually rigid way, as if we were listening too hard to one another, instead of to the song itself. Naturally, in interviews of the time we were full of pompous pronouncements about the aesthetic glories of this approach to recording; unfortunately, the result was something so sterile as to defy description. No one in the band was satisfied, either with our individual performances or with the total effect — six soloists, walking on eggs, taking no risks, and never, ever, playing together.

As Jerry isolated himself, the glue that held us all together began to dissolve. We were each more strongly connected to him than to each other, and now, offstage, we began to lead very separate lives. Billy had long been living up in Mendocino County with his third wife, Shelley, a tall blonde whose calm demeanor and firm support had enriched his life immeasurably. They had built a ranch together, and now the word came down that they were splitting up. She had kept him reasonably together, but now he was teetering on the edge.

Bobby's natural habitat had become the "Hospitality Suite" (the rest of us called it the "Hostility Suite"); a set of rooms that Bob took at each hotel for the duration of our stay — where show guests (including women that the crew had picked out of the audience, sometimes using binoculars) were invited to visit after the show. Here Bob would hold court, solving the problems of the world late into the night, while band members, crew, and random hangers-on came and went, sometimes only to grab a beer from the bathtub, which was always pressed into service as a cooler. Typically not wanting to be responsible for a decision, Bob would set it up so that at the end of the party, the female candidates could choose among themselves who would stay the night with him.

I was feeling less vulnerable to the ups and downs of the Grateful Dead because my personal life kept getting better and better. On September 4, 1989, our second son, Brian, was born, making our family complete. In a bit of all-American imagery, when Jill went into labor we drove the thirty miles to the hospital in San Rafael at speeds up to ninety miles per hour. I was actually hoping to be pulled over so I could utter the immortal words "Officer — my wife's having a baby!" Brian came into our lives like a ray of sunshine, with his outgoing personality and general exuberance for life. Grahame and Brian were part of a flock of "new generation" Grateful Dead kids — Brent's daughters, Jessica and Jennifer; Mickey's son, Taro; Bob and Maureen Hunter's daughter, Katy; Steve Parish's son, Tony, and daughter, Lauren; our monitor mixer Harry's daughter, Shana; and Jerry's daughter, Keelin. Jerry and Manasha, Keelin's mother, had met at a Garcia Band gig. She had found her way through the maze of roadblocks to connect with him, and they'd been a couple for some time now. Manasha was a pleasant, quiet, round-faced young woman who at times seemed a bit overwhelmed by the rock 'n' roll life.

Jill and I always brought both kids on tour with us; Jill had been touring with me since '83, and Grahame had been coming along since he was three months old (Brian joined the parade at three weeks). Now, here we are, touring with two kids, complete with all the associated paraphernalia — strollers, car seats, diaper bags, tons of clean clothes and dirty laundry. We must have been quite a spectacle as we struggled through airports and hotel lobbies, trying to keep the boys from diverting to the nearest roadside attraction (which wasn't hard while they were in strollers, but after they grew big enough to walk through the airport — look out!).

The boys took to it like pigs to mud. Even though other kids their ages would travel occasionally with the band, Grahame and Brian relied mostly upon each other for companionship, which strengthened the bond between them to a point where so-called sibling rivalry didn't exist. When Brian was still in his crib, he and Grahame would hang together in our hotel rooms, communicating with giggles or with scribbled drawings on scraps of paper. As they grew older, we began utilizing the various educational opportunities (aquariums, planetariums, science and art museums) available in the cities we were visiting, doing our best to enrich their lives somewhat beyond the confines of the hotel and the gig. I can take a certain amount of pride in my own personal evolution during this time, leaving the party room far behind to spend my offstage time arising early with my kids to explore the city.

As the audiences for our shows grew larger, so did the number of "friends" backstage. Hundreds of them roamed the halls, in desperate need of something (face time, mostly) from the band members. To avoid the growing pressure, the band would rarely leave the stage, and to make it more comfortable, we asked the crew to build separate areas (frameworks covered with curtain material forming the walls), incorporating all the stuff one would normally find in the dressing rooms. Here we would relax, eat dinner before the show, read, or visit with selected guests (my "room" featured a round table with a red-and-white checkered tablecloth and a candle in a wine bottle; our own little Italian restaurant). Here, too, the boys would read or play chess before and even during the shows, oblivious to the roaring noise and flashing lights.

Every so often, when there were more kids traveling, we would hire someone to entertain them in the kids' room — Bozo the Clown, a juggler, a singer. And then there's the time Barney the Purple Dinosaur came in to do his shtick. Barney's popularity had turned him into a very lucrative franchise for his creators, and Barney clones were turning up all over that year, at birthday parties and kindergarten graduations. This night, however, happened to be April Fools' Day — and Jill came onstage at the end of the break with a prank in mind. "You've got to put on the Barney costume for the first song of the second set," she whispered in my ear. Whoa — wait a minute; I couldn't possibly play with the Barney mitts on my hands, so we worked out a compromise: Barney would strap on my spare bass and take the stage, miming the motions of playing, while I would hide behind my speaker stack and play the song from there.

The band took the stage, tuned up, and Jerry kicked the band into "Iko Iko." Barney and I did the old switcheroo at the last minute, and when Jerry looked over and saw that ugly purple dinosaur playing bass in his band (mind you, he could hear what was unmistakably my playing), the expression on his face was that of a man who didn't believe what he was seeing — a *very* rare situation for him. After all the hallucinations he'd played through in his life, to be confronted by *this?* Barney, meanwhile, is having the time of his life — shaking it left and right, up and down — while I'm laughing so hard at the look on Jerry's face that I can hardly breathe, let alone play. The sheer cognitive dissonance of it all (seeing one thing, hearing another) finally tickled his sense of humor and brought forth a kind of shaky smile — OK, you got me this time, man — and we finished the song. Barney took a well-deserved bow and left the stage; I emerged from hiding only to be on the receiving end of another Jerry Look — "I owe you one, man" was the gist of it. The final twist in *l'affaire Barney* was the letter the Grateful Dead received from "his" lawyers — a demand that we cease and desist from using Barney's image and likeness, unless of course we wished to pay suitable compensation.

In March 1990 another guest, albeit a more musical one, joined us onstage: Branford Marsalis, surely one of the most inventive and warmhearted saxophonists in all music. On the first night of our three-show run, Branford showed up onstage to say hello. I knew that he was uniquely open-minded for a jazzer, having done acclaimed work with Sting and other rock musicians, so Jerry and I fell all over ourselves inviting him to come back the next night — and to *please* bring his horn. He came back with not one, but two — tenor and soprano.

We scrambled to figure out a set list that wouldn't bore him, and he joined us in the first set for "Bird Song," returning for the entire second set, which featured a spacy "Dark Star" and an "Eyes of the World" for the ages. It was truly marvelous to join with Branford as he wove his lines in and around ours with consummate artistry and total empathy.

Back at home, during a routine physical, I was given some disturbing news. My liver enzymes were elevated, and with further testing it was discovered that I had hepatitis non-A, non-B, which in a few years would be officially identified as hepatitis C. Hepatitis C is an incurable viral disease, blood-borne and usually spread through blood transfusions or sharing needles. I had probably been infected in the early sixties when my girlfriend Ruth and I experimented with needles for a period of a few months. I had already cut back drinking to the level of wine with dinner, but the diagnosis scared me badly enough so that by the end of 1990 I had quit completely. At that time, information was scarce about the virus, and there were few successful treatments, so I became a vegetarian, sought out alternative treatments to strengthen my immune system, and began to exercise daily. As a result, I felt and looked better than I had in years.

Brent, meanwhile, was wrestling mightily with his many demons; not the most self-confident of men, he never realized that the Deadheads were divided in their opinions of everything, not just of his work with the band. The Deadheads were quite vocal about every as-

pect of the Grateful Dead, from set lists to ticket prices to venue se-
lection to stage lighting; all of these things were subject to scrutiny
on the smallest level of detail, and every possible position staked out.
Brent took any criticism as rejection, hearing only negativity and ignoring the many messages of support and love beamed at him by the
Heads. The band had been bending over backward to assure him that
he'd secured his place, and he had contributed four fine songs to the
Built to Last album, only to be deeply disappointed by their critical
reception.

At the end of the 1990 summer tour, I stopped by Front Street to
pick up my instrument. As I got out of the car, soundman John Cutler ran into the parking lot, tears streaming down his face, to tell me
Brent had died from an overdose of cocaine and heroin the night before, during one last binge before he went into rehab for DUI. I
sagged against the fender of my car, the sadness and waste of it coming down on me like a wall of concrete.

Brent and his wife, Lisa, had split up for good in 1989, and Brent
was now alone in their former home. On the road, he spent late nights
hanging with Billy and Dan Healy. Billy had a tendency to get physical when he drank, and one afternoon Brent walked into sound check
with a nice black eye. After that, he began hanging out in low dives,
like the bar in New York where he would repair after the shows, bran-
dishing his gold Rolex watch like a badge. We all feared that one day
he would wash up along the river minus a hand (and the watch).
Alarmed by his self-destructive behavior, we tried an intervention in
the form of a band meeting, during the course of which even Jerry was
heard explaining why Brent's agony of self-medication was affecting
the music — all too aware of the irony of his words. Brent was defen-
sive, then apologetic, but nothing came of it.

Once again we gathered to attend the funeral of a fallen brother.
Our auras were suppurating with denial and detachment. We cracked
desperate jokes, hardly looking at one another, as Bob told us that his

sister Wendy was channeling Brent from the beyond. And boy, was he pissed: "All he did was go through the wrong door once, and it slammed shut behind him, and now he's dead, and he didn't really mean it." We struggled with the weight of the coffin. A recording of Brent singing his song "I Will Take You Home" played quietly while tears flowed.

Unbelievably, we had still not put any money aside in the event of an emergency that would keep us off the road for a long stretch. Our overhead was piling up on us — salaries to pay, rent, equipment maintenance, etc. We had no time to absorb our loss, and so we were forced to hire a new keyboard player quickly and get back on the road as previously planned. Auditions were scheduled; candidates were screened; the whole galumphing machine swung into motion. Meanwhile, Jerry and I discussed pursuing pianist Bruce Hornsby, a jazz buff and connoisseur of Ives and Bud Powell whose mainstream pop hits revealed a wide-open mind and a Coplandesque sense of sonority. Bruce, of course, had his own career to consider, but he agreed to help us out for a couple of tours. Nothing permanent. (He would play with us on and off for the next eighteen months.) The auditions were a rushed affair, as the tour was looming; we quickly decided on former Tubes and Todd Rundgren keys man Vince Welnick, as he also sang high harmonies. After several weeks of rehearsal with Vince, we resumed the road in September with Vince on board and Bruce due to join in at our New York gigs at Madison Square Garden. Then we would have three weeks off and take the band to Europe.

At the first gig, in Richfield, Ohio, I was heartened to see a sign in the audience reading HEY, VINCE, WELCOME BROTHER. Then the audience greeted Vince's first standout organ lick with a cheer, and I knew for sure that Vince was going to have an easier time of it than Brent had. It helped, too, that there would be two keyboard players; Bruce would help ease the transition for Vince, as well as provide us with another improvisational foil.

New York City has always been a haven and a cynosure for the Grateful Dead; ever since our first shows there in 1967, we've been able to draw a full house of wildly enthusiastic listeners who know what risks the band is capable of taking, and who demand nothing less than our very best. It's immensely satisfying and an honor to perform for such a crowd — it's somehow easier to let oneself go, to open up completely to the flow of energy and the feedback from the people. Never have I felt that reality more strongly than at our next MSG gigs, when Bruce Hornsby joined us as a member for the first time. These six nights were one of the longest sold-out runs ever recorded at the Garden; the next year, we would play nine straight sold-out nights, a record that would stand for ten years.

The combination of two keyboards, two guitars, two drummers, and bass gave the music a richness of texture and an ease of flow that felt as if the band had been reborn from its own ashes. The agility with which Bruce and Jerry played off of each other lit a fire under the whole band; everybody wanted to get into the act. Bobby's playing at these shows highlighted his originality, wit, and inventiveness, and Vince's tasteful and colorful contributions provided the icing on the cake. For me, the new lineup opened up whole new realms of potential; now there were more ideas to bounce off of, and more kindred spirits to integrate into the gestalt.

While recording *In the Dark,* we had hired Stevie Wonder's MIDI-man and synth programmer, Bob Bralove, to program and maintain Brent's new keyboards; he had remained on board after Brent's passing to work with all of us — Jerry, Bob, Vince, Mickey, and myself — in developing new instrument sounds. (Jerry had been using synthlike stomp boxes for years, notably an envelope follower that put a little *twang* on the attack of each note, and an octave divider, which added a lower octave to any note he played, resulting in a flatulent barnyard bassoon sound — I called it his "I Love New York" tone.) The resulting timbral combinations, especially in the "space" segment of our show, began to border on the surreal. Some excellent examples of this type of musical exploration can be found on our album *Infrared Roses:* Bob would be playing some kind of wheezing calliope sound, Jerry a trumpet tone that was just a little askew, and my favorite was a flute sound that when played in the very low register virtually defined the term "sub-contrabass piccolo."

Frustratingly for me, early MIDI basses were susceptible to delays in analog pitch tracking, causing the music to stutter and stagger as it was processed through the MIDI chain. Now, however, some hotshot engineers in Australia were offering a pickup and MIDI distribution system that could allow my bass to drive synthesizers in real time — except only the center four strings could read MIDI. OK, I'll start with that, I say to Bralove, but let's commission these guys to make a six-string pickup, too, since I had switched from a standard four-string to a six-string electric bass about ten years back.

I had been craving more range from my instrument for some time, and after scanning the instrument magazines for six months or so, I came across an ad for Modulus Graphite, a local company making six-string basses with fiber-graphite through-body necks. This one-piece neck allows both the bridge and the string nut to be attached to the same piece of material, be it wood, fiber graphite, or aluminum. The result is an instrument that speaks more articulately; beginnings and endings of notes can be precisely placed, and sustained tones can be extended longer and decay more slowly. Another attraction of the six-string instrument was its flexibility; it was possible to play patterns that had previously required running up and down the neck to be played in one position, for example, and the extended range both above and below the normal range of the bass provided virtually infinite gradations of texture, dynamics, and tonal weight.[1] Since that

---

[1] The same note will have a different weight played on different (thicker or thinner) strings.

discovery, I've played Modulus instruments pretty much exclusively, and they have served the music admirably.

In October '90, we flew to Stockholm to start a three-week European tour. Most of the band brought their families: Jerry came with Keelin and Manasha, Mickey brought his young son, Taro; and, of course, Jill and I brought Grahame and Brian, while some of the crew brought their kids as well. Usually on these trips, jet lag was the bane of our existence, but this time our family had a plan. We would get to our hotel, sleep for two hours, and then get up and stay awake somehow during the day until normal bedtime in that time zone. Getting out of that warm bed was one of the hardest things I ever had to do, but up I got and out we went, into the swirling gusts of a windswept Swedish autumn afternoon. We plodded through an art museum, looking at contemporary art. I played with Brian, then only one year old, in huge piles of gorgeous-hued leaves, throwing handfuls of them into the air again and again, watching the wind spin them away. Eventually, we were able to crash, sleeping deeply until a reasonable hour and waking ready to face the new day — that being the day that Brian broke his leg in the city's public playground. Somehow he had caught his leg between the side of the slide and his mom's leg as they slid down together. When he couldn't walk on it, we caught a taxi to the nearest emergency room, where we discovered from X rays that Brian had a hairline fracture of the shin and would need a cast. I had to leave to do the show; when I met the family back at the hotel after our performance, Brian proudly showed me his cast. And what a cast: a clunky, old-fashioned plaster cast that looked as though it weighed as much as Brian did. It didn't slow him down at all, though; the next day he was happily showing off the cast in return for signatures, garnering the John Hancock of everyone on the tour.

The morning after our first gig in Berlin, a group of us grabbed some taxis and cruised through Checkpoint Charlie into the former East Zone, looking for a piece of the Wall. The Berlin Wall, that is, the monstrous structure erected by Khrushchev in 1961 to prevent people from fleeing to the prosperous West. My little family group was accompanied by Gloria and Vince DiBiasi (who had come to play an important role in Jerry's life: Gloria as Keelin's nanny, and Vince as his personal assistant); their son, Chris; and Max R., a friend from outside Vienna who spoke fluent German. We plunged deeper into the desolate East Zone; huge gray apartment blocks flashed past, separated by boulevards wide enough for a tank regiment. We suddenly came upon a wide avenue of grassy open space, running as far as the eye could see in both directions. There was a depression running along the center, as if a drain or sewage channel had once flowed. Here and there along the depression huge chunks of concrete wall, thirty feet high at least, rose up like broken giant's teeth from the grass. Jill lifted Grahame in her arms, and in both hands he held the hammer that Vince had presciently brought along. He swung with all his strength, and a chunk of concrete fell to the ground; we shouted with exultation: "All right, Grahame!" Another chunk of the Wall bit the dust. I gave Grahame a big high five, and we picked up our souvenirs and returned slowly to the cars.

Berlin in late 1990, only weeks after the reunification of Germany, was as wired-up a city as I've ever visited. There was new construction everywhere, and as I gazed out from my hotel balcony over the hundreds of huge cranes looming like prehistoric birds across the landscape, I remember thinking incredulously, *This place is wound tighter than New York ever dreamed of being.* The atmosphere was crackling with energy, and we managed to sporadically capture some of that frenzied feeling in our concerts.

Berlin also has the most aggressive professional autograph seekers on the face of the earth. They acted as if they had a perfect right to hound us mercilessly from the moment we stepped out of the hotel. My kids were a little freaked by the in-your-face tactics — "Phil! You will sign my albums!" (All twenty of them.) When we were on our way out of town after the gigs, our group was followed to the airport, where a bunch of these guys literally cornered Bobby like a pack of dogs, barking orders at him. Bob was so outraged that he picked the nearest one up and threw him against the wall, precipitating a nice little session with airport security. Bob was nearly thrown in jail (in Germany? not a happy prospect) for assault. Luckily, calmer heads prevailed, and we got out of Dodge, not a moment too soon. We finished the tour with gigs in Paris and London. All in all, it was a pleasant family vacation for all concerned. We closed out 1990 with four wonderful New Year's shows. Branford opened with his band, and joined us for, among others, an incandescent "Bird Song."

Our 1991 summer tour was more of the same — stadiums and sheds, sheds and stadiums. Despite the loss of Brent, and Jerry's ongoing drug use, I enjoyed playing this tour. Bruce Hornsby brought an adventuresome spirit back into the band, pulling some great responses out of Jerry. With Bruce in the band, we could break the music down into little chamber-music subgroups: duets and trios. Before and after the drum duet, there would usually be a space for free playing, and many times Bruce and I, or Bruce and Vince and Jerry, or Bob and Jerry, would take this space and explore hitherto unknown territory.

But the band couldn't ignore the evidence of Jerry's backsliding, and while on the road the band members agreed that when we got home, another intervention would be necessary, this time with a professional counselor. Shortly after the tour I got the call: the meeting would be held at our Front Street studio. When I arrived, everyone was already seated, with Jerry by the mix board and the band and assorted others arrayed in a line facing him. It was clear from the look on his face that he knew what was coming and was not happy about it. After the counselor was introduced, Jerry sat there stone-faced while we voiced our concerns about his health — and then I brought up my frustration with the effects of his drug use on the music. For the first time, Jerry and I actually started to have a real dialogue about it. It must have been shocking for everyone in the room to see Jerry and me get into it with each other: His avuncular "Papa Jerry" mask fell away, and he angrily responded, which was like a ray of light to me. I didn't care that he was referencing my drunken, sloppy playing of previous years — I was past that now, and he knew it — but I was exhilarated that he could finally confront me about it.

Unfortunately, our drug-abuse counselor had come into the meeting with a backpack full of predigested notions about Jerry, the band, and the rehabilitation process. Almost as soon as Jerry and I started to get serious, he cut us off at the knees, steering the meeting into safer, less controversial waters. My frustration knew no bounds, and Jerry was even more incensed by this shift in emphasis, retreating into his shell and basically telling us to fuck off. I left, my thoughts in a shambles, feeling as if I'd actually opened a door only to have it slammed shut in my face.

Another opportunity blown, it seemed, although Jerry may have taken more away from the meeting than was immediately apparent. A short time later, he called and invited me over to his house, a sprawling pad in San Rafael. We sat by his swimming pool, and he told me that he'd been going to a methadone clinic in San Francisco. He said that he had wanted to do it his own way, chuckling with pride as he described standing in line waiting for his methadone. What a great solution for Jerry, I thought; he never wanted special treatment, and now he was just one of the guys. I went home elated; in his own sweet way, he had let me know that he'd heard what I had to say.

What wasn't working for him was our touring schedule — our huge overhead was draped around his neck like a yoke on an ox. In hindsight, maybe it would have been better if instead of helping to pull the load, I'd put the brakes on.

To cover our $500,000-a-month overhead, we would have to work — and keep working — so management was already booking

298 ~ Phil Lesh

shows through 1992. Around this time, we discussed the situation, not for the first time, in a board meeting. From the minutes:

> **JG:** We are a community, a family, a tribe. This pressure chokes off enthusiasm. It's killing [me] to keep doing the same tours. It has not much dignity. The pressure is so great that we can't stop. It's hard to be creative with a gun held to your head. It's a huge responsibility.
> **VW:** We need to take some time together to rework things. Doesn't want to stop — can hardly afford his house now.
> **JG:** Is talking about twenty-five years and is burnt out and wants to do what he wants to do.
> **PL:** It's your turn, man.
> **BK:** We should take six months off.
> **JG:** Can't guarantee the workers. We can make enough to take six months off without shutting down. We did it in 1986, from July to December. We can try to do it next year. Maximize on tours and organize the vault. Try to eliminate the fall tour.

I should have immediately called upon our management to create a six-month break from touring. I was concerned about constantly taking my kids out of school to travel with me, but I selfishly didn't want to tour without my family. As much as I loved playing the music, I too was burned out from years of nonstop touring. But I still couldn't pull the emergency cord and bring the train to a halt, knowing that even a six-month break would mean the layoff of most of our longtime employees, who depended on the band for their livelihood: house payments, medical insurance, etc. In the end nothing changed. We took the path of least resistance and kept touring.

For some years now, we had divided the responsibilities for our tours between two promoters: Bill Graham Presents and Monarch (later Metropolitan) Entertainment in New York. BGP generally handled anything from Denver west, and Metro everything east of the Rockies. Naturally, the two principals detested each other. That's why it was such a surprise to see Bill Graham backstage at our nine-show Madison Square Garden run — as a general rule he made it a point never to appear at a gig promoted by the competition. Bill was warm and open, giving both Jill and me big hugs, saying that he had just been "passing through," and couldn't pass up the chance to see part of our record-breaking run, etc., none of which mitigated the strangeness of his visit by one iota.

Less than a month later, Jill and I were reading in bed late one stormy fall night when a massive power failure put out the lights all over San Rafael. It wasn't until the next morning, with a call from our manager Cameron, that we discovered the cause: a helicopter carrying Bill Graham, his friend Melissa Gold, and his pilot, Steve Kahn, had crashed into a power transmission tower on Highway 37 en route from a show at Concord Pavilion; all aboard were killed instantly. It was fitting of Bill to go out in such a spectacular blaze of glory — according to witnesses, the crash lit up the sky, and it plunged two counties into darkness. Bill's death hit the Grateful Dead especially hard, as he had essentially given us our start, in the early years booking us over and over at his dance halls, later at festivals and on national tours, even managing us for a short time. He never lost faith in our music and our power to move audiences, frequently introducing us as "not just the best at what they do, but the only ones who do what they do."

Bill's death marked the exit from the stage of a type — an avatar, if you will — of visionary entrepreneur, the larger-than-life concert and tour promoter. Where can we see his like today, in an age of faceless corporate monopolies and predigested pop baby food? Had it not been for Bill, the San Francisco music scene would have taken a vastly different shape, and rock music itself might have had far less of an impact on global culture.

It was with leaden hearts that musicians from all over the country (among them Santana, Jackson Browne, Crosby, Stills, and Nash, Los Lobos, Tracy Chapman, and many others) gathered in Golden Gate Park to pay a final public tribute to Bill's memory. Our set was graced with guest appearances from John Fogerty and Neil Young, the latter channeling Dylan with a fervent rendition of "Forever Young."

As always when such a life is cut short, a feeling of emptiness and waste pervaded the atmosphere, but the performances and spoken tributes were inspiring enough to dispel the gloom and turn the day into what it was intended to be: a celebration of "music, love, and laughter."

I wasn't surprised when Bruce Hornsby gave notice after our spring tour in '92. He had said from the beginning that he wanted to help us through the transition period after Brent's death, and now that Vince was fully up to speed, Bruce wanted to concentrate on his own work and focus exclusively on his solo career. It was also clear to me that Bruce was unhappy with our inability to play his songs to his satisfaction, and that he also wanted to spend more time with his young twin sons, Keith and Russell.

The summer '92 tour was a long one, starting at Shoreline Amphitheater in California, passing through stadiums in Las Vegas, New Jersey, Chicago, upstate New York, and arenas and sheds all across the country. Playing stadiums had been exciting at first, but the thrill of projecting our music across such vast spaces evaporated rapidly in the face of the mind-numbing sterility of the stadium environment. It came to feel as if we were playing into a vacuum, with no possibility of feedback or response from an audience that was barely visible from the stage.

Our volume onstage had reached a level of loudness that made it impossible to hear what anyone else was playing through the sound of one's own instrument. In searching for a solution, we came across a promising concept: a stereo mix of the whole band (or whatever each individual musician considered relevant) mixed onstage and broadcast via RF (radio) to the players, each of whom was wearing a small receiver and stereo ear monitors (tiny speakers similar to hearing aids, custom-fitted to the ear canal). Other artists, notably Steve Miller, had been using these devices and reported good results, so we decided to give them a try, hoping at the same time to reduce the rate of hearing loss we'd been experiencing.

In typical Grateful Dead style, though, we took the concept all the way to the wall; we removed *all* onstage instrument monitor speakers, so that the drums were the only sound heard acoustically onstage. This would prove to be both a blessing (for the sound crew) and a curse (for the musicians) — running all the instrument signals directly into the PA and the subsequent elimination of their leakage into the vocal mikes made mixing in the front of house much cleaner; at the same time, the sound we were hearing through the little ear speakers was shrill, tinny, and sorely lacking in low-end warmth (as if it were "strained through a sheet," to quote the old traveling salesman joke). Over the last few years that we performed as the Grateful Dead, I spent at least as much time running back and forth between my stage position and the monitor board adjusting my mix as I did playing my instrument; on top of that, we had to run the little buggers so loud (to get some semblance of the instrumental sound we were used to) that our rate of hearing loss accelerated rather than slowed.

The tour blew by in the by-now-familiar blur of hockey rinks, hotels, basketball arenas, hotels, airports, and football stadiums. Jerry was playing and singing beautifully, but he wasn't looking good. I didn't think he was using again, but I wondered if perhaps his solitary life on the road was beginning to pall on him. His companion, Manasha, was a kind woman who loved Jerry and their daughter, Keelin, but she was withdrawing more and more with every tour. We could be staying in great cities with major art exhibits that we were invited to view exclusively, or we would be invited to attend a rehearsal of an opera, a symphony performance, or a late-night jazz show — all of those things that kept us sane while touring. No matter; Manasha refused to leave Keelin alone with their nanny and would not let Jerry go anywhere without them. I was concerned that Jerry was beginning to isolate himself again — he was gaining weight and looking unhealthy. The Grateful Dead as an entity can be cruel to the women in the family, and Manasha was not the first (or last) woman to want to retreat from it.

Shortly after we came home from the '92 summer tour, Jerry's assistant, Vince DiBiasi, called frantically to tell us that Jerry was having a serious health crisis. My insides went cold as he gave me the details; apparently it was a replay of the diabetic event of 1986. At that point Jerry was still extremely ill but refused to go to the hospital; an acupuncturist and a licensed physician were treating him at home. The next few days were pretty dicey, but with the care and support of Manasha, his medical team, and especially Vince and Gloria, Jerry survived yet another near-death experience.

Jerry was the kind of guy who had to get scared shitless to give up all his favorite junk foods and take up exercise. This incident gave him the incentive he needed. He lost a large amount of weight and became much more like his old self again. Jill and I would visit him while he recuperated at his fine new home. We cracked up when he showed us his closet; a large walk-in with a dresser in the middle and acres of hanging space — completely empty except for his neatly hung collection of seven or eight black T-shirts. He loved to swim, and now he could enjoy his new pool with his two beautiful Newfoundland dogs, frolicking and playing with them like a kid. He was most excited, though, about his garage, which he had converted into an art studio because it had wonderful natural light. I was relieved to see that Jerry seemed to be healthy once again and could maybe have a homelife, along with his creative renaissance.

We had no choice but to cancel the fall tour while Jerry recovered. My family celebrated Brian's third birthday in the Trinity Alps — staying in a rustic cabin on the Stewart Fork of the Trinity River. We spent two leisurely weeks hiking, swimming, and sweating out all of the past year's tour grime, cleansing ourselves in the cold, clear river water. It was a considerable relief to know I would be able to take the fall off and enjoy some of the ordinary moments in everyday life.

Meanwhile, management had been trying to figure out how to get through the rest of the year while Jerry recuperated. To that end, three plans were submitted to the band in a document entitled:

Ways to Survive the Next Few Months
So Jerry Can Get Better

Plan A: assumes local shows in October and December

1. cut back salaries immediately by ⅓ across the board
2. continue salary cuts through December
3. possible reallocation of a few people to other entities
4. cut back other expenses — equipment, outside contractors, etc.
5. give modest Christmas bonuses and hopefully go back to full salaries in January (or even December if a lot of shows in December)

Plan B: assumes no shows until December

1. same as Plan A except cut back salaries to 50 percent starting in November, back up to ⅔ or full in December if income in December is sufficient to cover December and January

Plan C: assumes no shows for remainder of 1992

1. salaries cut by ⅓ immediately, to 50 percent in October or as soon as it appears that shows unlikely for remainder of year
2. cut back expenses further by laying off everyone except for those necessary to maintain office and operations until we regroup in 1993

While we were all grateful for Jerry's quick recovery, once again we had missed an opportunity to make our schedule less strenuous by reducing our workload and taking a serious look at our overhead. To make up lost income, management booked more shows for '93 than we had played in any one year over the last five years.

Back on the road that December, I started hearing rumors that Jerry had reconnected with an old love, Barbara Meier, whom I remembered from back in Palo Alto. We had all hung out together then — Jerry was nineteen, and Barbara was fifteen going on sweet sixteen. For her birthday that year I composed a little melody, which I called "Theme for Barbara (on Her Sixteenth Birthday)." I briefly saw them together backstage at a Denver show, and they were so immersed in each other it was as if for them the last thirty years had never happened. Even so, I didn't really think he would leave Manasha and Keelin. He had had other girlfriends on the road, but he delighted in his role as a doting father and seemed to care deeply for Manasha.

On December 30 Maureen Hunter called, saying Barbara was flying in, Jerry was coming over, and would Jill and I join them. When we got there, it was thrilling to see Jerry so animated; we sat around the table in the Hunters' bright, flower-bedecked kitchen and reminisced, until the conversation turned to whether or not Jerry would be returning home or staying to see Barbara. He was sure that he wanted to be with Barbara but was afraid of the consequences of leaving Manasha. I think at one point he decided that he was already in such big trouble, by being gone so long without calling, that he might as well avoid all conflict and stay. Jill and Maureen convinced him that he needed to personally tell Manasha that he was leaving, so he sat at the kitchen table, with the women hovering, and wrote her a letter that was delivered by Vince DiBiasi later that night.

My family had planned to fly out to Maui after New Year's Day, and Jerry and Barbara and the Hunters decided to meet us there. We flew into Maui after Jerry and Barbara, and soon after our arrival I was walking along the path at Kaanapali and spotted Jerry walking alone in a Windbreaker and a floppy hat. I snuck up behind him, tapped him on the shoulder and said, "Hey, man, aren't you a rock star?" and he replied, laughing, "No, over here I'm just another elderly gentleman."

We had a wonderful time in Hawaii with Jerry, Barbara, and the Hunters. We were all staying in a condo complex, and we would stop by to visit each other. I even caught ol' Jer doing the dishes one night after dinner. Unlike the rest of the band, Jerry and I were never particularly athletic. Bobby played football, mountain biked, jogged; Mickey rode horses and had a black belt in judo; Billy also rode horses and went diving. Jerry and I were the nerds, taking pride in our aversion to athletic participation of any kind. Since he had taken up scuba diving years ago and crossed over to join the manly men, he insisted, and I do mean insisted, that on this trip I learn to dive in solidarity: "You'll love it, man — just give it a try." So Jerry, Barbara, Bob, Jill, and I awoke every morning at the crack of dawn to meet our instructor and learn to dive. Despite my apprehension, I enjoyed it thoroughly. It was cool to watch Jerry so at home in the ocean; he would pick up a small octopus and tickle it or excitedly point out a moray eel sticking its ugly head out of a hole in the coral. Bob Hunter also took to diving. In a fine moment of poetic truth, I saw him swimming sideways like a crab — a classic Cancer. The six of us got together every evening to sit on the beach with glasses of champagne and sparkling water, watching the sunset. It was a lovely interlude in our lives, and I told myself that I would make sure that more of these moments would happen.

During the first gigs of 1993, in Chicago, Jerry and Barbara split up after only three months together. Jerry remained in good spirits, hanging with M.G., with whom he had renewed the friendship that had lapsed during his time with Manasha. Later that spring, while doing shows in Washington DC, we were invited to the White House through the good auspices and connections of our publicist, Dennis McNally. A group of us, including Jill and myself, Jerry, M.G., Mickey and his wife, Caryl, and others met with Al Gore in his office. Al then took us into the Oval Office and showed us around. The impression that stayed with me was how small the room actually was — it didn't seem large enough to contain the immense importance attached to it. Mickey and Jerry sat down in two overstuffed wing chairs in front of the Oval Office fireplace and pretended to solve the problems of the world.

Later that year we were back playing in stadiums — and embroiled in controversy with our opening act. We had been booking name acts to open for us at the biggest stadium shows. This was tough on the openers, since most of our audience spent their time before our set in the parking lot vending area or partying on their own tailgates. This meant that the opening act was playing to a less than fully attentive crowd, while the people were attempting to find their seats, setting up their taping gear, etc. For Sting, our opening act in '93, this situation was aggravated by the discovery that Dan Healy, our soundman, had been running the PA at 75 percent capacity for the opening act. Dan's rationalization was that he didn't want to risk blowing up the system, but in reality he was making sure that the opener didn't upstage the Grateful Dead on any level. Sting was understandably upset, and I was personally so taken aback at this breach of professional courtesy that I sought him out at breakfast in the hotel restaurant, attempting to assure him that the Grateful Dead would never countenance such actions on the part of an employee, and that we would ensure it never happened again.

That was only one of the issues we'd all been having with Dan's mixing. Dan, an amateur guitarist, had special problems with Bobby. Bob's guitar would disappear from time to time, and strange electronic effects would be applied to Bob's voice or guitar. If Bob tried to say anything from the stage, Dan would drown his voice in artificial reverb so that nothing said was comprehensible. When this started happening during songs, Jerry and I decided to listen back to the recorded mixes to see what else was going on. We discovered far too many dubious mixing decisions for comfort, so we called a band meeting to discuss the problem. The band met at Mickey's ranch and listened back to some of the mix tapes, and all agreed that something had to be done. We dithered about for a while, admitting to ourselves that we were cowards who abhorred confrontation; no one wanted to be the one to tell Dan he was fired. So, wimps that we are, we had Cameron, our manager, do the deed.

During his short-lived reunion with Barbara Meier the previous year, Jerry had run into his old flame from the seventies, Deborah Koons, in a grocery store. After the breakup with Barbara, he continued to see Deborah, even going with her to Ireland on a location-scouting trip for one of her film projects. They became closer and closer over the next year, and on Valentine's Day '94, they were married in a nondenominational ceremony at an Episcopal church in Sausalito. The reception was held at the Tiburon Yacht Club, and for me it was like a flashback to Jerry's first wedding in Palo Alto so many years before: Most of his friends and bandmates had gone through their heavy-drinking periods, or rehab, by that time, and could be found clustered around the food tables or on the dance floor (where I managed to make a spectacle of myself and embarrass my wife with my strange birdlike dance, completely without the assistance of alcohol), while most of the drinking was done by the bride's family and friends.

In March, I'd been offered a unique opportunity. Kent Nagano, the conductor of the Berkeley Symphony Orchestra, called me and asked if I'd be interested in guest conducting the orchestra for their annual fund-raiser. I remembered how much fun it had been conducting in school, and said yes immediately, but added a caveat: I wanted to conduct some real music, not just an arrangement of some pop tune or an orchestral version of a Sousa march. Kent didn't even blink when I suggested "A Celebration of Some 100 x 150 Notes," an orchestral "fanfare" lasting some three and a half minutes by my friend Elliott Carter, whom I'd come to know as a result of the Rex Foundation supporting a new recording of his *Concerto for Orchestra.* Although Elliott is arguably America's greatest living composer, his orchestral music is rarely performed, and I wanted to do my bit to change that. Kent replied, "OK, but let's do more than one piece. How about some Stravinsky? The "Infernal Dance" from the *Firebird,* maybe?"

At the concert, Kent had programmed my pieces separately. The first segment of the concert featured the Stravinsky, and the Carter came after the intermission. As I walked to the podium for my first stint, I thought I saw a familiar face out of the corner of my eye, but I was too focused on the proper tempo for the opening bars to turn and look. The piece came off rather well, I thought, except for a miscommunication a few pages in; I'd gestured to the tuba player to play softer, but he said after the concert that he thought I was just "waving hello." As I returned to the wings, I looked down into the audience, and to my immeasurable delight, I saw Jerry sitting there alone, looking up at me with that ineffable quicksilver grin. My stint was the last before intermission, and when I walked out to meet my family, Jerry joined us, saying, "Hey, man, why didn't you tell anybody about this? I had to read it in the paper. You know, they played better for you than they did for their regular guy." (Kent had done a short piece with the orchestra earlier in the program.) "Jerry," I replied, a little embarrassed at such extravagant praise, "give Stravinsky a little credit, will ya?" "OK, OK, but still . . . ," and he patted me on the back and wandered away into the crowd. My heart swelled with love and gratitude; never in my wildest dreams had I imagined that he would come out on his own to support me. Several days after the concert, I received a phone call from Jerry: "I just wanted to tell you that I made some sketches of you conducting; I want you to have them after I work them up a little." "Wow — thank you, Jer, I'm really touched." "Hey, man — you done good."

When the spring '94 tour arrived in Orlando, Florida, for two shows at the Orlando Arena, Billy got some bad news: His father was very sick. He immediately hopped on a plane to California, where he found his dad weak but recovering. Just before we had to make the decision to cancel, Jerry suggested bringing in a drummer friend of his to play the show, but Mickey understandably refused to play without Billy.

The following day, Billy returned on an overnight red-eye flight for the second Orlando show. The venue was overwhelmed by thousands of ticketless Deadheads, who the night before had been shut out of the canceled show. They tried unsuccessfully to break into the arena before the show. The police responded with tear gas and dogs, and as we pulled up to the stage entrance, we were met by event security, attempting to get us out of the car and into the hall quickly. Unfortunately, my son Brian got his "King Arthur" wooden sword tangled up in the seat belt — and while we struggled to extricate him, a cloud of tear gas bore down upon us at great speed, causing general consternation: The idea of a four-year-old breathing tear gas was not comforting. We tried to get Brian to leave the sword in the car, but he refused — loudly and at length. At the last possible moment, everything came untangled; Jill swept Brian up (sword and all) in her arms, and we ran into the building, the tear gas seeming to follow us like some malevolent Disney monster. The rioters were eventually dispersed, and the show went on, but it made me wonder if the disconnect that was happening in the band was somehow transferring itself to the fans. Perhaps as the Grateful Dead moved farther away from our original vision of intimate communication and spiritual transformation, and we were playing in larger places to pay the bills, the crowds had become too large to sustain the closed circuit of consciousness that we'd always striven to achieve.

Back on tour in July, we again hit Washington DC for a couple of gigs, and the band was invited to lunch at the Senate dining room by Barbara Boxer, our senator from California, with whom several of us had a long-standing acquaintance. (I had met Barbara during her first political campaign, for Marin County supervisor, and had supported her ever since.) We took a quick tour of the Senate chamber (not forgetting the famous cloakroom, where many deals are cut), with the Senate historian in attendance, whispering factoids and historical obscurities all the while. We then repaired to the dining room, where our entrance turned many heads. Strangely, the warmest response came from an unexpected quarter; the segregationist Dixiecrat dinosaur Strom Thurmond, who rose from his table and shuffled over, offering his hand to Jerry, who, with a fleeting look of comic alarm, took it graciously and mumbled an inaudible response. We enjoyed a fine meal, though, notable for Jerry's enthusiastic description of his new song "Days Between" to a fascinated Senator Boxer.

Jerry wasn't alone in his delight with his new song. Jerry and Hunter had brought several songs in during our most recent flurry of serious rehearsals, and they were as fine as anything the pair had ever done. "Days Between" and "So Many Roads" stand out for me, because they seem to be almost a matched pair. In a sense, these two songs seem to encompass Jerry's life from a poetic perspective, and I suspect that Hunter may have written these lyrics as a loving tribute.

Achingly nostalgic, "Days Between" evokes the past. The music climbs laboriously out of shadows, growing and peaking with each verse, only to fall back each time in hopeless resignation. When Jerry sings the lines "when all we ever wanted/was to learn and love and grow" or "we gave the best we had to give/how much we'll never know," I am immediately transported decades back in time, to a beautiful spring morning with Jerry, Hunter, Barbara Meier, and Alan Trist — all of us goofing on the sheer exhilaration of being alive. I don't know whether to weep with joy at the beauty of the vision, or with sadness at the impassable chasm of time between the golden past and the often painful present.

"So Many Roads" unfolds like a farewell. The music is quintessential Jerry: so simple and tender, yet elegiac, and full of surprises. The weary singer yearns to travel on "along those roads of gold and silver snow," and for release "where ice-blue roses grow," telling of "so many roads/so many roads I know/all I want is one to lead me home/so many roads/to ease my soul." Jerry's voice — so ragged, yet somehow more expressive than ever — embodied the bone-tired acceptance of the lyric so completely that a listener almost wouldn't need words to understand the song.

On the road, Jerry didn't look well, even though he was halfheartedly working with Deborah on an exercise regime. One morning, Jill and I were in the health club at our hotel, she on the stair machine and I on the treadmill. Deborah and Jerry came in — he dressed in sweats and a T-shirt, she ready to go out on the town. She put him on a treadmill next to me, set the timer for thirty minutes, and left. After allowing enough time to make sure of her departure, Jerry got wearily off the treadmill, shrugging sheepishly, and made a little face at us on his way out the door. I didn't know whether it was drugs, his health, or his marriage, but he seemed to be aging before my eyes.

In November '94 we went into the Site, a local recording studio, with the vague idea of making an album to commemorate our upcoming thirtieth anniversary. The studio was located on a hilltop in rural Marin, not far from Jerry's old digs where he'd lived with Manasha — a truly spectacular location, with panoramic views and frequent wildlife sightings. We had what we thought of as some pretty strong material — three songs from Jerry and two each from Bob, Vince, and myself.

We started the recording process with high hopes, but day by day our moods darkened, as Jerry frequently didn't make it at all, and when he did, it was clear he was using yet again, and that he'd rather be anywhere but in the studio. He actually only played for a few minutes during the three weeks we were there, and not one note was usable. The rest of us struggled on to finish out our time there, but Jerry's apathy spread among us like a virus, and in the end we packed up and split, agreeing halfheartedly to try again next year.

Anarchy wasn't working: With no one willing to take a stand, there seemed to be no way to stop the endless tour. We ramped it up again in spring '95, despite the fact that Jerry looked and sounded worse than ever. A little sunshine was provided by my son Grahame, who at eight years of age had become more aware of the music itself. Instead of spending most of his time in the kids' room or playing chess with his brother in my onstage hideout, he began watching and listening during the show. He had formed a special connection with Jerry, and on many a night could be found sitting cross-legged on a road case directly behind Jerry's amps, listening intently through headphones; from time to time Jerry would turn around and play directly to him. The look on Grahame's face at that moment could have melted stone; he looked up, or opened his eyes, and saw Jerry playing to him — and his whole being lit up. He flashed that killer grin of his, and Jer just dug in harder, rocking his head back and forth as he played, while Grahame practically lifted off from the road case in delight.

Grahame was also directly responsible for the belated live unveiling of my 1974 song "Unbroken Chain" at one of our Philadelphia shows in March '95. The song is, as are many of my efforts, so complicated and difficult to play that I was not inclined to play it live. Grahame, after listening to the recorded version, was so enthusiastic about hearing it performed that I just couldn't refuse — and lo and behold, it came off so well that I was encouraged to continue slotting it into our sets.

Just before our summer tour we learned of the firing of Vince and Gloria DiBiasi, who had been Jerry's domestic assistants for several years. The DiBiasis were a steadfast, loving couple, with grown children, who had formed the only real constant in Jerry's life (other than his music) throughout the turbulent comings and goings of girlfriends, his illnesses, and the demands on his time and energy from every direction imaginable. Vince acted as Jerry's personal assistant, as well as his liaison for the commercial end of his artwork projects — lithographs, ties, etc. Gloria was the rock around which all the currents swirled; she would make sure that Jerry had some decent nutritional value in what he was eating, and even watch over him as he slept to make sure he didn't stop breathing (Jerry suffered from sleep apnea). The departure of Vince and Gloria meant that Jerry was again living alone, as he and Deborah maintained separate residences. This situation was extremely worrisome for me, especially after Vince told me that Jerry's blood sugar had recently tested at an astronomical level.

So it was that with great apprehension I played the first gig of summer in Highgate, Vermont. The previous year we had played to about fifty thousand people in the same bucolic outdoor setting, and the gig had gone off without a hitch. This time, the crowd turned out to be much bigger than planned for — more than one hundred thousand people showed up, over a third without tickets. We only averted disaster by opening the gates to allow everyone entry.

From Highgate the tour rolled on to Giants Stadium and then to Albany, New York, where there were more gate-crashers, arrests, and injuries. Next came RFK Stadium in Washington DC, where some fans were struck by lightning before the show. It seemed as if every day we were getting reports of serious problems relating to our fans. Even more worrisome was Jerry's physical and mental condition. The sight of Jerry — clammy and gray, always out of breath, incommunicado onstage as well as off — was frightening to us all. The other band members' response was to play our asses off trying to engage him. Our efforts were largely unsuccessful; we watched, heartbroken, while he isolated himself from the brothers who loved him. On what was our official thirtieth anniversary, while playing to a sold-out crowd of sixty thousand at Giants Stadium, he turned his guitar volume down so low that we were essentially playing without him; on the next night, we had to start "The Other One" without him. Both there and in Albany, he had to be constantly reminded of what tune we were playing.

It got worse: before our gig at Deer Creek Amphitheater, in Indiana, I was in my hotel room and management called to give me some frightening news. Someone had threatened to kill Jerry during the show. The irony is that the death threat was redundant. Jerry looked, acted, and sounded as if he were already at death's door. It made me feel physically ill watching him try to get through each show. I sat on my bed, my mind in turmoil, and decided: This is it. I went to the band and management and told them that I was already packed and I didn't want to finish the tour. The promoters led the cheerleading — the show *must* go on. Jerry was adamant in his decision to go ahead and play, so I wearily acquiesced. Metal detectors, armed police, attack dogs, etc., were put in place, and the band did what we always did. We took the stage.

While we played, there were armed police clustered in the aisles spread out in front of the stage. Even during the show, the bright houselights remained on, and each person who came down the aisle to claim a seat was intensely scrutinized by security and cops. The atmosphere was a choking miasma of foreboding and defeat. The death threat did seem to bring back some of Jerry's sense of humor; in the first set he sang his song "Dire Wolf," including the refrain "Please, don't murder me."

I finally settled into the music. Bob was singing Dylan's epic "Desolation Row." Looking out into the amphitheater, I saw the bright houselights illuminating the happy faces of kids dancing and swaying to the music and the grim-faced armed police alike. Right after Bob sang the line "the riot squad is restless, they need somewhere to go," I was distracted by chaos at the back of the venue: Before my eyes, hordes of ticketless fans, assisted by others inside on the lawn, kicked down the security fence and poured in while police with tear gas and dogs fought to keep them out. We looked at one another in horror and kept playing; somehow we all knew that if the music stopped the rioting would escalate. The fighting continued while the band played on. The security for Jerry's safety was a joke at this point.

As I stood there playing, watching darkness fall on our long strange trip, I had to ask myself, How did we let it get this crazy? This isn't what music is about; this isn't what our community is about; this isn't the sweet, kindly, avuncular anarchy of the Acid Tests; this is black chaos.

Somehow, we managed to finish the set, and then the show; at that point we were faced with a decision about the second of the two sold-out shows: cancel, or no? The question became moot after the police informed the promoters that they would direct traffic but would not work inside the facility, and so the second show was canceled.

Even then, it wasn't over. At the show's end, as a security precaution, management had sent the band out of the venue in a production bus, perhaps fearing the reaction of the people if they saw us leaving in limos. We inched through the parking lot, sitting in stunned silence as our fans raged around the bus, shouting and banging on the sides. After finally winding through to the exit, we slunk away along a very narrow back road, as far away from the main road as we could get.

Just then the bus, which had been attempting to negotiate a ninety-degree turn on this tiny road, ran into a ditch — *veerrry* slowly. So out we all poured, infinitely relieved to have something to jive about — anything rather than think about the nightmare back down the road. The local farmer whose front yard overlooked the whole turn emerged from his garage with the cutest little tractor. It was so sweet — he came out in the middle of the night and tried to haul this huge tour bus out of the ditch. Maybe he felt that the sooner he got these freaks out of his driveway, the sooner he'd get some sleep that night.

At Riverport Amphitheater in St. Louis for two shows, the houselights were again left on because of residual concern about the death threat. We were still in shock from the horrific events at Deer Creek when we learned of more tragedy. After the show, some ticketless campers had sought shelter from pouring rain in an open pavilion, while others climbed to the roof, thereby causing the structure to collapse and injuring more than 150 people.

The tour was scheduled to wind up with two shows at Soldier Field in Chicago, where the media descended upon us in anticipation of more drama. In the end, however, the shows went off without incident, except for the crumbling consensus onstage. At the last show, I watched in despair as Jerry — whey-faced, hunched over with chin on chest, fighting for breath before singing every line — struggled his way through an incredibly moving performance of "So Many Roads" — "to ease my soul." His guitar never sounded so pure and touching as it did in that song, on that night. Jerry had always been able to connect with the essence of every song he sang, but it was apparent now that his life-force was at a low ebb; he seemed to respond only to the slowest, saddest songs.

At the end of "Unbroken Chain," toward the close of the set, Jerry tried to go into "China Doll," but Bobby had something else in mind, and took the reins, rocking to the fore with the first notes of "Sugar Magnolia." It took Jerry an unusually long time — sixteen bars or so — to pick up the thread of the tune, while my heart went out to him. For the encore, Jerry sang "Black Muddy River," and then I launched into "Box of Rain" at the last minute because I couldn't stand the thought of ending the tour with one of Jerry's most sorrowful songs.

After the music ended, there was a gigantic fireworks display set off from the backstage wall; over the PA, Jimi Hendrix played "The

Star-Spangled Banner"; and for once at a stadium, instead of bolting for our cars as the display distracted the audience (and kept the exits clear), we all stood silently together and watched the brilliant light show. My son Brian, only five at the time, was entranced by the lights even as he clapped his hands over his ears to shut out the explosions, which were louder than the band ever was.

Two days after the tour ended, we met at our offices for our post-tour board meeting. While discussing tour bonuses, Jerry piped up with a request: "Hey, man, I want an extra twenty dollars per gig for dodging bullets"; with a shout of laughter and a resounding vote of approval, the meeting broke up with hugs all around. We all scattered to the four winds, and that was the last time I saw Jerry.

I have spent my life
Seeking all that's still unsung
Bent my ear to hear the tune
And closed my eyes to see
When there were no strings to play
You played to me.

— Hunter/Garcia, "Attics of My Life"

In July '95, much to everyone's relief, Jerry checked into the Betty Ford clinic in Pasadena, in an attempt to clean up. This, unfortunately, lasted only two weeks, not enough to do the trick, but it left him with a very strong motivation to finish what he had started. He then decided to continue the process at Serenity Knolls, a rehab center in Lagunitas, California. Curiously, this facility was located in a house the band had rented for a month or so back in '66 — it was then known as "Camp Lagunitas."

Meanwhile, I had settled back into my routine at home: walking, relaxing, listening to music, reading — and driving my son Grahame to a summer day camp at the Bay Area Discovery Museum in Sausalito. On the morning of August 9, Grahame and I were cruising down the Waldo Grade en route to the camp when the car phone rang; Jill frantically informed me that a mutual friend had called from the East Coast and reported hearing a news bulletin saying that Jerry had died. She had then called our manager, Cameron Sears; he too had heard rumors, but not confirmation.

My first hope was "another death rumor" — but with my heart in my throat I called Steve Parish, Jerry's roadie. My conversation with Steve was brief. "Is it true?" "Yes." I was struck numb; I had lost my oldest surviving friend, my brother.

Someone once characterized my musical relationship with Jerry as "like a sandworm in heat," describing the way the bass lines twined around those of the guitar — a perfect metaphor for the way I loved that man. His many gifts, his delight in life, and his gusto for experience were balanced by an endearing humility of spirit and an almost obsessive refusal to take himself seriously. His conversation could range from the deeper meaning of the I-Ching to the latest science fiction, and he never failed to deftly skewer ballooning egos. It was the warmth of his heart, though, that just pulled everybody in. Even though, like most of us, he didn't suffer fools gladly, there was room there for just about every-damn-body. Then, too, his insatiable curiosity and range of interests were like a breath of fresh air — at last, someone I can talk to!

The morning after the news came down, Jerry was laid out in state at a funeral home in San Rafael. Mickey called to let me know, and we agreed to meet there. We walked in together, and there he was, lying in his coffin with a smile on his face. He looked so good, so at peace, with all the cares of this world lifted from him, that I wanted to hug him, or try to wake him up. But stark reality suddenly hit me — hard — and I staggered under the impact. A thousand feelings chased themselves through the black hole that opened up in the center of my heart.

Grateful Dead family members started calling around to one another, wanting to connect and be together, so Jill and I invited everyone to our home for an impromptu old-fashioned wake. That night, almost everyone showed up — and we all celebrated Jerry, each in his or her own private way: eating, drinking, singing, laughing, and crying.

Two days later, his funeral service was held at St. Stephen's church in Belvedere. Gathered there were most of the Grateful Dead extended family, including Hornsby, Bill Walton, and Bob Dylan. In a glimpse of what was to come, Jerry's widow, Deborah, refused to allow

M.G. or Manasha, the mothers of his children, to attend the service. David Grisman, Jerry's old friend and collaborator, played a haunting rendition of "Amazing Grace," and many friends and family members, including Hunter, Kesey, Parish, and Jerry's daughter Annabelle, spoke of Jerry with touching eloquence and passionate love. I myself spoke of the transcendental joy I'd experienced making music with him. The service ended with a deafening standing ovation in celebration of his life, one of the most moving tributes imaginable to this truly unique spirit.

After the service, Jill and I stopped by Bill Graham's old house in Corte Madera, now owned by Bobby's friend Michael Klein, where another wake was being held; we had planned to stop by the Hunters' on our way home, where M.G. and other family members were gathering, but we were so completely drained by then that we decided to go home and hug our two boys.

Deadheads had been gathering spontaneously at the Polo Fields in Golden Gate Park, organizing themselves into memorial mode. The folks at Bill Graham Presents had then organized something more formal. A stage of sorts had been erected, featuring a thirty-foot portrait of Jerry, grinning hugely as he ripped off an inaudible guitar lick. Hundreds, maybe thousands, of flower arrangements, mementos, gifts, and photographs were piled up around the periphery, and some microphones were set up so we could address the crowd, some twenty-five thousand strong. As our family walked in from the street, I could hear the band playing over the PA system, with Jerry's guitar soaring heavenward. I almost broke down then and there, once again overwhelmed by the magnitude of our loss. Each of the band members addressed the crowd briefly; I spoke of Jerry being a "wounded warrior" and expressed my hope that he was "done becoming, now he is being." Mickey told the Heads, "It's up to you now; take what he gave you and do something with it!" and then handed out drums to all of us, and we marched out through the crowd, drumming for all we were worth, my son Brian riding on Jill's shoulders and Grahame drumming hard with the rest of us. The people in the crowd were dancing, clapping their hands in rhythm, or just standing there with tears streaming down their faces; we had to stop every few steps to hug or acknowledge someone, but the groove never faltered. As we left the field, the music welled up from the shrine, and I was hammered again by the enormity of Jerry's absence.

In early April '96 Bobby and Deborah took some of Jerry's ashes to India and poured them into the sacred Ganges River. Then, on a cloudy, windswept day in late April, we gathered at a boat dock in Sausalito to commit what remained of Jerry's ashes to the deep, as per his last wishes. Deborah refused to allow M.G. to board the boat, even after Bobby begged her to reconsider. As we pulled away from the dock, our last sight was of M.G. standing there, the mother of two of Jerry's children, shut out of paying her last respects to the man she'd been with for the better part of twenty years.

The waters of the bay were whipping up into a fine, choppy froth as we sailed under the Golden Gate Bridge, and an unbroken bank of fog was rolling in from the west. We eventually reached the spot that our captain had suggested would be the best place to scatter the ashes so that the tide could carry them out to sea. Unfortunately this area of the Gate was particularly turbulent, and as Jerry's ashes were tipped into the water, some portions were caught by the wind and blown back against the side of the vessel. Bobby, clutching a cloth napkin that Jill had handed him, leaned over the gunwale and scrubbed poor Jerry off the hull, almost going overboard in the process. If I hadn't grabbed him by the belt, he would have been swimming for his life in very rough waters. Bobby managed to clean most of the ashes from the hull before he was unceremoniously hauled back into the boat and dumped on the deck, soaked and shivering.

Some time later, Jill, while on a school field trip to an organic farm with our son Grahame, was weeding a garlic patch when she reached into a pocket and found a napkin, still encrusted with some kind of light-gray, flaky material. At a loss at first, she soon recognized it as the very napkin that Bobby had been clutching as he was heaved back over the side of the boat that day, and the material as some of Jerry's ashes. Offering up a quick prayer, she buried the napkin there in the field; Jerry now rests in the earth as well as in the waters.

A month after Jerry's funeral service, partly to help deal with my grief and despair at his passing, I go into the studio with our sound team and begin listening to tapes from the vault, searching the past for music we can release. Listening to each concert is like returning to a room in a house where I had lived for many happy years. Show after show passes through the tape machine, and my mind roams freely back through time. Fragments of disconnected memory rise to the surface of my consciousness:

Las Trancas Woods, Palo Alto, 1965: Bobby and I run breathlessly up a fire road toward the top of a hill — we'd been playing with the echo in a tree-lined gorge below. Ahead, I see a strange shape scuttling along the ground on all fours: Jerry, who's channeling some animal totem or spirit — a squirrel? A raccoon? A wolverine? He sees us; his face breaks into a sheepish grin and he stops short, rolling over on his back and staring at the sky. We join him, and an endless parade of cloud forms passes over us, each one unique and beautiful, like a snowflake. No one speaks; we simply are.

California Hall, San Francisco, 1966: We've just finished one of the most burning sets of our young lives as a band. We're all still vibrating like bells from the energy of the music and the responses of the dancers. Jerry comes over and hugs me, saying in my ear, "Way to go, *Flash.*" I'm confused at first — is he busting me for rushing? No, he's just sharing his joy at the quality of what we're doing. I find myself surprised at how pleased I am; he rarely expresses himself in that way.

The In Room, San Carlos, 1965: We're playing our final set of the evening — it's about 1:30 a.m. (We normally play forty-five minutes and take a fifteen-minute break, five sets a night.) This set consists of one song, "Midnight Hour." The first jam has ramped up and back, Pigpen has done his first rave, and we're off into the more exploratory segment of the tune. Larry, the bartender, has been playing little tricks on the patrons lately, "Just to keep them on their toes," he says, although "Just to get their hands out of their pockets" is how Pig might put it. I look over at the bar and see that Larry, tiring of his conversation with the two or three barflies, is making mysterious waving passes over the back of the bar, holding a small can of — lighter fluid? I look at Pigpen, signaling with my eyebrows — what's that weirdo bartender doing now? Pig shrugs — who knows? — takes a long drag on his cigarette, and flicks the glowing butt in a spark-showering arc across the dance floor, where it makes a perfect landing on the bar and rolls slowly into the trough at the back. Whump! The back of the bar goes up in a sheet of flame, as the patrons scramble to safety. The band imitates an air raid, while Larry rolls on the floor shaking with helpless laughter.

It's funny, these memories don't have any connection to the particular shows I'm listening to; it's as if the music opens the door to a space where all memories have the same access code and are equally accessible.

Now, we were trying to deal with both our grief at Jerry's loss and the mess that his passing had left behind him. Each of us had our own way of coming to terms with the trauma, and we were frequently at odds when discussing what we would do next.

The shock was still reverberating several months later as we met at Grateful Dead headquarters to address the most pressing question: Are we going to go on as a band without Jerry? We had been receiving increasingly intense inquiries from management and promoters, who were already looking to the next year's touring schedules.

We gathered in the old boardroom. A painting of Jerry had already been hung on the wall behind one end of the long conference table, something he'd never have permitted if he'd been around to be asked. We gloomily took our seats, and Billy, who had already closed up his place in Mendocino and moved to Hawaii and was attending by telephone, spoke first. "I don't want to tour anymore," he said. I felt as if the weight of the world had been lifted from my shoulders — because neither did I. So, the decision was made.

Simple enough, one might think — but that didn't address the dire financial straits in which GDP found itself. The ironies were overwhelming: We had never taken any time off, even in view of Jerry's failing health, and now we were forced to do everything we'd tried to avoid by continuing to tour. Employees were laid off wholesale, beginning with touring personnel. We were now faced with a Herculean task — converting an entity that had been created to support our touring and which had run on tour money, into a merchandising firm funded by the sale of T-shirts and CDs of our concerts. Despite the wave of layoffs, we still had a large staff to support.

One of our promoters put forth the offer of a "definitive" documentary film; we bandied that about for several months, but since the offer didn't include financing for production, we had to pass on that one. Then there was "Terrapin Station," the catchall term for a museum, merchandising outlet, and music store, where we would make our live concert recordings (the Vault) available to our fans. This idea was a great deal of fun while we were in the brainstorming stage, but in typical Grateful Dead fashion it became inflated in scale beyond all practicality — evolving from a simple storefront, where a rotating display of memorabilia would enhance the buying experience, to a ten-thousand-square-foot exhibition/concert hall in San Francisco. Who could afford to build such a thing? Not us.

I began to be the odd man out when I opposed a grand plan to start a new corporation with a huge influx of venture capital money. All we had to do was put up the Vault — our sole legacy — as the major asset. Try as I would, I couldn't get any concrete information from the investors as to how they were planning to recoup their investment. Most disturbing was the fact that the Vault would be totally under the control of the new company for at least ten years. In essence, we were gambling with our legacy — giving control to investors whose intentions were obscure at best. Despite my adamant protests, GDP spent hundreds of thousands of dollars that we couldn't afford trying to get this deal going. The dot-com bust of 2001 finally put an end to the plan — fortunately, before the Vault was given away.

I was also upset by the decision of the other band members to contest Jerry's will, in which he had clearly stated that he wanted his custom guitars to be returned to their maker, luthier Doug Irwin. Management advised us to fight the will, since according to them GDP had bought the instruments for Jerry. It was such a classic Jerry gesture — wanting to return his instruments to their maker — that I couldn't in good conscience be part of a lawsuit to subvert his last wishes.

The irony was inescapable: The Grateful Dead, which for over thirty years had given me so much joy and meaning, had turned into a source of frustration. Without Jerry's presence to pull us together, we were spinning farther and farther apart.

The stress of being in the minority regarding these decisions was taking its toll on my health. I had assumed my hepatitis C was under control, as I hadn't had a drink for eight years. I exercised regularly and maintained a healthy diet, but at the same time, I was imperceptibly losing weight, and strange little quirks started appearing. I was tired all the time, and always cold, no matter what the weather.

In September '98 I suddenly hemorrhaged internally while at dinner with my sons. I sagged to the floor, and my vision slowly faded to gray; through the haze, I saw the frightened shock on their faces. I flashed on Jerry, losing his father at age five, and was filled with despair; I didn't want to leave my boys behind without their father.

As I lay in the hospital, with strange faces hovering over me, I remember feeling curiously detached, as if I wanted to deny the seriousness of my condition. I soon learned that I had end-stage liver disease and would need a transplant, if I were lucky enough to survive the wait for an organ.

In a frightening twist of fate, Jill had recently been told during a checkup that a lump on her neck felt like thyroid cancer. The doctor wanted her to have surgery immediately, but it was agreed that since thyroid cancer is usually slow-growing, we would deal with one crisis at a time — first my liver transplant, then Jill's thyroid surgery and radiation treatment.

The next three months passed in a blur of semiconsciousness — an endless parade of hospital rooms, gurneys, blood draws, tests, procedures, and conferences. Some moments, however, stand out clearly from the fog:

> I'm on a gurney, being wheeled down a corridor to yet another test — this one to see if a shunt will work for my

blocked liver vein. We enter a large room that's being used as a staging area for the many patients who are undergoing some sort of medical procedure. There's a row of stalls along the wall — almost like pits at a racetrack — each holding one gurney. While waiting, Jill and I pass the time storyboarding a little fantasy: "Transplant: The Musical." We've reached the point where the big dance number should come in, and we mentally choreograph a chorus line of gurneys, each bearing a gowned patient; simultaneously they sit up and sing "It's Not an Operation, It's a Pro-ceee-dure!" Not that funny, but it's one way to ignore the cold fear that's lurking like a clenched fist in my gut. It only works for a while, though, and soon we fall silent and just wait, hand in hand.

I'm lying in my hospital bed. Lights are flashing, and there's a lot of frantic movement. Everything seems very far away, although my mind is still lucid. Jill's face flashes into my vision, and then is swiftly replaced by several masked medicos. I vaguely understand that something is *very* wrong, but I can't quite grasp what. Funny, I can't hear anything — with all this action, shouldn't there be noise? Instantaneously, sound comes crashing in, and I hear "Code blue! His blood pressure's crashing!" Curiously, I feel no fear; it's at this moment that I bow to my fate, whatever it may be, and put my trust in the good Lord — and in the professionals who are trying to save me.

After kissing Jill, I'm wheeled into the operating room. I wonder briefly if the music I'd brought would be playing: Before I can ask, strains of Mozart fill my ears. Ahhh. I'm too doped-up to be afraid, so I lie there passively as what seems like a dozen tubes are plugged into me here and there. The anesthesiologist puts a mask over my nose and mouth, and asks me to count backward from 100. I don't get much past 99 before a black velvet curtain descends over my mind, blotting out all consciousness.

I awake in my bed. I'm in some kind of intensive care unit. My back is killing me, but I feel absolutely no pain in my abdomen, where there surely must be a fresh incision scar. I ask for a nurse, and try to tell her about my back. She simply smiles, turns a little valve on my IV tube, and says calmly, "Have some more morphine." Shit. I don't even *like* morphine, and it's not doing anything for my back. Oh, well, at least I must have survived the operation. Somehow I don't think being dead hurts this much.

It's less than twelve hours after my surgery. For the first time in what seems like months, I'm on my feet. I'm walking — shuffling, rather — very slowly down a hospital corridor. To my right: the head nurse on the recovery floor, an imposing woman affectionately known by all as "Sarge." To my left: my new best friend, a wheeled IV drip tower. Not much of a conversationalist, but truly a faithful companion. I hobble to the end of the hall, turn, and make my way back to my bed.

It all comes home to me when, midway through my first week of recovery, Jill wheels me outside the hospital front door to see a stunning sunset. I break down completely in a flood of gratitude; deep down inside, I haven't been sure I'd see anything that beautiful ever again. I now know that the simple joys of being alive — breathing, seeing, hearing — are infinitely precious, and I'll never take them for granted again.

My confrontation with mortality, it seems, had given me an in-valuable gift: the ability to live in the moment, without yearning toward the past or the future. It's difficult to describe the extent of my joy in simple actions: walking our dogs, doing dishes after dinner, taking Grahame and Brian to Little League practices, or going with them to "guy movies."

Then it was my turn to take care of Jill, when in June 1999 she had surgery to remove her cancerous thyroid. The subsequent radiation treatment started in the fall and continued through the end of the year. I'm very proud of our family for being so strong for one another during this very traumatic period. As adversity sometimes will, this experience brought us closer together and gave us all a renewed commitment to each other.

After my recovery, I started to play music again as "Phil Lesh & Friends," drawing upon a pool of local musicians — invited to collaborate because of their flexibility, love for the songs, and empathy with the improvisatory freedom that was the hallmark of the Grateful Dead at its best.

For the first expedition after my transplant I asked Trey Anastasio and Page McConnell from the fine jam band Phish to join me and other musicians for a few nights at the Warfield Theatre in San Francisco. We gathered at the Grateful Dead studio to rehearse; from the first notes, I knew we could have big fun, and we did. Over the next few years, I toured as Phil Lesh & Friends with many different musicians — at colleges and at festivals, in sheds, and in theaters all across the country — sharing the stage with established legends such as Bob Dylan, the Allman Brothers, and Willie Nelson, and younger bands like Widespread Panic and String Cheese Incident. I resurrected Grateful Dead classics, covered rock and jazz tunes I'd always wanted to do, and wrote new stuff, working again with Bob Hunter in a serendipitous renewal of our old partnership.

My vision of music has always been informed by a desire to explore the full potential of every musical idea. Songs seem to me to act as springboards to transformative improvisation, whether in an instru-

332 ∞ Phil Lesh

mental break between verses, or in expanded intros or out-choruses. As a bandleader, I like nothing better than to plan shows in which I can string songs and improvisations together thematically, like a garland of pearls, and then encourage the musicians to step outside their standard way of thinking and play — completely in the context of the moment.

I continue to seek out multiple musical partners, in a quest for that elusive chemistry that comes and goes as it wishes. Sometimes "it" happens onstage, or sometimes in rehearsal, but it always leaves me breathless and wonder-struck: The music is still *there,* waiting for us to approach, to open ourselves, to let it pass through us. In Jerry's absence, the music will lack "The very spirit . . . of whatever is muddy river at its core and screams up into the spheres," as Bob Dylan put it in his elegy — but fresh approaches can still be brought to it by new combinations of musicians.

By spring 2002, all the surviving members of the Grateful Dead were touring with their own bands: Bobby with his perennial Ratdog, me with Phil & Friends, Mickey with his latest world music aggregation Bembe Orisha, and Billy with his new band the Trichromes. It seemed like the right thing to combine our different tours with a big reunion festival — a two-day event featuring all the individual bands, plus all the remaining members playing a whole show together for the first time since Jerry's death. This took place in August at Alpine Valley, in Wisconsin; we called it "Terrapin Station," and it was a wonderful rebonding experience for everyone.

For two days, the whole Grateful Dead family gathered together at Alpine. We brought memorabilia to exhibit, and guest artists played on a second stage. For the closing set each night, Bobby, Billy, Mickey, and I took the stage to play our best-beloved music. Members of Phil & Friends and Ratdog joined us onstage, and the level of energy and commitment from everyone present was truly astonishing. I knew then that our community would not only survive, but prevail. What form it would take, I knew not, but I felt the future — and it felt good.

Terrapin Station began a period of collaborative music-making that's still intermittently ongoing. At the same time, business challenges abound that we're still struggling to deal with. But today, it's more than ever a pleasure to be making music, both as an individual and together with my brothers.

The Grateful Dead group mind was in essence an engine of transformation. As such, it had no morality of its own — it made no judgments, took no positions — it merely opened valves for music to pour through. As long as the only things we cared about were exploration and ecstasy, that's how long it remained pure.

There will never be another band like the Grateful Dead. It was born at a time when magic and change were in the air, and it felt then as if we were an integral part of some cosmic plan to help transform human consciousness.

Like family members who still celebrate with one another after the patriarch of the family has passed on, my brothers and I play on, and I always feel Jerry's presence at our shows. No one can be replaced in the hearts of those who love them, but I still feel the necessity to play — for those who come to dance and those who hope to find magic, communing together with friends and family.

I rest not from my great task!
To open the Eternal Worlds, to open the immortal Eyes
Of Man inwards into the Worlds of Thought: into
Eternity
Ever expanding in the Bosom of God, the Human
Imagination

— William Blake, "Jerusalem"

A F T E R W O R D

There have been many excellent books about the Grateful Dead, written from many different points of view: management, road crew, historical-scholarly, song analysis, etc. In the process of writing this book, I discovered that to include everyone who contributed to the progress of the band would have expanded the text to unmanageable proportions, and it became necessary to limit the scope of the book to my memories and experiences of the band members themselves, together with key technical and support personnel.

That said, I would like to acknowledge the invaluable assistance of many dedicated souls — pride of place among them goes to my wife Jill, who has been my first reader, my muse, and my inspiration. My sons, Grahame and Brian, have been constant sources of warmth, support, and humor.

To Bob, Bill, and Mickey — my deepest love and gratitude for forty years of music and magic.

To my literary agent Sloan Harris, and to the team at Little, Brown — Michael Pietsch, Zainab Zakari, and Shannon Langone — my profound thanks for your kindness to a first-time author; your help made it seem easier than it was.

Thanks to Jay Blakesberg for his sterling efforts as photo editor, gathering together the photos for the book, and to Herb Greene and Jim Marshall, who have been especially generous in opening their archives — and in some instances creating new work — for this project. My thanks also go out to the many other artists whose images chronicled the Grateful Dead throughout the decades.

Cameron Sears, David LeMieux, and Jeffery Norman at Grateful Dead Productions have provided important historical records, and I have Tina Carpenter and Steve Hussman, from Dye in the Sky, and especially Gary Houston to thank for the stunning cover art.

Thanks to Eric Greenspan, whose attention to the most minute detail made dealing with contractual issues more transparent than I could believe.

Finally, my undying gratitude to the Phil Lesh & Friends team — Robbie Taylor, Kathy Sunderland, Dennis Leonard, Ian DuBois, Candace Brightman, Lauretta and Duane Walkup, J.C. and Audrey Juanis, Brian Connors, and Jonathan Levine — for their all-embracing hearts and unlimited devotion to the music.

ABOUT THE AUTHOR

Phil Lesh has been the bass player for the Grateful Dead since their formation in 1965. He lives in California with his family.